LITERACY AS PRAXIS: CULTURE, LANGUAGE, AND PEDAGOGY

Edited by

Catherine E. Walsh

ABLEX PUBLISHING CORPORATION
NORWOOD, NEW JERSEY

Copyright © 1991 by Ablex Publishing Corporation

Printed in the United States of America.

Library of Congress Cataloging-in-Publication Data

Literacy as praxis : culture, language, and pedagogy / an edited
    volume by Catherine E. Walsh.
        p.   cm.
    Includes bibliographical references and index.
    ISBN 0-89391-648-X
    1. Literacy.   2. Sociolinguistics.   3. Language acquisition.
    4. Literacy programs.   5. Educational sociology.   I. Walsh,
    Catherine E.
    LC149.L4983   1990
    302.2'244—dc20   90-38886
                                                                          CIP

Ablex Publishing Corporation
355 Chestnut Street
Norwood, New Jersey 07648

Table of Contents

PART III. Pedagogy, Empowerment, and Social Change

Preface

This book highlights the sociopolitical nature of literacy and illuminates the potential in literacy for the empowerment of individuals and communities subordinated by race/ethnicity, culture, language, gender, and class. It is an attempt to address the specific reality of literacy for "language minority" populations—that is, for individuals and communities of color who utilize languages other than English in their daily interactions and relations. In many cities throughout the United States, these communities are now the majority in numbers, but clearly remain the minority in terms of power.

The initial conception of this text grew out of a series of literacy symposiums that the Multifunctional Resource Center at the University of Massachusetts at Amherst and Brown University sponsored during 1987–1989, and at which a majority of the authors of this text participated. As coordinator of some of these symposiums, I endeavored to give voice to a more critical view of literacy, one that recognizes how traditional forms of instruction can work to maintain literacy deficits and support the differential positioning of students within the social structure. In compiling readings and bibliographies for the symposiums, I was always dismayed at the lack of critical literature that specifically addresses language minorities. This book helps fill that void. Its goal is to challenge the ways bilingual, English as a second language, multicultural, and adult educators typically think about and practice literacy instruction, and to expand the dialogue about literacy and language minority students. In most cases, the essays herein are original to this volume and are not papers previously presented.

The text is organized into three major sections; my introduction in Chapter One affords an overall framework from which these sections follow. In the development of this chapter, I applied Mikhail Bakhtin's belief that literature cannot be understood outside the "total context of the entire culture of a given epoch" (Emerson & Holquist, 1986, p. 2) to literacy. I situate discourses of literacy within the sociohistorical and political moment in which we live, analyze the demographics of and approaches to "illiteracy," and examine the understandings which frame particular discourses and approaches. The focus is on elucidating what is meant by "literacy as praxis."

Part I, *Literacy, Culture, and Schooling*, considers how students' socially and culturally constituted identities and experiences differentially impact school success. In Chapter Two, "Cultural Diversity and School Experience," John U. Ogbu provides insight into the complex sociocultural realities of minority students and the ways these realities, historically, have been divergently positioned within the broader society. Through a comparative analysis of the primary and secondary cultural differences that exist between and within

v

particular racial/ethnic groups, Ogbu demonstrates that language and culture alone do not determine minority students' difficulties in school. Rather, he argues that poor school adjustment and academic performance are more closely connected to a subordinate status. Citing examples from local, national, and cross-cultural studies, Ogbu illustrates how primary and secondary cultural differences and societal attitudes work to promote academic success among immigrants and educational problems among subordinate or "involuntary" minorities (e.g., Puerto Ricans, Mexican Americans, Native Americans, and African Americans). And, it is the involuntary minorities who, because of frequent oppression, establish postures and identities of resistance.

One can certainly argue, however, that not all Puerto Ricans or Mexican, Native, and African Americans have academic or adjustment difficulties in school, exhibit oppositional identities or behaviors, or necessarily experience overt domination. Moreover, immigrant students are not monolithically successful, passive, nor impervious to racism, classism, and other forms of subordination. Yet, the fact that involuntary minorities continue to face higher rates of illiteracy, lower educational achievement, and leave school in greater numbers than do immigrants suggests the viability of Ogbu's analysis. This chapter is important precisely because it encourages an awareness of and discussion about ethnolinguistic minority students, not simply in terms of language or cultural identity (e.g. Latino or Hispanic), but in relation to the intersection of language, culture, race/ethnicity, and class with a socially, historically, and politically inscribed "status." Furthermore, it points to the need to raise this awareness among educators, students, parents, and communities, and to promote practices in schools, homes, and communities which can assist with encouraging academic success without demanding linear acculturation.

Gordon Wells' "Apprenticeship in Literacy" (Chapter Three) examines the relationship between young children's understanding of and experience with literacy and subsequent school achievement. As Wells details, within the social and cultural orientation of the home and community, children build initial conceptions of literacy which, in the case of minority children, frequently do not coincide with the implicit assumptions embodied in the curriculum and assumed in texts. While school success is partially contingent upon how reading and writing instruction is matched to children's understanding of print, it is also tied to "the inclusiveness of the model of literacy they have constructed on the basis of their experience of literacy events in the community." Wells thus contends that although culture informs literacy, it should not dictate or limit the functions of reading and writing. Conversely, school literacy practices should not discount divergent experience, nor should they conceptualize literacy solely in terms of skills or informational processes. Wells proposes a four-level taxonomy for categorizing the ways literacy should be defined operationally in education, and argues for the implementation of multidimensional modes of learning that derive from the relationship of speaking, thinking, and writing and that permit all students to become creative and critical thinkers and communicators.

Adeline Becker's Chapter Four affords a more intimate look at the inter-relation of literacy, culture, and schooling within one ethnolinguistic group. Through an ethnographic study of Portuguese children at home as well as in school, she discovered elements in operation, even in nonliterate households, which contributed to differential success in early reading. High parental expectations for children, in terms of household responsibilities, were found to promote higher expectations among children and to relate to reading achievement. It seems that the ability to successfully perform tasks rein-forced at home helped these children acquire the confidence to perform the tasks required within the school environment. However, enrollment in a Portuguese bilingual classroom with a native Portuguese teacher precluded cross-cultural and cross-class competition and the fulfillment of Anglo-teacher expectations. Yet, the divergencies in the manner the students ap-proached literacy and particularly reading demonstrate the multifarious na-ture of experience, even within common linguistic, cultural, and class group-ings. By looking at what these children actually did at home and relating these interactions and responsibilities to reading group assignment, Becker concretely illustrates the critical connection between lived experience and school performance.

Part II, *Towards the Development of Language, Reading, and Writing*, moves from the broader sociocultural analysis of student experience to a focus on pedagogy and classroom practice. The three authors in this section address ways to encourage the development of literacy for language minority chil-dren which build upon their knowledge, cultural, and linguistic base and which actively engage and challenge them in the process.

In "Creative Reading: A Relevant Methodology for Language Minority Children" (Chapter Five), Alma Flor Ada ideologically situates reading in-struction and contends that the overemphasis on isolated skills, irrelevant content, and on the English language has inhibited language minority stu-dents' literacy acquisition. She presents an alternative methodology that is theoretically grounded in the work of Paulo Freire and in a dynamic view of reality. In this method, reading is understood as a pleasure producing process which fosters oral language development, extends cultural, linguistic, and social confidence, is meaningful and engaging, and serves as a means for effecting positive changes in children's daily lives in school as well as in the community. She advocates that instruction be conducted in the native language, that materials be culturally relevant and interesting, and that parents be actively involved in the literacy process.

While native language literacy should be nurtured throughout students' education, the ability to read and write in English is crucial to success in school. In Chapter Six, "Contexts for Literacy Development for ESL Children," Sarah Hudelson helps translate current research and theory on the processes of reading and writing to English as a second language (ESL) classroom practice. By means of a continuum of ESL literacy experiences, she underlines the multiple aspects of literacy which ESL children must develop in order to achieve in school and outlines specific classroom instructional strategies which can advance this development.

Roser Salavert's discussion in Chapter Seven similarly draws from whole language theory and research. The focus, however, is the design and implementation of an innovative literacy approach which incorporates computer technology. Through the use of language experience and process writing strategies, she encouraged first- through third-grade Puerto Rican children to experiment with print and with text development on the computer. And, by means of a connected computerized speech output, the children received immediate auditory feedback in the same language in which they had written. Detailed in her chapter are individual examples of how the use of speech output (both in Spanish and in English) enhanced bilingual children's metalinguistic awareness, motivation and interest, literacy behaviors, and actual reading and writing. Samples of children's writing are included.

Part III, *Pedagogy, Empowerment, and Social Change*, locates literacy, learners, and schools/educational programs within the social structure. The authors in this section all explicitly recognize the connection between literacy, knowledge, and power, the potentiality of agency, and the transformative possibilities of pedagogy.

In Chapter Eight, for instance, Maritza Arrastia, Sara Schwabacher, and Ana Betancourt argue that reading and speech are individual processes, but that literacy and language are collective. For them, illiteracy is not just the inability to read—"it is the silence of a community's voice in print." Their chapter describes an approach to literacy which is based on the collective creation of a community literature in the classroom. Drawing from the work of Freire and of whole language educators, they detail the process by which culturally and linguistically diverse women come to dialogue about aspects of their lives and then, in conjunction with the teacher/participants, transform this dialogue into text. The numerous writings in the chapter reveal the power and significance of a literature constructed from the spoken word. Not only does this approach give valor and authority to the lived lives of the women, but it also enables them as learners to author the process of literacy.

In "Teaching How to Read the World and Change It: Critical Pedagogy in the Intermediate Grades" (Chapter Nine), Robert Peterson offers a practical discussion of how, in a public school context, upper elementary students might also assume control and ownership of learning and of their own lives. While Peterson similarly references Freire and whole language theory, this chapter brings us into his fifth-grade bilingual classroom. There, he explicates, through actual examples, how dialogue and reflection can replace lecture and repetition, how pedagogy can be situated in student- and community-based generative themes that are then used as the base for critical discussion, writing, reading, and exploration, and how students can be encouraged to think about the social nature of knowledge, question the contexts and contents of their lives, and take transformative action.

Finally, Rosa Torruellas, Rina Benmayor, Anneris Goris, and Ana Juarbe provide a powerful analysis of the impact of a literacy-for-empowerment program on the lives of poor, disenfranchised women from New York's El Barrio (Chapter Ten). Detailed are the philosophy and pedagogy which inscribe the Popular Education Program and its ethnographic, participatory research component through which ongoing documentation and reflection are made possible. It is in the interpretive narratives of four Puerto Rican women, however, that the real-life potential of critical literacy is evidenced. Through these testimonies, the women offer not only a subjective glimpse of what literacy has meant to them personally, but insight into the processes through which cultural, community, and gendered knowledge is affirmed and constructed and a collective, cultural citizenship is affirmed and expressed. Their voices speak to a coming to consciousness about their subjective conditions as well as the subordinated condition of their community, and they reflect the desire to do something about it. It is these women who, in conjunction with Torruellas, Benmayor, Goris, and Juarbe, give definition and hope to a pedagogy of literacy for social change—a pedagogy of praxis.

Catherine E. Walsh

REFERENCE

Emerson, C., & Holquist, M. (Eds.). (1986). *M. M. Bakhtin. Speech genres and other late essays.* Austin, TX: University of Texas Press.

1
Literacy as Praxis:[1]
A Framework
and an Introduction

Catherine E. Walsh
University of Massachusetts at Amherst

Me dicen que soy analfebeto, que no hablo inglés y no leo ni escribo, que soy estupido . . .
Después de oirlo tanto, ya estoy empezando a creer.
(They tell me I am illiterate, that I can't speak English or read or write, that I am stupid. . . . After hearing it so often, I am beginning to believe it.)

a Latino High School Student

In the last 15 years, literacy has come to be viewed as an issue of major national concern. We are told that schools are not properly teaching, that students are not adequately learning, and that too many adults lack functional skills. Increasing numbers of immigrants, refugees, Puerto Ricans and Chicanos are thought to further exacerbate the problem. Indeed, "literacy" is the new catchword in the educational literature, in the public media, and even in casual conversation. Reports abound on the "literacy crisis" of our nation and on the need to both refocus educational instruction on the "basics" and to enforce administrator, teacher, and student accountability. Television commercials encourage us to become "literacy" volunteers by either joining state or national campaigns or by just reading to our children. Newspaper articles frequently make direct associations between the high rates of crime, unemployment, and lack of literacy. Recently, I overheard two white, obviously middle-class teenagers on a Boston subway train talking about the "literacy problem" and their teacher's suggestion that they try and do something to help "them." It is this perceived difference between "them" and "us"—the illiterates and the literates—that, at least in part, positions the literacy crisis and shapes its dominant discourse.

But what is this crisis actually all about? Who are the "illiterates"? How

---

[1] The term *praxis* originated in the theoretical works of Karl Marx and was further developed by the Italian Communist Antonio Gramsci (1971). It refers to a combined reflection and action, the goal of which is a transformation of reality (Freire, 1970); that is, a critique of the status quo and an effort to build a more just society (Lather, 1986).

1

has the federal government positioned the problem? And what are the ambiguities in its focus and approaches?

Literacy has long been considered the cornerstone for educational as well as economic success. Yet, in the last 10 years, the United States has witnessed a decline in rates of literacy and an increase in the percentages of school dropouts and of poverty. The United States currently ranks 49th among the 158 United Nations' members in literacy level (Kozol, 1985) and, as compared to other world nations, has fallen into the double digit numbers in terms of rank in standard of living (Cohen & Rogers, 1983). Estimates suggest that approximately 33 percent of all adults are functionally or marginally illiterate; one million teenagers aged 12–17 cannot read above a third-grade level; and 15 percent of all high school graduates cannot read above the level of sixth grade (Kozol, 1985). The Committee for Economic Development reports that nearly 13 percent of 17-year-olds in school can be categorized as functionally illiterate while an additional 44 percent are marginally literate.[2] Furthermore, among those who drop out, approximately 60 percent cannot read or write.

In December 1988, then-President Ronald Reagan declared 1989 as the year of the young reader, extolling the importance of literacy and the government's supposed commitment to its promotion. His proclamation speech heralded reading as "a key to past, present, and future—a path into virtually limitless treasures of knowledge and inspiration" and an instrument of consciousness and of cultural transmission:

> Reading encourages wonder about the world, broadens awareness of others, and offers clues about the meaning of life. It helps transmit our cultural legacy and fosters inner resources of spirit, intellect, and imagination. . . . Now, as always, America needs a literate and knowledgeable citizenry fully conversant with and determined to defend our heritage of liberty and learning.

These comments make evident some of the contradictions which underlie the federal government's positioning of the literacy problem. For example, neither the state of literacy nor the minimal support given to literacy initiatives and to education in recent years are mentioned. Instead, a universal cultural legacy is suggested where reading becomes an issue of individual desire, interest, and good intentions rather than a process inextricably linked to broader structural concerns. By putting forth a common heritage of liberty and learning, Reagan ignores historical inequalities (of schooling and of social participation), the ethnic and linguistic diversity of the populace, as well as the differential literacy experience students bring to the classroom. According to him, there is no reason why any child who wants to read should not be able to do so.

---

[2] The Bureau of the Census defines functional illiteracy as demonstrative of less than a fifth-grade education.

Meanwhile, numerous commissioned and private reports continue to document difficulties among children and adults with regard to reading and writing. Implied is that schools used to teach these skills well but somehow got distracted during the 1960s and 1970s. These reports make clear that the economic stability of the nation is dependent upon the production of a literate workforce; the concerns voiced and the directives suggested are generally toward supplying corporate and business needs rather than the individual and collective needs and goals of students and their communities (e.g., National Commission on Excellence in Education, 1983; Carnegie Forum, 1986). Bastian, Fruchter, Gittell, Greer, and Haskins (1985) point to the problem with this focus:

> Given the disjuncture between economic and educational rewards, the effort to link school reform to the market value of education threatens to abandon large segments of American youth. If one argues that schools should reflect the logic of a polarizing labor market, the necessary conclusion is that we must reinforce competitive schooling—raise elitist barriers, add new stratification mechanisms, reward only the most exceptional or advantaged. (p. 55)

The pedagogical orientation of this school reform effort has been a back-to-basics curriculum coupled with minimum competency testing. Shor (1986) contends that this emphasis on basic skills under the guise of a "literacy crisis" and educational reform has served as a facade to cover up the real failure of the economy. Indeed, basic skill programs emphasize and display students' deficiencies and weaknesses, placing the blame on them for being unable to go after good jobs. The resultant effect is, as Shor points out, that until you read, write, speak, add, subtract, and divide like *cultured* citizens [my emphasis], you can not expect decent employment. Culture is thus removed from the realm of lived experiences; it is reified as the skills, abilities, and values of the white middle class (e.g., Hirsch, 1987). Hence, it is not by chance that the adult and child candidates for basic skill programs are most often low-income and minority. As Torruellas (1989) indicates, these individuals' and communities' difficulties with literacy are probably more a manifestation of oppression than the cause of economic exclusion.

Few if any reports on the literacy condition have addressed the changing racial/ethnic and linguistic character of U.S. schools and adult education programs or of the problems generated by the race, class, and gender divisions of the broader society. Current estimates suggest that approximately one-third of the U.S. school population are students of color. Roughly three million of these are students for whom English is a second language, a majority of whom are of Latino background.[3] Latino students are disproportionately poor—40 percent compared to 17 percent for Anglos (Hispanic

---

[3] Only an estimated one-third of linguistic minorities nationwide, however, receive any language support services (National Coalition on the Advocacy of Students, 1985).

Policy Development Project (HPDP), 1988)—and in urban areas, as many as 80 percent leave school before graduation. Fifty-six percent of Latino 17-year-olds are classified as functionally illiterate compared to 47 percent of African Americans and 13 percent of whites (Fueyo, 1988). Latino students are more likely to be retained in-grade and to enter high school overage (HPDP, 1988). Language is frequently cited as the major cause for Latino students' academic difficulties (e.g., see Business Council for Effective Literacy, 1989). However, the conservative mood of the nation has also provoked a resurgence of arguments of genetic inferiority.[4] Bilingual education programs address the linguistic needs of a small proportion of Latino youth and of other linguistic minorities, yet increasingly negative attitudes fostered by xenophobic movements like U.S. English coupled with waning federal support limit these programs' implementation, expansion, and effectiveness. Numerous studies indicate that language is not the primary cause for Latino students difficulties (e.g., see Cummins, 1986, 1989; Walsh, 1987, 1990). In fact, a large proportion of the Latino youth classified as illiterate and of those counted as dropouts are actually proficient speakers of English. While issues of language are clearly of significance, poverty is probably a greater predictor of educational failure, particularly for students of color.[5]

As with school-age students, the vast majority of illiterate adults are also poor; perspectives differ, however, as to compositions by race/ethnicity and linguistic status. These variant perspectives, important more for their illustrative than research value, demonstrate how the composition of who is illiterate can serve to differentially position the literacy problem. Kozol (1985), for example, contends that while 44 percent of blacks and 56 percent of Latino adults are either totally or partially illiterate, Latinos and all other

---

[4] The most recent proponent of the genetic inferiority argument is Lloyd Dunn, principal author of the Peabody Picture Vocabulary Test. In a monograph on the scholastic aptitude of Hispanic children he states: "Most Mexican immigrants to the U.S. are brown-skinned people, a mixture of American Indian and Spanish blood, while many Puerto Ricans are dark skinned, a mixture of Spanish, black, and some Indian. Blacks and American Indians have repeatedly scored about 15 IQ points behind Anglos and Orientals on individual tests of intelligence" (1987, p. 64).

[5] This is true for all groups. Asians, for example, the second largest ethnolinguistic minority group in the United States, have been repeatedly hailed as the model minorities because of their higher educational attainment and greater economic success. Disparities exist, however, among individual Asian groups. In an analysis of the 1980 Bureau of the Census figures, Vietnamese were found to have the highest poverty rate among Asian groups and one of the lowest levels of high school graduation. Moreover, the influx of poor and predominantly rural Vietnamese, Cambodian, and Laotian refugees in the 1980s have further challenged the Asian success myth. Between 1982 and 1985, dropout rates for Southeast Asians virtually doubled (Brand, 1987). While adult Asian immigrants are twice as likely as native-born Americans to have attended college, illiteracy is also a reality for many. Southeast Asian refugee men, for example, average six-and-a-half years of previous education and women less than four years. Hmong tribespeople from the highlands of Laos average less than a year-and-a-half of formal schooling and for the most part have no experience with a written code (Bliss, 1986).

"nonwhite" illiterates together comprise only a fifth or sixth of the 60 million illiterate or semiliterate adults in this country. He thus maintains that the frequent association by the media and others of the literacy crisis with immigration (either voluntary or forced through political conditions or slavery) is incorrect and serves to shift the burden of this problem away from a "national" (i.e., white, English-speaking) cultural legacy and heritage. Bliss (1986), on the other hand, cites figures from the U.S. Government Bureau of the Census which suggest that over a third of adults classified as illiterate do not speak English at home. Eighty-two percent of these are said to be born outside the United States with 21 percent entering the country within the last six years. An overwhelming 86 percent of non-English speakers illiterate in English are also characterized as illiterate in their native language (which means that 14 percent *can* read and write in their vernacular). Almost half are said to live in neighborhoods where languages other than English predominate. In this case, the literacy problem can be perceived as constituted by foreigners and non-English speakers and as brought on (and maintained) by the illiterates themselves, that is, they came without literacy and have not attempted to integrate into the English dominant society. Moreover, literacy seems to be defined only in reference to one language; those who cannot read and write in English (because they do not know the language) are considered illiterate regardless of literacy level in their native language. The remedy, as prescribed in most government-funded adult literacy programs, is intensive English instruction, job readiness, and acculturation. This remedy negates the pedagogical postulate that individuals illiterate in their mother tongue will learn to read and write best in a language they understand and that literacy skills are transferable across languages. Furthermore, it denies the rich cultural and linguistic experience students bring to the learning situation.

Literacy is and should be an issue of national interest. Yet in its common usage, literacy has become associated with an enigma requiring some kind of action or resolution. The illiterates which comprise the enigma are conceived as thorns in the backside of progress even though, as the Latino student's words at the outset of this chapter indicated, they may not even know they are part of the problem. This chapter presents a broader understanding of literacy, one that goes beyond a simple, measurable, have/have not condition. It situates literacy within the social dynamics of the society, the pedagogy of schools and adult education programs, and within the consciousness of educators and learners. It is oriented around several questions: What does the term "literacy" actually signify? What practices, approaches, and actions does it promulgate or engender? And how are these practices shaped by race/ethnicity, class, and language? These questions afford a framework for analyzing the ways society and its principal institution—schools—define, promote, and perpetuate discourses of and approaches to literacy. In other words, it is by examining the discourses and practices of literacy (and illiteracy) that we can begin to understand how pedagogies are socially constructed, ideologically positioned, and enabling or disempowering to their participants.

LITERACY—ITS MEANINGS AND PEDAGOGICAL PRACTICES

Literate adults may seldom contemplate how they came to literacy or what literacy might mean in daily life. For those who are literate, literacy is so much a part of existence that it is taken for granted. Thus, when we think about literacy it is generally in regard to an "other," to someone involved either in the learning or teaching process, or to someone who has been left out. There is an assumption that literacy somehow has a beginning and an end, that it is related to formal schooling, and that once it is acquired, the individual can get on with life or move on to higher studies. The mainstream definition of literacy in fact helps to produce these assumptions. Webster's Dictionary describes the condition of being literate as educated or cultured; able to read and write. Yet, as the Brazilian educator Paulo Freire details below, the attainment of literacy can signify much more than a reading and writing ability.

> To acquire literacy is more than to psychologically and mechanically dominate reading and writing techniques. It is to dominate these techniques in terms of consciousness; to understand what one reads and to write what one understands; it is to "communicate" graphically. Acquiring literacy does not involve memorizing sentences, words, or syllables—lifeless objects unconnected to an existential universe—but rather an attitude of creation and re-creation, a self-transformation producing a stance of intervention in one's context. (Freire, 1973, p. 48)

Paulo Freire's words illuminate a view of literacy which is purposeful, contextual, and transformative. It places the learner rather than the teacher or the text at the center of the literacy process. The learner is understood as an active, socially constituted agent—not a "patient recipient"—who comes to literacy through first "reading" the surrounding world and then reading and writing the words which help to define and express it. Literacy, in Freire's view, thus encompasses more than the skills associated with reading and writing per se; literacy is a creative activity through which learners can begin to analyze and interpret their own lived experiences, make connections between these experiences and those of others, and, in the process, extend both consciousness and understanding. In this sense, literacy is intimately connected to language itself, grounded in the historical and cultural background of the learner, and centered in the personal and social construction of meaning.

Freire is not alone in his belief that literacy and language are intertwined and that both are based in the development and communication of meaning. Whole language educators also argue that literacy is an integral component of language; that literacy has to do with our ability to use language in our negotiations with the world (Cambourne, 1988) and in making sense out of this world both inside and outside of schools. Whole language theory is constituted by the belief that language is actually learned from whole to part, through its use in real, functional, and meaningful situations (Altwerger, Edelsky, & Flores, 1987; Goodman, 1986a, 1986b). While reading and writing are part of this language so are a number of other behaviors (e.g., talking, listening, thinking, problem solving, and reflecting) that are related to learning in general. Whole language educators thus maintain that literacy cannot be broken down into separate subskills nor can it be judged by artificially contrived measurements. Instead it is best promoted through authentic events that stimulate, motivate, challenge, and engage the learners in their own development.

These perceptions of literacy obviously go counter to that which underlies the dominant discourse at work in most U.S. schools and educational programs. Emphasized in this discourse of literacy are discrete, mechanical skills, that are thought to be separately learnable and separately teachable (Altwerger, Edelsky, & Flores, 1987; DeFord, 1985). It is these skills and the instruments used to impart them (i.e., teachers, basal texts, and tests) which reduce the complexities of literacy to a single problem of reading instruction. Students are relegated to the position of objects, expected to repeat, memorize, and absorb prepackaged information in measured doses while teachers act as the technicians of this delivery system (Goodman, 1979). Standardized tests determine the extent of absorption and delivery.

The institution of schooling explicitly defines literacy as reading and writing. Yet students are often kept from the latter until the teacher or test determines they are "ready" to handle the material (itself usually foreign to students' experiences and realities). In elementary schools, for instance, literacy becomes synonymous in instructional terms with the commercial basal reader and its accompanying scripted guides, workbooks, charts, tests, and ditto masters, at use in over 90 percent of U.S. elementary classrooms (Shannon, 1989a).[6] Homogenized stories come replete with questions, activities, vocabulary lists, and tests to move students along sequentially through as many as 48 levels of literacy development (Smith, 1986). This "seatwork" takes up to 70 percent of the time allocated for reading instruction (Ander-

---

[6] Recent studies have found that over 74 percent of teachers using basal series overwhelmingly rely on the teachers guide for all of their literacy-related instruction. By so doing, teachers believe they are fulfilling administrators' expectations (e.g., see Educational Products Information Exchange, 1977; Shannon, 1989a). As Shannon (1989b) points out, "basals promise teachers, administrators, and state officials success in making every student literate with the ease of fingertip planning" (p. 630).

son, Hiebert, Scott, & Wilkinson, 1985). Bilingual students are often doubly subjected to this production in both English and their native language. Because of its levelized focus, basal instruction subsumes a major portion of the teachers' school day and of direct instruction. McDermott and Gospodinoff (1981) suggest that teachers' behavior is also shaped by basal reading groups, with quality and quantity of instruction increasing with group level. For students, identity is even frequently coupled with and shaped by the specific level and book of the basal series (e.g., Rainbows, Tigers, etc.).

By secondary school, students are expected to be "literate" and no longer in need of specific reading instruction; if they are not, reading remediation is sometimes provided—often through a special education referral (and label) and with an English language instructional approach of discrete skills orientation. Writing is formally introduced through classes in grammar and composition. Reading continues, however, to serve as the primary basis for all academic grouping with those who can demonstrate competence in reading generally in the college-bound track and those who cannot in basic or vocational education. As in the elementary school, poor and minority students overwhelmingly comprise these low-track groups. Jeannie Oakes (1985) contends that the objective of low-tracked classes is to prepare students for low-status jobs.

Adult literacy programs tend to resemble a combination of the elementary and secondary formats repeating, on a more individual basis, the instructional methods that contributed to the problem in the first place (Fingeret, 1984; Fueyo, 1988). Learners are placed on levels determined by multiple choice and fill-in-the-blank tests and instruction frequently follows a "drill-the-skill" methodology with competency measured by commercially developed worksheets. Again English is the most frequent language of instruction and the only language in which the federal government and most states will fund programs.

In the elementary, secondary, and adult contexts presented above, the creative potential for literacy is most often constrained as is an understanding of literacy's purposefulness and meaning in real life situations. Literacy, in both theory and practice, is treated as an isolated, hierarchical, and measurable entity, a commodity that is at once deemed necessary for school and later economic success in an English-dominant society but holds no immediately apparent connection to lived experiences and daily struggles.

The meaning of literacy as proffered by the traditional practices of formal education conflict with that framed in whole language classrooms and in Freire's work and writings. At issue here is not the identification of a generalized definition or, as Brian Cambourne (1988) cautions, the reification of the term. Rather, it is to illustrate how perspectives of and approaches to literacy are shaped by theoretical and ideological concerns which extend beyond the classroom walls. These concerns are related to beliefs and assumptions about the nature of knowledge, of people (i.e., teachers and students), and of experience and to the relations of power and of social and cultural control which these beliefs and assumptions both construct and incorporate.

The literacy orientation of traditional programs, for example, derives from a positivistic conception of knowledge (e.g., see Adorno & Horkheimer, 1972; Giroux, 1983; Roth, 1984), a rationality which situates knowledge as separate from the individual and from his/her actions, experience, and social context. It is considered quantifiable, verifiable information that is beyond students and which must be formally acquired. Implicit in this conception is a theory of how individuals learn and, as a result, how teachers should teach. The acquisition or "learning" of knowledge is treated as deductive and deterministic; instruction breaks "it" down into discrete pieces and feeds it to students in a systematic way. Learning thus becomes synonymous with an unquestioned absorption. Consequently, teaching is relegated to a transmission-oriented task, dependent not on the teacher's creativity or engagement with the students and the material but on the skill of imparting decontextualized matter so that students might replicate it in "standardized" tests of achievement. The acts of teaching and learning come to be stabilized through measurable productivity; the people who are the subjects of these acts, that is, teachers and students, come to be the objects of knowledge considered unable to act with or upon it. Students and teachers are controlled by the curriculum, its content, and methodology. The enigmatic processes involved in how one comes to know and in what is to be known are ignored because of the emphasis on a certainty that can be measured. As a result, learning and the iteration of textbook knowledge are rendered identical.

The dictates of this positivist rationality can also be witnessed in the ways experience is treated and understood. In a positivist pedagogy, little or no connection exits between knowledge and its practical, human purposes (Roth, 1984). Knowledge (as literacy) is treated as separate from lived experiences, as transcendent of culture and of history (Lather, 1986). As such, the diverse socioeconomic, cultural, and linguistic realities of students are thought to be extraneous to the "scientific" task of teaching (and of learning) and to the acquisition of "neutral" and "universal" content. The exception to this rule is, of course, if the students are young, white, middle class (and probably male) for it is this cultural capital that is a valued commodity in school settings. Shirley Brice Heath (1983, 1986) and Anderson and Stokes (1984), for example, found the literacy-related experiences commonly initiated and supported in white middle-class homes (e.g., book reading, labeling and describing, recounting and recasting past events, list making, etc.) to be recognized, supported, and expected in the early grades. Conversely, the divergent literacy experiences of poor and minority children were judged irrelevant, deficient, and even detrimental to learning in traditional classrooms. These studies as well as numerous others document the range of practices and supports for literacy development in working-class, minority, and immigrant homes (e.g., Auerbach, 1989; Delgado-Gaitan, 1987; Diaz, Moll, & Mehan, 1986; Taylor & Dorsey-Gaines, 1988). Yet schools tend to discount this experience as inferior or "impoverished." When students' cultural capital is compatible with that which schools disseminate, educational and life success is thought to be enhanced. However, when this capital differs from the prerequisite knowledge legitimized in school, school failure, academic difficulty, or problems with literacy are the result.

Within a positivist approach, instruction conveys that there is one desirable and "standard" language, culture, and class; only the experiences of this dominant group are consistently portrayed in texts, consistently reinforced in instruction, and consistently linked to "legitimate" knowledge. While other languages may, such as in bilingual education, for instance, be used for instruction, the knowledge they present and the methods they present it through are no different than that which occurs in the "mainstream." Moreover, their use is only transitional; the goal is to move students quickly into the "regular" or "standard" classroom. The underlying assumption of the positivist approach is, as Mortimer Adler (1982) points out, that "despite their manifold individual differences, the children are all the same in their human nature" (p. 42). This version of universality translates into a white, middle-class bias. Teacher practice becomes subsumed with how students can best master a given body of knowledge, a mastery dependent on certain predispositions which derive from an intimate familiarity with the dominant culture (Bourdieu & Passeron, 1977). For poor students, students learning English as a second language, and for many students of color, access to knowledge is thus mediated through cultural capital and curricular content and organized through grouping and tracking. Knowledge never exists independently of the interests and the individuals that produce and use it although positivists would have us think otherwise. Hence, in dismantling their discourse, we must question "neutral" and "universal" knowledge and its "scientific" directive, question who determines and maintains its impartiality and significance, and question how it is that schools so readily obtain, distribute, and sustain it.

Schools do not freely "choose" the knowledge to convey nor do they freely select its theoretical and practical orientation. School knowledge derives, at least in great part, from commercial texts whose content and approach is, in turn, designed to represent and sustain particular socioeconomic and political interests. The production of these texts is geared towards mass education through the realization of the largest possible profit. Five publishing companies controlled the yearly $400,000,000. U.S. basal market in 1989 (Goodman, in press). By the end of this same year, mergers of two of the companies further consolidated their monopoly. The context and content of basals is thus oriented toward how this industry constructs the "majority"; the orientation is overwhelmingly white, middle-class, and suburban although, in newer versions, faces may be colored, names changed, and city scenes added to increase distribution.[7] Its guidebook controlled presentation attempts to deskill teachers and students, while at the same time trying to insure standardization in practice and effective and efficient delivery. This adaptation of scientific management allows administrators to maintain strict control over teachers' work, and teachers to maintain control over students' increments of progress. In his study of reading instruction in the U.S., Patrick Shannon (1989a) connects this dependence on commercial texts to reification, formal rationality, and alienation.

> School personnel understand and describe reading instruction in a manner similar to how workers in other occupations discuss their work because they are all subject to the same societal influence—the process of rationalization. . . . [They] believe that commercial reading materials can teach because they have reified reading instruction as commercial materials. This illusion of instructional power is supported by school personnel's reification of the scientific inquiry concerning reading instruction as the directions for lessons in teacher's guidebooks and by the use of formal rationality in the organization of reading programs . . . This combination of reification and formal rationality alienates school personnel from a central feature of their work . . . —the development of students' literacy. Thus administrators expect the use of commercial reading materials and teachers use them because they have internalized the process of rationalization; and like other workers, they apply its business and scientific principles to the task of teaching reading. (p. 60)

Shannon's analysis outlines the explicit relations of control at work in schools and makes reference to the implicit power wielded by commercial materials but realized through the actions of teachers. This power lies not in the materials themselves but in the wider relations their use engenders, in the assumptions they promote, in the meanings they fashion, and in the actions they encourage. The emphasis on teachers as the agents and managers of commercial texts and students as the passive consumers, for example, may promote better classroom "control" only because it discourages questioning, creativity, teacher and student agency, and shuts out all forms of difference. The intent is to render students and teachers both voiceless and powerless by

---

[7] Basal publishers have also been quick to exploit bilingual education and the growing Spanish-speaking population. This reality was made clear recently in a conversation I had on an airplane with a representative of one of the major textbook publishing houses. While speaking of her company's advances in the production of Spanish language texts (translations of the English), she emphasized the large profit the southwest Hispanic population provided. "All we have to do is translate the texts and change the names," she said, "and the schools are buying them up like crazy."

encouraging conformity and a legitimation and maintenance of the status quo.

A different understanding of knowledge, people, and experience is inscribed in whole language-oriented pedagogies. In contrast to those organized by positivistic approaches, whole language educators present an integrated view of knowledge that is intimately connected to the individual, her/his social context, and personal/social needs. Knowledge acquisition, understood from a humanistic-scientific base (Goodman, 1986a), is thought to take place as part of a natural meaning-making process. Understanding in this view is an interaction between the prior knowledge and lived experience all learners bring to understanding and the new knowledge and experiences constructed and confronted in the school environment. Students are considered active participants rather than passive consumers, creating meaning through actual involvement; teachers facilitate, encourage, and position this construction through the promotion of purposeful activities of interest to students and through real writing and reading. Texts serve not as the sole source of knowledge but instead afford a supplement to and an extension of students' own experience and discovery.[8] Skills are an afterthought, developed in context when the need arises.

Whole language approaches construct a different kind of power relations. The mechanisms of control and the relations of power characteristic of material management and direct instruction are diffused in whole language classrooms. Without prescriptive mandates to follow, teachers are given the authority and responsibility to link theory with practice, to create the conditions for authentic, productive knowledge and language development, and to relinquish direct control over students' learning. As Ken Goodman (1986a) details, it is the learners themselves who build the "knowledge, knowledge structures, and strategies from the enriched environment the teacher helps to create" (p. 39). As independent and active learners students assume a more authoritative and responsible stance. Moreover, in the experiences which they bring and in the meanings which they construct, a sense of valor, authority, and personal power is also developed.

In practice, whole language pedagogies derive from the "natural" interconnectedness of knowledge, people, and experience and, in theory, portend to lack the relations of power and of control that inscribe more positivistic approaches. The discourse of whole language consists of a focus on learners and on the processes they go through in the classroom in constructing

---

[8] True whole language classrooms utilize student-created texts, real literature, and functional works as the core "text" material. Commercial publishers, however, have caught on to the developing teacher interest in whole language and now produce "whole language" basals, teachers' guides, and a host of accompanying materials. This pedagogical cooptation has resulted in the institutionalization of what are being called whole language approaches in a number of school districts throughout the country. Their focus and methodology, however, remains instrumentalist both in practice and in theoretical orientation.

knowledge and interpreting experience. However, this discourse does not necessarily consider as essential the social and cultural dynamics, realities, and struggles involved in the interpretation, definition, and understanding of the experiences. Experiences in most whole language classrooms are treated as neutrally lived and unequivocally understood and accepted while action is treated as meaning rather than praxis (Roth, 1984). And this is a problem because the power relations of the broader society are seen as benign as are the social inequalities which frame life outside the classroom.

Although some whole language teachers make the wider political connections among school, community, and society, the theoretical and practical perspective portrayed in the literature on whole language and organized in most classrooms presents this connection as primarily humanistic in nature (e.g., Cambourne, 1988; Goodman, 1986a; Newman, 1985). People's ability to act is thus conceived in limited terms, restricted to free will and to individual meaning making within and under what are considered to be optimal and nonproblematic conditions. Subjectivity is positioned as unitary and noncontradictory. In addition, the whole language orientation assumes that schools are insular and instructional rather than the political and ideological institutions that they are. Consequently, broader structural concerns are absent. Students are not usually exhorted or invited to question the contexts of their lives, the curriculum, or the inequities of the social structure nor are the meanings they produce usually revealed as partially shaped by societal power relations (Giroux, 1983). Instead, power inequities of race/ethnicity, language, class, and gender are generally played down while an idealistic, cohesive plurality is celebrated (e.g., Harmon & Edelsky, 1989). Language is conceived as a neutral medium of expression and a way to present knowledge rather than as a constitutive medium for instruction and for thought and as a site of struggle (Volosinov, 1973). Non-native speakers of English, for example, may be permitted to read and write in their mother tongue but the differential meanings and experiences which underlie language use and the differential ways these meanings and experiences are both struggled with and perceived at home, in the community, and in the wider society tend to go unrecognized. Culture comes to be depoliticized, severed from the social and class relationships that inform it. In this context, culture is addressed, as Eric Wolf (1982) describes, as "integrated totalities in which each part contributes to the maintenance of an organized, autonomous, and enduring whole." The problem is that such depiction of culture, as well as of language and of power inequities in general, can only work to dismiss the antagonisms we live in. Moreover, the treatment of all perspectives, contributions, and forms of knowledge as valid, despite the fact that in the social world they are not, works to conceal and deny the lived lives of the students and of their communities.

Holistic theory and technique offer much for actively involving learners in literacy as a form of meaning/knowledge production. Yet taken alone, whole language's action/meaning orientation threatens to isolate learners, teachers, communities, and schools from structural components of society and from the changing power relations that are explicitly and implicitly present in everyday living.

Critical theory provides the foundation for a more vital view of knowledge, people, and experience—one that is connected to practical human needs, that is, to the individual and structural influences that operate both upon and within society (Giroux, 1983; Roth, 1984). The postpositivist theoretical understanding that underlies what are sometimes referred to in the United States as critical pedagogies or in Latin America as programs of popular education characterizes knowledge as socially and culturally constructed, historically generated, and ideologically based (see Habermas, 1971, 1979; Hesse, 1980; Lather, 1986).[9] This contrasts with both the "given" notion of knowledge framed in the positivistic discourse of literacy and its interpretation in the humanistic-scientific discourse of whole language as the mere reflection of interaction and experience (i.e., meaning). Critical approaches recognize knowledge as always partial and as bound in complex ways to the social, cultural, and linguistic conditions and to the actions that position meanings and interpretations (Walsh, 1990). In coming to know, learners draw both from their personal histories and their lived experiences, and from what they have taken on as their own within particular social, cultural, and economic formations. The meanings and interpretations that emerge in this production are not singular, complete, or stable; they beckon those which have come before and are constantly shifted, modified, and reworked as experiences become lived and organized in the individual's consciousness. Bennett and Pedraza (1984) suggest that in this ongoing social process is a different view of culture.

Embodied in knowledge itself are relations of power and of control. Michel Foucault (1980) speaks of this power as present not only between those who know and those who do not but as more concretely grounded in the conditions which make possible this dichotomy. Knowledge is inseverably tied to the social, political, cultural, and economic conditions of the

---

[9] While the conceptual roots of popular education derive in part from Paulo Freire's early work in and writings about Brazil and Chile (referred to at the time as "Education for Liberation"; e.g., Freire, 1969), its development and present connotation are linked to more explicit political dimensions, that is, to class conflict and to the actual organization of popular power among peasants and Indigenous movements.

Some authors have attempted to link popular education theoretically to the action and democratic-oriented pedagogy of what is sometimes called the New School Movement, characterized by the writings of, among others, Dewey, Freinet, Montessori (see Paiva, 1982; Matthews, 1980). (Similarly, some U.S. educators assume a direct connection between critical pedagogy and whole language.) As Freire points out, although these attempts offer much to improve methodology and teacher/student relations, they clearly lack an analysis and "critique of capitalist production" (in Torres, 1988, p. 41, my translation).

society; and the ways it is organized in educational institutions reproduces and maintains dominant interests. Critical educators' recognize these interests as present in schools and in adult education programs and as having a disproportionate and limiting effect on poor students, women, English-as-a-second-language (ESL) learners, and students of color.[10] Recent work demonstrates that people are not passive to this domination but develop active forms of resistance and of counter knowledge production (e.g., Attinasi, Pedraza, Poplack, & Pousada, 1982; Aulestia, 1990; Britzman, 1986; Ellsworth, 1989; Everhart, 1983; Fine, 1987; Giroux, 1983; McLaren, 1989; Sola & Bennett, 1985; Walsh, 1987, 1990; Weiler, 1988; White, 1984; Willis, 1977).

The discourse of critical literacy has come to be largely associated in the Western world with Paulo Freire. Although Freire's actual work in literacy has been with peasants in his native Brazil and with adult literacy campaigns in other parts of Latin America and Africa, U.S. educators have attempted to adapt his pedagogical tenets and draw from his theoretical understanding (e.g., see Chapters 5, 8, 9, & 10, this volume). The pedagogical tenets and theoretical understanding derive from a view of learners as people who bring to the learning situation the contexts and contents of lives lived within communities that are positioned by and situated within a wider social structure. Illiteracy is tied to the unequal exercise of power and to the oppressive relations within this structure. Literacy, according to Freire, is a political project: It involves as much a theorizing about these lived lives—a "reading of the world"—as it does the reading and writing of words to describe it. Freire refers to this process of coming to think critically about the world and the place of people within it as "conscientization." The political nature of literacy also requires action within the world. For Freire, learners are sociohistorical, creative, and transformative beings, and literacy is the process through which these learners can come to critically reflect on reality and take actions to change oppressive conditions. The ultimate goal of literacy is thus empowerment and social transformation.

In its practice, the critical approach to literacy draws extensively (although not exclusively) from Freire. In orientation, it is both dialectical and participatory. It challenges learners and teachers to question the contexts and contents of their lives both inside and outside the classroom and to theorize about experiences and the contradictory nature of their subjectivities, cultural expectations and identities, actions, interpretations, and ideologies (i.e., their consciousness). Because knowledge is considered in critical theory as

---

[10] This is not to suggest that middle-class youth are not also affected by the relations of power and control which define our technocratic society. As Larkin (1979) explains: "[Middle-class] students experience a two-fold alienation: from adult society wherein lies the power, and from each other as invidious competition and mobility undercut authenticity and understanding of each other" (p. 210).

always problematic, teachers involved in critical pedagogies invite learners to question and to examine, in light of their own experiences and understandings, both individually and collectively, the overt and the hidden knowledge that schools present. "Minority" students might ask, for instance, why it is that texts never adequately present the histories of their ancestors or portray the realities in which they currently live and why their languages remain as devalued cultural capital. They might also take action to document an alternative perspective. Of necessity then, is as Freire points out, a requisite understanding on the part of teachers of "the act of knowing," including "knowing for what, with whom, in favor of who, against who . . ." (in Torres, 1988, p. 60, my translation). This understanding permits in dialectical terms, a constant creation, mediation, and refashioning of practices and of pedagogy through a process that encourages a personal and collective reflection (by teachers as well as students) on the differing (and sometimes conflictive) meanings, views, and experiences that underlie both lived and portrayed realities. Moreover, this approach requires an awareness of the imperfections, incompleteness, and potentialities of meanings (Held, 1980), and a realization of people's role in creating and using meaning. This awareness is particularly important for students and teachers involved in the negotiation of second language culture learning and raced, classed, gendered, and aged-inscribed perspectives.

The participatory nature of a critical literacy derives from the interaction among teachers, students, and methodology. It is students and teachers who together are in control of and actively engaged in shaping the pedagogy, in learning about themselves, their realities, and the social world, in developing collective analyses, and in working towards structural transformation (Hall, 1981). This requires a rebalancing of student/teacher relations and an acceptance by teachers that they too have much to learn. The fact of power clearly cannot be negated. However, as Maxine Greene (1986) explains, educators must seek ways to relax the controls.

> We can undertake a resistance, a reaching out towards becoming persons among other persons . . . To engage with our students as persons is to affirm our own incompleteness, our consciousness of spaces still to be explored, desires to be tapped, possibilities still to be open and pursued. (p. 440)

Involved is a recognition of the reciprocity between the knower and the known—a mutual negotiation of meaning and of power (Lather, 1986) that is tied not just to what teachers teach but also to the productive meanings that culturally and socially diverse students bring to and produce within classrooms (Giroux, 1988).

Students and teachers are understood in this discourse as actors engaged not only in the building of personal meanings or in the production of meaning in schools but also in the production and organization of the means and the conditions necessary for learning itself. Their agency and power, in other words, is as much social and cultural as it is individual. It is grounded in community ways of knowing and in the vernacular forms of thought and linguistic expression. And it is the experience that emerges because of agency that constitutes the pedagogical base from which knowledge and power are constructed and from where social and cultural control can be struggled with and interrogated. Literacy is an integral part of this process, providing not just the basic skills but the elements necessary to comprehend, to critique, and to intervene in the world. Such a perspective of literacy requires a creative practice which can be personally and socially meaningful and empowering to the participants. In theory, the contents and orientation of this practice is directed toward challenging the power relations of traditional schooling. In practice, it therefore should relate to the contexts of the learners' lives, be interesting, purposeful, and engaging, incite dialogue and struggle around meanings, interpretations, and identities (Simon, 1987) and promote among the learners a critical understanding of their relationship to the broader society, and of their and its political nature, and transformative possibilities. Herein lie potentialities that positivistic and whole language approaches to literacy fail to recognize or imagine.

A critical approach to literacy by no means offers a recipe list for educators to follow, nor does it suggest a singular pedagogy or method. It is also not my intention to present a possible one. However, because the theoretical direction of this volume is toward a critical view of literacy, I think it important to present in more concrete terms the major understandings that both inform and position this discourse and, shape its practice.

First and foremost is the realization that there is no neutral education and, as such, no neutral approach to literacy instruction. Education involves people who in the act of knowing and creating, draw upon their histories and on the meanings and experiences which derive from life lived in a world imbricated with social, cultural, economic, political, and ideological interests. Education should always signify interventions.

Second, the critical approach begins with the recognition of the complex and often contradictory dynamics of and relations among learners, teachers, communities, schools, and society. Entailed here is the development of an understanding and a discourse that can address the multifarious meanings of experience and of knowledge production. An awareness, in other words, that the social, cultural, and ideological conditions which shape the development of meaning at home, in the community, and at school are influenced by structural forces at work in society. These conditions are also fashioned by and mediated through the learners' own linguistic, cultural, and social observations, interactions and struggles in settings which are by no means monolithic, homogeneous, or static in substance or in composition. Cultural communities, for instance, do not simply inscribe singular perspectives, learning styles, or linguistic forms in their members nor do schools unproblematically impart the dominant ideology by means of compliant teachers and to passively receptive students. As institutions composed of human beings, communities and schools are constituted by and through relations of production and resistance as well as reproduction.

Third, a critical approach has the potentiality for generating social knowledge forms which can challenge the categories through which individuals perceive, understand, and evaluate social reality (Bennett & Pedraza, 1984). Patti Lather (1986) refers to this as an emancipatory knowledge which "increases awareness of the contradictions hidden or distorted by everyday understandings and . . . directs attention to the possibility for social transformation inherent in the present configuration of social processes" (p. 259). This involves a critical reappropriation of knowledge outside immediate experience (Simon, 1987). Through this generation and reappropriation, individuals can begin to theorize about the divergent understandings different groups have of the world and of their and their community's place within it. They can also come to understand the way these understandings are positioned by race, ethnicity, class, and gender, shaped by relations of power, and constrained or enabled by the learners' abilities to express their understandings either in written or oral form.

Fourth, a critical approach depends upon helping students interrogate, challenge, and diffuse the power wielded by and organized within the educational institution. This entails developing strategies to analyze the multiple ways race, ethnicity, class, gender, and language are used in school to serve dominant interests, to examine what textbooks lack as well as what they contain, and to investigate how particular instructional discourses, practices, and policies work to silence certain class and cultural groups. It also requires an understanding of power as an active process in which there is a "continuing shifting balance of resources and practices in struggle for previously specified ways of naming, organizing, and experiencing social reality" (Giroux, 1985, p. 35). This shifting of power makes possible new relationships among teachers, students, and their communities. These relationships are characterized by mutual respect and reciprocal, dialogic exchange.

And fifth, the emphasis in a critical approach is on a heightened awareness and enlightened action. This approach makes possible an expansion of what it means to be literate beyond a functional capacity to read and to write. In other words, it fosters a reading of reality itself which goes beyond merely producing or reproducing the existing social relations and the "legitimate" knowledge which schools frame but instead encourages learners to look at the world around them in critical ways, to think "loudly" (Ada, 1989) about this world, and to know that their actions and involvement can make a difference.

The discourse of critical literacy challenges the theoretical foundations and the practical effectiveness of the "official" discourses at work in most public schools and adult education programs. It challenges the power relations that differentially position teachers, minority learners, and minority communities and it breaks down the "them" and "us" categories that frame the "literacy crisis." Most importantly, it permits a pedagogy that gives space to traditionally silenced voices and gives credence to the languages students speak and the cultural and social conditions in which they live and struggle. This discourse allows the possibility of "literacy as praxis" and offers hope for a more equitable world to come.

REFERENCES

Ada, A. F. (1989, June 2). *Empowering minority students: Critical pedagogy perspectives.* Presentation given at Long Beach, CA.

Adler, M. (1982). *The Paideia proposal.* New York: Macmillan.

Adorno, T. W., & Horkheimer, M. (1972). *Dialectic of enlightenment.* New York: Seabury Press.

Altwerger, B., Edelsky, C., & Flores, B. (1987). Whole language: What's new? *Reading Teacher, 41*(2), 144–154.

Anderson, A., & Stokes, S. (1984). Social and institutional influences on the development and practice of literacy. In H. Goelman, A. Oberg, & F. Smith (Eds.), *Awakening to literacy* (pp. 24–37). Portsmouth, NH: Heinemann.

Anderson, R., Hiebert, E., Scott, J., & Wilkinson, I. (1985). *Becoming a nation of readers: The report of the Commission on Reading.* Washington DC: National Institute of Education.

Attinasi, J., Pedraza, P., Poplack, S., & Pousada, A. (1982). *Intergenerational perspectives on bilingualism: From community to classroom.* New York: Center for Puerto Rican Studies.

Auerbach, E. R. (1989). Toward a social-contextual approach to family literacy. *Harvard Educational Review, 59*(2), 165–181.

Aulestia, J. (1990). *From the voices of the oppressed: Cultural and educational experiences of indigenous peoples in the Andean region of Ecuador.* Unpublished doctoral dissertation, University of Massachusetts at Amherst.

Bastian, A., Fruchter, N., Gittell, M., Greer, C., & Haskins, K. (1985). *Choosing equality: The case for democratic schooling.* New York: New World Foundation.

Bennett, A., & Pedraza, P. (1984). Discourse, consciousness, and literacy in a Puerto Rican neighborhood. In C. Kramarae, M. Schulz, & W. M. O'Barr (Eds.), *Language and power* (pp. 243-259). Beverly Hills, CA: Sage.

Bliss, B. (1986, June 6–7). Literacy and the limited English population: A national perspective. In *Issues of Parent Involvement and Literacy.* Proceedings of the Symposium held at Trinity College, Washington DC.

Bourdieu, P., & Passeron, J. C. (1977). *Reproduction in education, society, and culture.* Beverly Hills, CA: Sage.

Brand, D. (1987, August 31). The new whiz kids. *TIME Magazine,* p. 49.

Britzman, D. (1986). Cultural myths in the making of a teacher: Biography and social structure in teacher education. *Harvard Educational Review, 56*(4), 442–456.

Bureau of the Census. (n.d.). *We the Asian and Pacific Islander Americans.* Washington, DC: U.S. Department of Commerce.

Business Council for Effective Literacy. (1989, April). *Newsletter.* New York: Author.

Cambourne, B. (1988). *The whole story. Natural learning and the acquisition of literacy in the classroom.* New York: Ashton Scholastic.

Carnegie Forum on Education and the Economy. (1986). *A nation prepared: Teachers for the 21st century.* New York: Carnegie Forum.

Cohen, J., & Rogers, J. (1983). *On democracy: Toward a transformation of American society.* New York: Penguin Books.

Cummins, J. (1986). Empowering minority students: A framework for intervention. *Harvard Educational Review, 56,* 18–36.

Cummins, J. (1989). *Empowering minority students.* Sacramento: California Association for Bilingual Education.

Delgado-Gaitan, C. (1987). Mexican adult literacy: New directions for immigration. In S. Goldman & H. Trueba (Eds.), *Becoming literate in English as a second language* (pp. 9–32). Norwood, NJ: Ablex.

DeFord, D. (1985). Validating the construct of theoretical orientation in reading instruction. *Reading Research Quarterly, 20*(3), 351–367.

Diaz, S., Moll, L., & Mehan, K. (1986). Socio-cultural resources in instruction: A context-specific approach. In California Department of Education (Ed.), *Beyond language: Social and cultural factors in schooling language minority children* (pp. 187–230). Los Angeles, CA: Evaluation, Dissemination and Assistance Center.

Dunn, L. (1987). *Bilingual Hispanic children on the U.S. mainland: A review of research on their cognitive, linguistic, and scholastic development.* Circle Pines, MN: American Guidance Service.

Educational Products Information Exchange (EPIE). (1977). *Report on a national survey of the Nature and Quality of Instructional Materials Used by Teachers and Learners* (Tech. Report #76). New York: EPIE Institute.

Ellsworth, E. (1989). Why doesn't this feel empowering? Working through the repressive myths of critical pedagogy. *Harvard Educational Review, 59*(3), 297–324.

Everhart, R. (1983). *Reading, writing, and resistance.* Boston: Routledge and Kegan Paul.

Fine, M. (1987). Silencing in public schools. *Language Arts, 64*(2), 157–174.

Fingeret, A. (1984). *Adult literacy education: Current and future directions.* Columbus, OH: ERIC Clearinghouse on Adult, Career and Vocational Education.

Foucault, M. (1980). *Power/knowledge.* New York: Pantheon Books.

Freire, P. (1969). *La Educación como practica de la libertad.* Mexico: Siglo Veintiuno Editores.

Freire, P. (1973). *Education for critical consciousness.* New York: Continuum.

Freire, P. (1970). *Pedagogy of the oppressed.* New York: Seabury Press.

Fueyo, J. M. (1988). Technical literacy versus critical literacy in adult basic education. *Journal of Education, 170*(1), 107–118.

Giroux, H. A. (1983). *Theory and resistance in education.* South Hadley, MA: Bergin and Garvey Press.

Giroux, H. A. (1985). Critical pedagogy, cultural politics, and the discourse of experience. *Journal of Education, 167*(2), 22–40.

Giroux, H. A. (1988). *Schooling and the struggle for public life. Critical pedagogy in the modern age.* Minneapolis: University of Minnesota Press.

Goodman, K. (1979). The know-more and the know-nothing movements in reading: A personal response. *Language Arts, 56,* 657–663.

Goodman, K. (1986a). *What's whole in whole language.* Portsmouth, NH: Heinemann Educational Books.

Goodman, K. (1986b). Basal readers: A call for action. *Language Arts, 63*(4), 358–363.

Goodman, K. (in press). Access to literacy: Basals and other barriers. *Theory into Practice.*

Gramsci, A. (1971). *Selections from prison notebooks.* New York: International Publishers.

Greene, M. (1986). In search of a critical pedagogy. *Harvard Educational Review, 56*(4), 427–441.

Habermas, J. (1971). *Theory and practice.* Boston: Beacon Press.

Habermas, J. (1979). *Communication and the evolution of society.* Boston: Beacon Press.

Hall, B. (1981). Participatory research, popular knowledge, and power: A personal reflection. *Convergence, 14*(3), 6–19.

Harmon, S., & Edelsky, C. (1989). The risks of whole language literacy: Alienation and connection. *Language Arts, 66*(4), 392–406.

Heath, S. B. (1983). *Ways with words: Language, life, and work in communities and classrooms.* New York: Cambridge University Press.

Heath, S. B. (1986). Sociocultural contexts of language development. In California Department of Education (Ed.), *Beyond language: Social and cultural factors in schooling language minority students* (pp. 143–186). Los Angeles: EDAC.

Held, D. (1980). *Introduction to critical theory: Horkheimer to Habermas.* Berkeley: University of California Press.

Hesse, M. (1980). *Revolution and reconstruction in the philosophy of science.* Bloomington, IN: Indiana University Press.

Hirsch, E. D. (1987). *Cultural literacy: What every American needs to know.* Boston: Houghton Mifflin Company.

Hispanic Policy Development Project (HPDP). (1988). *Closing the gap for U.S. Hispanic youth.* Washington, DC: Author.

Kozol, J. (1985). *Illiterate America.* Garden City, NY: Anchor.

Larkin, R. W. (1979). *Subordinate youth in cultural crisis.* New York: Oxford University Press.

Lather, P. (1986). Research as praxis. *Harvard Educational Review, 56*(3), 257–273.

Matthews, M. (1980). *The Marxist theory of schooling, a study of epistemology and education.* Sussex: Harvester Press.

McDermott, R., & Gospodinoff, K. (1981). Social contexts for ethnic borders and school failure. In H. Trueba, G. P. Guthrie, & K. Hi Pei Au (Eds.), *Culture and the bilingual classroom: Studies in classroom ethnography* (pp. 212–230). Rowley, MA: Newbury House.

McLaren, P. (1989). *Life in schools. An introduction to critical pedagogy in the foundations of education.* New York: Longman.

National Coalition on the Advocacy of Students (NCAS). (1985). *Barriers to excellence: Our children at risk.* Boston: NCAS.

National Commission on Excellence in Education. (1983). *A nation at risk: The imperative for educational reform.* Washington, DC: U.S. Department of Education.

Newman, J. (Ed.). (1985). *Whole language: Theory in use.* Portsmouth, NH: Heinemann.

Oakes, J. (1985). *Keeping track: How schools structure inequality.* New Haven, CT: Yale University Press.

Paiva, V. (1982). *Paulo Freire y el Nacionalismo Desarrollista.* México: Editorial Extemporáneos.

Roth, R. (1984). Schooling, literacy acquisition, and cultural transmission. *Journal of Education, 166*(3), 291–308.

Shannon, P. (1989a). *Broken promises. Reading instruction in twentieth-century America.* South Hadley, MA: Bergin and Garvey.

Shannon, P. (1989b). The struggle for control of literacy lessons. *Language Arts, 66*(6), 625–634.

Shor, I. (1986). *Culture wars. School and society in the conservative restoration 1969–1984.* Boston: Routledge and Kegan Paul.

Simon, R. (1987). Empowerment as a pedagogy of possibility. *Language Arts, 64*(4), 370–380.

Smith, F. (1986). *Insult to intelligence. The bureaucratic invasion of our classrooms.* Portsmouth, NH: Heinemann.

Sola, M., & Bennett, A. (1985). The struggle for voice: Narrative, literacy, and consciousness in an East Harlem school. *Journal of Education, 167*(1), 88–110.

Taylor, D., & Dorsey-Gaines, C. (1988). *Growing up literate. Learning from inner-city families.* Portsmouth, NH: Heinemann.

Torres, R. M. (1988). *Educación popular. Un encuentro con Paulo Freire.* Buenos Aires: Bibliotecas Universitarias, Centro Editor de América Latina.

Torruellas, R. (1989). Alfabetización de adultos en 'El Barrio,' ¿Destrezas básicas o educación popular? *CENTRO de estudios puertorriqueños bulletin, 2*(6), 66–70.

Volosinov, V. N. (1973). *Marxism and the philosophy of language.* Cambridge, MA: Harvard University Press.

Walsh, C. E. (1987). Schooling and the civic exclusion of Latinos: Toward a discourse of dissonance. *Journal of Education, 169*(2), 115–131.

Walsh, C. E. (1990). *Pedagogy and the struggle for voice: Issues of language, power, and schooling for Puerto Ricans.* South Hadley, MA: Bergin and Garvey.

Weiler, K. (1988). *Women teaching for change: Gender, class, and power.* New York: Bergin and Garvey (an imprint of Greenwood Publishing Group).

Willis, P. (1977). *Learning to labour: How working class kids get working class jobs.* New York: Columbia University Press.

White, E. F. (1984). Listening to the voices of Black feminism. *Radical America, 18*(2–3), 7–25.

Wolf, E. (1982). *Europe and the people without history.* Berkeley: University of California Press.

Part I
Literacy, Culture, and Schooling

2

Cultural Diversity and School Experience*

John U. Ogbu
Department of Anthropology & Survey Research Center,
University of California, Berkeley

INTRODUCTION

This chapter addresses two interrelated issues. First, the belief that there are different types of minorities who are distinguished by different types of cultural and language differences; second, that an understanding of the cultural and language differences characteristic of each type of minority provides the basis for more effective educational services. Before I elaborate on these issues I will explain the types of research we do in anthropology on minority education and how they have led me to focus on the comparative aspects of minority culture and education.

Anthropologists do different kinds of research in education. Some address the question of cultural and language differences and the consequences of these differences for the school experience of children, especially minority children. Many anthropologists have conducted excellent ethnographic studies showing how cultural and language differences lead to cultural and communication conflicts in school and classroom and how the conflicts, in turn, adversely affect minority children's schooling outcomes. Other anthropologists start from the point where the first type of research ends to search for solutions. This second type of research is basically an intervention research: It asks the question, what can be done to eliminate the cultural and language conflicts encountered in teaching and learning in classrooms and schools serving minority children? The purpose of this type of research is to discover what works for minority children's education through cultural understanding and the use of cultural knowledge and materials for curriculum, teaching, communication, social interaction, and the like. This has sometimes involved the cooperative efforts of anthropologists and teachers.

---

* This chapter is a revised version of a keynote talk given at the N.E, Multifunctional Resource Center Literacy Symposium, Boston, MA, May 18, 1987.

The third type of anthropological research is what may be called *comparative research*. It is not concerned primarily or immediately with finding "solutions" to the problems that minority children have in school and in the classroom, although the results of such comparative studies can be used to provide solutions to the problems. But the main objectives of this third type of research are, first, to understand the nature of the problem encountered in the education of minority children; second, to understand how these problems originated; and, third, to understand how and why they persist among some minority groups but not among others.

My own work on minority education has been largely of the third type. In analyzing my ethnographic data on minority school experience as well as in analyzing other researchers' studies of minority school experience in the United States and elsewhere, I have been impressed by the variability in the persistence of cultural and language conflicts and in the school performance among minority groups. This discovery has led to a number of questions, such as: Why do some minorities experience more learning problems in school than others because of cultural and language differences? Why do some minorities do relatively well in school in spite of cultural and language differences, while other minorities do not do so well? What kinds of problems are experienced because of cultural and language differences by those minorities that do relatively well in school? These and related questions are addressed in the following pages.

EVIDENCE OF VARIABILITY IN SCHOOL PERFORMANCE

What evidence do we have that there are differences in the school performance of minority groups who face cultural, language, and other barriers in school and who also face social and economic barriers in the wider society? Evidence for the variability exists both for minority groups in the United States and for minority groups in other countries. In the United States the evidence comes from local studies (Gibson, 1983; Ogbu, 1974) and national studies (Coleman, et al., 1966; Heller, Holtzman, & Messick, 1982; Slade, 1982; Wigdor & Garner, 1982). Several studies in other countries provide good evidence that the variability exists outside the United States (Guthrie, 1985; Mat Nor, 1983; Ogbu, 1978; V. B. Penfold, 1981, personal communication; Skutnabb-Kangas and Toukoma, 1976; Tomlinson, 1982; Wan Zahid, 1978; Woolard, 1981).

Evidence from Local Studies:

Ogbu (1986) reports that in the 1930s in Stockton, both Asian students (Chinese and Japanese) and Mexican-American students experienced difficulties in school because of limited proficiency in English. A study by the local school district in 1947, however, showed that the language problems had disappeared among the Asians but persisted among Mexican-Americans (Stockton Unified School District, 1948). In fact, Asian students were by this time doing so well academically that their representation at the junior college level had risen to 250 percent of their expected rate. In contrast, less than five percent of the Mexican-Americans in the seventh and eighth grades made it to the junior college. Local blacks did not do much better. In my own ethnographic study in the same community between 1968 and 1970, Chinese and Japanese students were found to be doing considerably better in school than blacks and Mexican-Americans (Ogbu, 1974, 1977).

Similarly, Gibson (1983) found that Punjabi students in a Californian high school were doing well academically in spite of their cultural and language differences. As she notes: "Almost all Punjabi youths graduate from high school—regardless of how recently they arrived in the United States— Punjabi children raised and educated from first grade in Valleyside (do better than those who came to America later). Many do quite well academically, as well as in fact their mainstream counterpart, or, in the case of boys, even better" (p. 3). She sums up the Punjabi school success as follows:

> Punjabi youngsters are successful in school, by and large, in spite of sharing group characteristics which many researchers have found to correlate with school failure—parents with low income, low status jobs, little formal education, little or no proficiency in English, and a cultural tradition regarded as "backward" and un-American by some in the larger society. Not all Punjabis in Valleyside fit this description, but enough do that their success strategies merit serious analysis. (p. 3)

Gibson also addresses *comparatively* some issues of cultural differences and cultural discontinuities. Take, for example, the problem of differences in the meaning of "eye contact" between teachers and minority students. Byers and Byers (1972) have used this to explain why Puerto Rican children have learning difficulties in school. According to them, Anglo children are brought up to look at an adult directly when being reprimanded; if they fail to do so, it means an admission of guilt and a sign of disrespect. Among Puerto Ricans, on the other hand, children learn to look respectfully down when they are being chastised. It is suggested then that problems arise for Puerto Rican children when teachers who are not familiar with their culture interpret their behavior—looking respectfully down—as disrespectful or as an admission of guilt. It is concluded that since what is polite for the Puerto Ricans is considered rude by Anglos, teachers and Puerto Rican children may unwittingly "misinterpret one another's behavior, thus jeopardizing learning transactions."

Punjabi students in Valleyside seem to face similar problems in coeducational classrooms because they are brought up to avoid eye contact with members of the opposite sex. This means that Punjabi girls may experience problems addressing male teachers and male classmates and Punjabi boys may also face similar problems addressing female teachers and female classmates. Cultural discontinuities also arise for the Punjabis with respect to class discussions. This is because in Punjabi culture children are taught to defer to adult authority. Such a training, it is reasoned, does not prepare Punjabi students to participate in classroom discussions where they have to express ideas different from those of teachers. Other examples of cultural discontinuities include decision making, wage earning, and financial management. In spite of these and other differences in culture, values, and attitudes, Punjabi students are quite successful in school and, as Gibson (1983) reiterates, "in the case of boys, (the Punjabis are even) more successful" than Anglos.

Evidence from National Studies

At the national level, Coleman et al. (1966) report that Asian-American students do better than blacks, Mexican-Americans, Native Americans, and Puerto Ricans in reading, verbal ability, and math tests. *The New York Times* (Slade, 1982) also reported that Asian-American students did better than other language minorities on the SAT administered by the Educational Testing Service in 1980–81 (see also Tsang & Wing, 1985). School success, however, is not limited to Asian-Americans. Hispanic cultural and language minorities from Central and South Americans as well as from Cuba are also relatively successful (Davis, Haub, & Willette, 1983; Hispanic Policy Development Project, Inc., 1984; Suarez-Orozco, 1987).

Evidence from Cross-Cultural Studies

Cross-cultural studies indicate that this variability also exists outside the United States. In Britain, for example, East Asian students do considerably better than West Indian students even though the former are less fluent in English (Ogbu, 1978; Tomlinson, 1983). In New Zealand, the native Maori language minorities do less well in school than immigrant Polynesians who share similar language and culture with the Maoris (Penfold, 1981).

Instances where cultural and language minorities do better than the majority groups have also been reported from Spain (Woolard, 1981) and Malaysia (Mat Nor, 1983; Wan Zahid, 1978). Although the Catalan language in Spain was repressed and legally banished for a long time from the public domain, including education, and Catalan children were "trundled off to Castilian language schools, treated as if there were no other language than Castilian, and (made to learn) to 'speak Christian.' " Woolard (1981, p. 10) reports that Catan students were "by and large successful in school. At the University of

Barcelona, for example, 60 percent of the students are native Catalan speakers." In Malaysia educational reforms have resulted in the elimination of the English language as the medium of instruction in the public schools. English has been replaced at all levels (including the university) with Malay, the language of the dominant group or numerical majority. In spite of this, Chinese and Indian students—the language and cultural minorities—continue to do better in school than native Malay speakers.

ADDITIONAL EVIDENCE THAT THE PROBLEM OF SCHOOL ADJUSTMENT AND PERFORMANCE IS NOT DUE TO MERE CULTURAL/LANGUAGE DIFFERENCES

Differences in school performance appears to be not due to mere differences in culture and language: Some minority children do well in school even though they do not share the language and cultural backgrounds of the dominant group that are reflected in the curriculum contents, instructional style, and other practices of the schools. Mexican students in the United States, for instance, appear to be more successful than Chicano students (Fernandez & Nielsen, 1984; Matute-Bianchi, 1986; Woolard, 1981), although a majority of the Chicanos are native English speakers. In Britain, East Asian students for whom the British language and culture are totally new do considerably better in school than West Indian students who have been privy to the British language and cultural domains (Ogbu, 1978).

It thus seems that in some instances, a minority group does poorly in school in its own country or country of origin where its language and culture are more or less similar to the language and culture of the dominant group. However, when members of the same minority group emigrate to another society, they tend to do quite well in school even though their language and culture are now less similar to the language and culture of the dominant group controlling their education in the host society. A good example of this phenomenon is the case of the Japanese Buraku outcaste. In Japan itself, Buraku students continue to do poorly in school when compared with the dominant Ippan students. In the United States, however, the Buraku do as well as the Ippan immigrants (DeVos, 1973; Ito, 1967; Shimahara, 1983). Another example is the case of the Japanese Koreans. In Japan, where they went originally as colonial subjects in forced labor, the Koreans do very poorly in school. But in the United States, Korean students do as well as other Asians (DeVos, 1984; DeVos & Lee, 1981; Rohlen, 1981). The Koreans in Japan also serve as a telling example of how cultural similarities do not necessarily lead to minority school success. Due to a common Confucian worldview, Japanese and Koreans share many cultural features, including those relevant to formal education. For example, they share similar intrafamily relationships, child-rearing practices, values and attitudes toward education, and respect for teachers. But in spite of these similarities in culture, Korean minorities in Japan do not do well in school. Finally, West Indians are reported to be poor students in Britain (Ogbu, 1978; Tomlinson, 1982) but they do quite well in the United States (Fordham, 1984) and in St. Croix in the U.S. Virgin Islands where they consider themselves immigrants (Gibson, 1982). While these studies all demonstrate the variability in the school experience and performance of minority groups, none examined the complex reality of minority status in the various societies. It is to a discussion of this status and its impact in schooling that I now turn.

TYPES OF MINORITY STATUS AND VARIABILITY IN SCHOOL PERFORMANCE

Academic performance problems of minority children are due to complex forces not only in schools and classrooms but also in broader historical, economic, and sociocultural domains. In my effort to understand the historical and sociocultural forces, I have undertaken comparative or cross-cultural studies in the United States and other societies. One of may main findings thus far is that persistent and disproportionate problems of school adjustment and academic performance are associated with some minorities but not with others. This finding has led me to classify minority groups into three types described briefly here.

1. *Autonomous minorities* consist of people who are minorities primarily in a numerical sense. They may possess a distinctive ethnic, religious, linguistic, or cultural identity. However, although they are not entirely free from prejudice and discrimination, they are not socially, economically, and politically subordinated. Autonomous minorities do not experience disproportionate and persistent problems in learning to read and to compute partly because they usually have a cultural frame of reference which demonstrates and encourages school success. This type of minorities is typically represented in the United States by Jews and Mormons.

2. *Immigrant minorities* are people who have moved more or less voluntarily to the United States because of a desire for more economic well-being, better overall opportunities, and/or greater political freedom. These expectations continue to influence the way the immigrants perceive and respond to schooling in the host society. For this reason they do not experience lingering, disproportionate school failure, even though they often encounter initial difficulties due to cultural and language differences. Another reason, to be explored later, is that the immigrants are often characterized by a type of cultural difference which does not discourage crossing cultural boundaries. The Chinese and Punjabi Indians are representative examples.

3. *Castelike or involuntary Minorities* are people who were originally brought into the United States society *involuntarily* through slavery, conquest, or colonization. Thereafter these minorities were relegated to menial positions and denied true assimilation into the mainstream of American society. American Indians, black Americans, Mexican-Americans, Native Hawaiians, and Puerto Ricans are examples. The Burakumin in Japan and the Maori in New Zealand are examples outside the United States. It is involuntary minorities or nonimmigrants that usually experience more difficulties with social adjustment and academic achievement in school.

My focus of comparison is the cultural features characteristic of immigrant and involuntary minorities. When I compare these two types of minorities I find that they not only differ in features that distinguish their cultures from the culture of the "mainstream" America, but also that their cultures embody contrasting cultural or collective identities, folk theories of how to succeed in the United States, and degrees of trusting relationships with the public schools and the white Americans who control them. These differences accompany minority children to school and contribute to their patterns of social adjustment and academic performance.

TYPES OF CULTURAL DIFFERENCES

Comparative analyses of cultural differences that minority children in urban industrial societies like the United States and children from non-Western societies attending Western-type schools bring to educational experience suggests that we should classify cultural differences into three types: universal, primary, and secondary.

Universal cultural differences are universal in the sense that for *all children*, transition from home to school involves adjusting to new cultural and language behavioral requirements, to new social relations, and to new styles of language use or communication as well as to new styles of thinking (Cook-Gumperz & Gumperz, 1979; Scribner & Cole, 1973). This type of cultural difference is not necessarily associated with minority school adjustment and academic performance problems.

Primary cultural differences are differences that existed before two groups came in contact, such as before immigrant minorities came to the United States. Thus, the Punjabi Indians in Valleyside, California, spoke Punjabi, practiced the Sikh, Hindu, or Moslem religion, had arranged marriages, and males wore turbans before they came to the United States. Here, they continue these beliefs and practices to some extent.

The Punjabis also brought with them their distinct way of raising children. For example, they differ from whites in Valleyside in the way they train children to make decisions and to manage money. White parents begin early to train their children to make their own decisions and rationalize their actions by saying that they are preparing their children for independence. From a very early age they give their children options and help them consider each option and by adolescence the children are mostly on their own in decision making. As Gibson (1983) explains, "By the end of high school, many parents see their role as reduced largely to that of loving concerned advisor." The Punjabis, on the other hand, feel that parents make better decisions, that parents have the responsibility to make decisions for their children, and that children learn to make good decisions by examples set by parents.

In money management, Punjabi parents control the money earned by their children and use it for the running of the family. When children want something they ask their parents who decide whether it is a wise or appropriate expense. Punjabi parents believe that their control over the children's earning ensures that the money is wisely spent and maintains authority. In contrast, most white teenagers own and control the money they earn and do not contribute to the financial running of the family.

The nature of primary cultural differences is even better appreciated when we examine the situation of non-Western children who attend Western-type schools in their own countries. The Kpelle of Liberia in West Africa serve as a good example. The Kpelle situation was studied by Gay and Cole (1967) who wanted to find out how Kpelle culture and language affected children's ability to learn mathematics in school. The study examined the kinds of mathematical concepts and activities that existed in Kpelle culture: arithmetic concepts, knowledge of geometry, indigenous systems of measurement, and logic or reasoning, and do on. Findings demonstrated that arithmetic concepts of the Kpelle were in some ways similar to and in other ways different from those used in the American-type school. For example, like Westerners, the Kpelle classify things; this classification, however, is neither explicit nor conscious. The Kpelle counting system does not include concepts like "zero" or "number." And they do not recognize abstract operations like addition, subtraction, multiplication, and division, although in their actual mathematical behaviors they add, subtract, multiply, and divide things. Kpelle culture also does not have many geometrical concepts and the ones it has are used very imprecisely. For example, things which are described as a circle include shapes of a port, a pan, a frog, a sledge hammer, a tortoise, a water turtle, a rice fanner and so on. A tortoise shell, an arrowhead, a monkey's elbow, a drum, and a bow are all said to represent the shape of a triangle. Similarly lacking in the culture are measurements of weight, area, speed, and temperature, although present are measurements of time, volume, and money. These differences in mathematical concepts and use existed before the Kpelle were introduced to Western-type schools.

Secondary cultural differences are those differences which arise *after* two populations have come in contact with each other or *after* members of a given population have begun to participate in an institution controlled by members of another population, such as the schools controlled by the dominant group. In other words, secondary cultural differences develop as a response to a contact situation, especially a contact situation involving the domination of one group by another.

Although at the beginning of a contact period the minorities and the dominant group may each be characterized by primary cultural differences, the minorities begin to develop secondary cultural differences after the initial phase of the contact as they attempt to cope with the treatment at the hands of the dominant group. The new development in the minority culture may simply be a reinterpretation of their primary cultural differences or development of new types of cultural forms and behaviors.

There are five specific features of secondary cultural differences that play an important role in the school experience of minority children. First, the description of the cultural differences faced by nonimmigrant or involuntary minorities usually stress differences in *style*, not differences in *content* as in the case of immigrant minority children or children from non-Western societies attending Western-type schools. The cultural differences of the non-immigrants have been described with regard to differences in cognitive style (Ramirez & Castenada, 1974; Shade, 1982), communication style (Gumperz, 1981; Kochman, 1982; Philips, 1972, 1983), interaction style (Erickson & Mohatt, 1982), and learning style (Au, 1981; Boykin, 1980; Philips, 1976).

The second important feature of secondary cultural differences is the element of cultural inversion. *Cultural inversion* is here defined as a tendency for members of one population, in this case, the minority group, to regard certain forms of behaviors, certain events, symbols, and meanings as *not appropriate* for them because they are characteristic of members of another population (e.g., of white Americans); at the same time, however, the minorities claim other (often the opposite) forms of behaviors, events, symbols, and meanings as appropriate for them *because these are not* characteristic of members of the dominant group (i.e., not characteristic of white Americans). Thus, what is appropriate or even legitimate behavior for in-group members is defined in opposition to the practices and preferences of the members of an outgroup, say, the dominant white Americans.

Cultural inversion is sometimes used by the minorities to repudiate negative stereotypes or derogatory images attributed to them by white Americans. Sometimes cultural inversion is used by the minorities as a strategy to manipulate whites or for getting even with whites, or, as Holt puts it in the case of black Americans, "to turn the table against whites" (Holt, 1972).

Cultural inversion may take several forms. For example, it may include hidden meanings of words and statements (Bontemps, July, 1969, personal communication); different notions of time and its use (Weis, 1985); or different emphasis on language dialects and communication style (Holt, 1972; Baugh, 1984). It may simply be an outright rejection of the white American preferences or what whites consider appropriate behavior in a given setting like the school (Fordham & Ogbu, 1986; Petroni, 1970). Cultural inversion, along with other oppositional elements, thus result in the *coexistence of two opposing cultural frames of reference* or ideals orienting behavior, one considered by the minorities as appropriate for themselves and their members, and the other appropriate for white Americans.

A third feature is that bearers of secondary cultural differences seem to be characterized by ambivalent or oppositional social identities vis-á-vis the white American social identity. Nonimmigrant or involuntary minorities appear to develop a new sense of social identity *in opposition* to the social identity of the whites *after they have become subordinated* and they do so in reaction to the way that white people treat them in economic, political, social, and psychological domains. The treatment by the whites may include deliberate exclusion from true assimilation or the reverse, namely, forced assimilation (Castile & Kushner, 1981; DeVos, 1967, 1984; Spicer, 1966, 1971). Involuntary minorities also develop oppositional identity because they perceive and experience their treatment by the dominant group as collective and enduring. They tend to believe that they cannot expect to be treated like members of the dominant group regardless of their individual differences in ability, training, or education, differences in place of origin or residence, or differences in economic status or physical appearance. Furthermore, these minorities know that they cannot easily escape from their birth-ascribed membership in a subordinate and disparaged group by "passing" or by returning to "a homeland" (Green, 1981). The oppositional social identity combines with new cultural coping mechanisms described above to make cross-cultural learning or "crossing cultural boundaries" more difficult than it is for immigrant minorities or bearers of primary cultural differences.

In the context of minority status and schooling, the fourth feature is that the bearers of secondary cultural differences tend to be characterized by folk theories of getting ahead in the United States that differ from those of the whites and from those of the immigrant minorities or bearers of primary cultural differences. The connection between people's folk theory of getting ahead and their school perceptions and strivings can be better explained by introducing the concept of a *status mobility system*. A status mobility system is the socially approved strategy of getting ahead in a society or its segment (LeVine, 1967). Every society or population has its own folk theory of getting ahead; each theory tends to generate its own ideal behaviors and ideal successful persons or role models—the kinds of persons widely perceived by members of the population as people who are successful or people who can get ahead because of their personal attributes and behaviors. the personal attributes of the role models tend to influence the values of childrearing agents and the attitudes and behaviors of the children themselves as they get older and begin to understand the status mobility system of their group. Thus, if performing academically well in school and thereby getting good school credentials is a quality that enables members of a population to get ahead, say, to get good jobs that pay well, then those who have good jobs with good pay will usually be found to be people who are well educated and who possess the qualities or competencies that enhance academic success. In such a society or population, the child-rearing values and practices of parents and other agents will tend to emphasize the transmission of the competencies, qualities, and strategies that promote academic success.

But when external barriers are imposed to prevent people from getting ahead according to a prevailing folk theory, people will initially try to eliminate, lower, or circumvent those barriers. If the barriers persist they will tend to alter their folk theory to incorporate other strategies of getting ahead. Both immigrant and involuntary minorities in the United States, for example, have faced barriers to the American folk theory of getting ahead, barriers that have prevented them from using education to get good jobs with good pay. But the two types of minorities have differed in their response to these barriers and to the pursuit of education. The immigrants have tended to pursue education in spite of the barriers, whereas involuntary minorities appear to have responded by developing somewhat different versions of the folk theory of getting ahead that do not necessarily emphasize the strategy of academic pursuit in practice. In other words, involuntary minorities have developed "survival strategies," some of which do not necessarily promote academic efforts and success. Examples of the survival strategies among black Americans include collective struggle, uncle tomming, hustling, and the like. Other involuntary minorities have their own forms of collective struggle and survival strategies.

Finally, minorities who are bearers of secondary cultural differences tend to be distrustful of the members of the dominant group and the societal institutions the latter control. There is a deep distrust that runs through the relationship between the minorities, on the one hand, and white Americans and the public institutions they control like the public schools, on the other. And there are real historical reasons for the distrust. In the case of black Americans, for instance, one finds many episodes throughout their history that seem to have left them with the feeling that white people and the institutions they control cannot be trusted (Ogbu, 1986). Public schools, particularly in the inner city, are generally not trusted to provide black children with the "right education." This distrust arises partly from perceptions of past and current treatment of blacks by the schools as discriminatory which, in their view, is more or less institutionalized and permanent. This discriminatory treatment has, of course, been documented in several studies throughout the United States and throughout the history of black education (see Bond, 1966, 1969; Kluger, 1977; Ogbu, 1978; Weinberg, 1977).

Blacks reject segregated education because it is inferior education in inferior schools. Blacks distrust desegregated schools because they suspect the perpetuation of inferior education in such schools through such subtle devices as "biased testing," misclassification, tracking, biased textbooks, inappropriate and inadequate counseling, and because they doubt that the public schools understand the educational needs of their children or even understand the children themselves. This is particularly true in the case of black male students. Black Americans tend to attribute the lower school performance of black males to the schools' inability to "relate to Black males in ways that will help them learn" (Scherer & Slawski, 1978).

Similarly, distrust characterizes the relationship between Mexican-Americans and the Anglos or whites and the public schools the latter control. Mexican-American distrust of the Anglos dates back to the former's forced incorporation by conquest in Southwestern United States and subsequent economic and social subordination. These treatments led to bitterness, resentment, and distrust. As Acuna points out (1981, pp. 3–20), the conquest of 1848 left a legacy of hate which has exerted a powerful influence shaping contemporary Mexican-American response to their subordinate status. And Grebler notes that one consequence of the land dispossession and economic subordination brought about by the conquest was "widespread and lingering distrust and suspicion of the new, powerful population by the indigenous settlers and their descendants" (Grebler, Moore, & Guzman, 1970, pp. 50–51).

In contemporary urban United States, land dispossession is no longer at issue; instead, the conflict between Mexican-Americans and the Anglos centers around the issue of discrimination in employment, wages, housing, political representation, and education (Blair, 1971; Carter, 1970; Grebler et al., 1970; Schmidt, 1974). In the domain of education, Mexican-Americans began actively to "fight" against the public schools for better educational opportunity after World War II (Carter & Segura, 1979; Ogbu & Matute-Bianchi, 1986). Their collective struggle against the schools is not only about segregation and inferior education, but also about how they are treated in formal school curriculum and in textbooks, about inadequate counseling, disproportionate discipline, and the use of language.

To complicate matters, in the conflicts between the minorities and the public schools, the latter tend to approach the education of the minorities defensively—through control, paternalism, or "contest"—strategies which seem to divert attention from the real task of educating the minority children. Furthermore, because the relationship between the minorities and the schools is so characterized by conflict, distrust, and skepticism, blacks and

Mexican-Americans may not interpret school requirements as whites do. Thus, white middle-class parents and their children may endorse school rules and standard practices as necessary, desirable, and compatible with their educational goals. The minority parents and their children may interpret the same requirements as deceptions or as an unnecessary imposition of white culture and language that does not meet their "real educational needs."

PROBLEMS ASSOCIATED WITH SECONDARY CULTURAL DIFFERENCES HAVE MORE ADVERSE PERSISTENT EFFECTS

Problems Associated with Primary Cultural Differences

What kinds of problems in school are associated with primary cultural differences and why do bearers of primary cultural differences overcome these problems and more or less do well in school—That is, why do they successfully cross cultural boundaries? Primary cultural differences may initially cause problems in school both in interpersonal and intergroup relations or understanding and in terms of academic work. There are several reasons for the occurrence of these problems. One is that children from different cultural backgrounds may begin school with cultural assumptions about the world that are different from those of the schools, the teachers, and their fellow students from other cultural backgrounds. Another is that the minorities may come to school lacking certain concepts that are useful in school learning because their own native cultures do not have or do not make use of such concepts and therefore children had no need to learn them before entering school. However, there are features of the primary cultural differences which help immigrant children and non-Western children in Western-type schools to eventually overcome the initial problems, adjust socially, and learn more or less successfully.

One factor is that most of the cultural differences existed *before* the immigrants came to the United States and entered the public schools and *before* non-Western children like the Kpelle began to attend Western-type schools in their own country. Consequently, the cultural differences are not part of boundary-maintaining mechanisms that are in opposition to equivalent features in the culture of the dominant group and the schools controlled by the latter.

Because the primary cultural differences did not develop in opposition to their counterparts in the culture of the dominant group and the schools they control, and because they did not develop to protect the social identity and sense of security of the minorities under domination and subordination at the hands of white Americans, the awareness of the minorities of the differences is not emotionally charged. Nor do immigrant minorities and non-Western peoples perceive and interpret learning the cultural features of the schools required for social adjustment and academic achievement as threatening to their own culture, language, and social identities. Instead, they perceive and interpret such learning as additive, as acquiring, in addition to what they already have, the standard English language and those aspects of the culture of the mainstream and the schools which they think will help them succeed in school and later in the labor market. Non-Western and immigrant minority students thus tend to adopt what Gibson (1983) calls a strategy of "accommodation without assimilation." That is, while they may not give up their own cultural beliefs and practices, the immigrants are willing and may actually strive to "play the classroom game by the rules" and try to overcome "all kinds of difficulties in school because they believe so strongly that there will be a payoff later" (Gibson, 1983). With this kind of attitude the immigrants are able to cross cultural boundaries and do relatively well in school.

Non-Western people and immigrant minorities often perceive the cultural and language differences they encounter as *barriers to be overcome* in order for them to achieve their long-range goals of obtaining good school credentials for future employment. They do not expect the schools to teach them in their own culture and language. Rather, they go to school expecting and willing to learn the new culture and language of the schools in spite of difficulties in learning them.

Finally, primary cultural differences and the problems they cause for minority or non-Western students are often specific and can usually be identified through careful ethnographic research. This specificity and identifiability make it possible to develop appropriate educational policies, programs, and practices to eliminate differences or reduce their negative impact. For example, educational planning and programs can take into consideration the fact that some children come from cultures with styles of learning and teaching different from those of the schools, or that they come from cultures which do not have the same range of mathematical concepts used in school or do not use these concepts in the same manner the school requires.

Problems Associated with Secondary Cultural Differences

What kinds of problems do secondary cultural differences cause for social adjustment and academic achievement of nonimmigrant or involuntary minority children?

Cultural miscommunication, for example, is a problem that occurs in the education of Indian children which is said to lead to school failure. Dumont (1972, p. 365) reports that Oglala Sioux children are usually "noisy, bold, daring and insatiably curious" outside the classroom, but in the classroom they remain almost totally unresponsive to teachers' questions. He concludes that the children do not respond to teachers' questions because the way classroom communication is organized and controlled by teachers is not familiar to the children, that is, is different from the way the children were brought up to expect.

Similarly, Philips (1972) found in her study of Indian children on reservations that the "rules" which guide the use of speech in the Indian community and in the schools controlled by white teachers differ; cultural expectations of behavior were also differential. In classrooms where white teachers required Indian students to behave in "white ways" or according to the "standard," Indian children did not do well academically. But in classrooms where Indian teachers let the children initiate their own behavior or allowed them to work in small groups or otherwise act as they would in the Indian community, children's academic performance was considerably better.

The cultural organization of reading lessons provides another example. Au (1981) found that native Hawaiians' difficulties in learning to read were associated with a conventional approach to classroom organization. By reorganizing the reading activity to reflect the social and communicative interactions of the children's home and community (e.g., strategic use of "a talk story" or a "rambling personal experience narrative mixed with folk materials involving adults and children"), children's reading and overall school performance improved.

McDermott's study of an inner-city classroom affords further insights into secondary cultural differences. He found that there were two opposing forms of classroom organization, one by the teacher and the other by the children. The teacher grouped her class in the conventional manner, including ability grouping; black children who made up the bulk of the students, on the other hand, organized themselves differently, mainly according to peer relations and interests. Theirs was thus an alternative to the teacher's conventional organization. The children attended to peer "games," ignoring the teacher's lesson presentation most of the time. And they adopted street language rather than the language of instruction, that is, they avoided using the standard English. The result was a constant battle between the teacher and her students, with no real teaching and learning taking place. It seemed that the teacher and the student perceived and interpreted the classroom situation differently.

In general, researchers attribute the persistent, high rates of school failure among nonimmigrant or involuntary minority students to cultural and other discontinuities reflected in the foregoing cases. Sociolinguists stress differences in communication styles; cognitive anthropologists emphasize discontinuities in cognitive style or styles of thought, as well as mismatch between teacher and students in cognitive maps; interactionists and transactionists think that the problem of school failure and adjustment among involuntary minority students lies in differences in interaction style; and so on.

What needs to be stressed is that secondary cultural differences do not mererly cause initial problems in social adjustment and academic performance of nonimmigrant minority children but that the problems they cause appear to *persist*. Moreover, it is difficult for bearers of secondary cultural differences to cross cultural boundaries. There are six reasons for this.

First, secondary cultural differences developed initially as a part of boundary-maintaining and coping mechanisms between the minorities and those who dominante them in the case of the United States, i.e., white Americans. Since these cultural differences were developed as boundary-maintaining mechanisms they do not necessarily disappear or change just beause nonimmigrant minorities and whites are brought together as in desegregated schools or other societal settings.

Second, because the secondary cultural differences produce opposing cultural frames of reference or ideal ways of behaving, the cultural and language differences the minorities perceive are intercepted by them as markers of their social identity to be maintained, not as barriers to learning to be overcome.

Third, among minority bearers of secondary cultural differences, school learning is equated with the learning of the culture and language of the dominant group, i.e., the learning of the cultural frame of reference of their "enemy" or their "oppressors." (Note that for their part, the dominant group also defines the school learning for minority children as learning the culture and language of the dominant group that will eventually displace those of the minorities.) Thus, the minorities interpret school learning as a displacement process detrimental to their social identity and sense of security. By learning the white cultural frame of reference they fear that they will cease to act like minorities as well as cease to identify with minorities, thus losing a sense of community; the consequence being that they would begin to "act white" and lose their sense of community. Reality has demonstrated, however, that those who successfully learn to act white or who succeeded in school are not fully accepted by the whites; nor do such people receive equal rewards or equal opportunity for advancement open to whites with similar education.

There are both social and psychological pressures that discourage individuals from adopting the standard attitudes and behavior practices of the schools that enhance good school adjustment and academic achievement because such attitudes and behaviors are considered "white." In the case of black Americans, for example, the social pressures against "acting white," that is, against adopting the standard attitudes and behavior practices conducive to good school adjustment and academic achievement, include accusations of uncle tomism or disloyalty to the black cause and the black community, fear of losing one's friends, and fear of losing one's sense of community. The social pressures discourage bright black children from adopting serious academic attitudes and from investing sufficient time in their schoolwork to do well.

Petroni's study (1970) provides a good example of how social pressures work among black American students. At the beginning of the study black students in the high school told the researcher that they were excluded from certain courses and extracurricular activities by "white racism." But later Petroni found that black students stayed away from the courses and extracurricular activities in part because of pressures from fellow black students; furthermore, black students who participated in the so-called "white activities" like student government, madrigals, senior play, and the like, were called "Uncle Toms" and rejected by other black students. The following interview excerpt showed the dilemma of one black male student who had all As in his courses. This student told the interviewer:

> Well, I participate in speech. I'm the only Negro in the whole group. I find it kind of interesting that I'm the only Negro. I'm always contrasted in pictures of the group. The Negroes accuse me of thinking I'm white. In the bathroom one day, some Negroes wrote in big letters, "B.B. is an Uncle Tom." It's this kind of pressures from other Negro kids which bothers me most.

A female black student in the same school told the researcher that other black girls in her class threatened to beat her up because she was involved in "too many white activities." Indeed, it seemed that in general black students in this school who were doing well or trying to do well were classified by other black students as "white" or "trying to be white." And "White Negroes" who tried to succeed academically were considered disloyal and "not for the Negroes; they're for the whites. They've learned white ways" (Petroni, 170, pp. 262–263). Petroni suggests that the fear of being called "Uncle Toms" or being accused of "acting white" may prevent black students from working hard to do well in school. On the other hand, black students who excelled in nonacademic activities or in "black things," like sports, were highly praised by fellow blacks. Petroni's findings are supported by findings from other studies, including my own work in Stockton, California.

The same phenomenon has been described in a number of studies on American Indian students, demonstrating their tendency to "resist" adopting and following school rules of behavior and standard practices (Dumont, 1972; Philips, 1972, 1983). According to these studies, Indian students enter the classroom with a sort of cultural convention which dictates that they should not adopt the classroom rules of behavior and standard practices expected of public school students. A good illustration is Philips' study of Indian children in Warm Springs Reservation in Oregon referred to earlier. She found that the Indian students and their white teachers in an elementary school held different views about how students should interact with teachers and among themselves; they also held different views about how students should participate in classroom activities. Although the teachers' views apparently prevailed, they were not particularly effective in classroom management and in getting the children to learn and perform. The impression one gains in reading Philips' description of the situation is that the Indian children resisted learning how to go to school according to the definition of the school and the wider society perhaps because they defined such behavior as "acting white."

There are also psychological pressures not to act white in the absence of obvious social pressures and they equally discourage minority students from striving for academic success. The psychological pressures come about because the minority individual who desires to do well in school also may define the behavior enhancing school success and the success itself as "acting white." Knowing that striving for academic success and the success itself may result in loss of peer affiliation and support and at the same time uncertain of white acceptance and support if he or she succeeded in learning to act white creates a personal conflict for the student. Put differently, the minority student desiring and striving to do well in school is faced with the conflict between loyalty to the minority peer group and the sense of community and security it provides on the one hand, and on the other, the desire to behave in ways that may improve school performance but are defined by the peer group as the white way.

The dilemma of minority students who bear the secondary cultural differences then, is that they have to choose between "acting white" (i.e., adopting appropriate attitudes and behaviors or school rules and standard practices that enhance academic success but which are perceived and interpreted by the minorities as typical of white Americans and therefore negatively sanctioned by them) and "acting minority," as it were (i.e., adopting attitudes and behaviors that minority students consider appropriate for minorities but which are not necessarily conducive to school success.) Thus, unlike bearers of primary cultural differences, such as immigrant minorities, the bearers of secondary cultural differences, or the nonimmigrant minorities, do not seem to be able or willing to distinguish between attitudes and behaviors that result in academic success and school credentials for future employment and attitudes and behaviors that may result in linear acculturation or replacement of their cultural identity with the cultural identity of white Americans.

A fourth reason why the school adjustment and learning problems of minorities characterized by secondary cultural differences persist is that, as researchers have repeatedly pointed out, secondary cultural differences are more diffuse and less specific in nature when compared to primary cultural differences. It is therefore more difficult to eliminate the problems through conventional school policies and practices or programs. More specifically, as stated earlier, secondary cultural differences are not just differences in manifest contents of cultural attitudes and behaviors. The differences in contents are not the overriding problem, although they exist as in the case of primary cultural differences. *Rather, the differences that are problematic are in style and in the quality of opposition and ambivalence in relation to white or mainstream culture.*

Because of the oppositional nature of the cultural frame of reference upon which nonimmigrant minorities operate (rather than differences in content) students from these groups do not perceive and do not respond to learning "standard" English and other aspects of the curriculum in the same way as do immigrants.

Instead, nonimmigrant minorities tend to equate school learning with linear acculturation, which is threatening to their cultural identity, language identity, and sense of security. This situation creates a serious barrier to school adjustment and academic performance beyond the barriers caused by primary cultural differences.

The fifth reason for the difficulty has to do with the folk theory of how to get ahead in the United States for members of the minority group. Unlike the immigrants, involuntary minorities characterized by secondary cultural differences did not choose to come to the United States, nor were they motivated by hope of economic success or political freedom. They also do not have the dual frame of reference of the immigrants. That is, the nonimmigrant minorities do not have a comparative reference to conditions or to peers "back home" or to a less favorable former status or standards in regard to their present condition. If they make any comparison, they tend to consider their former state or preminority status period as considerably better than what they are now. The main comparative frame of reference they have, though, is the dominant white Americans, and when the minorities compare themselves with the whites they feel far worse than they think they ought to be and this makes them resentful. For these nonimmigrant minorities their poorer conditions appear to be enduring due to what they perceive as institutionalized discrimination perpetuated against them by white people and the institutions they control, such as the public schools. Thus, for the future these minorities also seem to have difficulty seeing things better than they are at present "without struggle."

The sixth and final reason I will consider is the relationship between minority bearers of secondary cultural differences and white Americans and the institutions the latter control, such as the public schools. This relationship, as noted earlier, is characterized by conflict and distrust. One consequence of the distrust of white people and the public schools appears to be that the minorities are more or less skeptical over whether they can trust the schools to educate their children in the same way they educate white children. Furthermore, because of the distrust, minorities may not necessarily accept and interpret school rules and school standard practices the same way that white middle-class people do. The latter seem to endorse school rules and standard practices as necessary, desirable, and compatible with their own educational goals. The minorities, on the other hand, appear to interpret the same rules and standard practices as an imposition of white culture that does not necessarily meet their "real educational needs." For their part the schools, as noted earlier, appear to approach the education of these minorities defensively—through control, paternalism, or even contest—strategies which divert attention from efforts to educate the children.

Because of the distrust of white people and the public schools and because of the skepticism over the school rules and standard practices, I suggest that it is probably more difficult for these minority parents and communities to teach their children convincingly to accept, internalize, and follow the school rules and standard practices that lead to academic success; it also seems that it is probably more difficult for involuntary minority children, than for other minority children (especially as the former get older), to accept, internalize, and follow the school rules and standard practices (Ogbu, 1984).

In summary, minority children with primary cultural differences and minority children with secondary cultural differences appear to experience difficulties in learning to read and to compute, at least initially. Some of the reasons both types of children experience initial difficulties is that the two forms of cultural differences equip the children with cognitive styles, interactional styles, and learning styles that are different from those of the mainstream and the public schools. Furthermore, the contents of the curriculum may be foreign to both groups of children. However, what seems evident from a close and comparative analysis of ethnographies of minority school experience is that children from small-scale societies who attend Western-type schools, such as the Kpelle of Liberia, and children of immigrants who attend the public schools in the United States (i.e., the bearers of primary cultural differences) do not manifest the kinds of attitudes and behaviors commonly found among nonimmigrant or involuntary minority children in the public schools (i.e., among bearers of secondary cultural differences).

One real issue in the school adjustment and academic performance of minority children is not whether the children possess a different language or dialect, a different cognitive style, a different style of socialization and upbringing, although all these are important. But the real issue is twofold: First, whether or not the children come from a segment of society where people have traditionally experienced unequal opportunity to use their education or school credentials in a socially and economically meaningful and rewarding manner; and, second, whether or not the relationship between the minorities and the dominant group members who control the public schools has encouraged the minorities to perceive and define school learning as an instrument of replacing their cultural and language identity with the cultural and language identity of the dominant group but with no equality of reward or true assimilation.

WHAT CAN BE DONE

Prerequisites

1. Recognize that there are different kinds of cultural/language differences and that these types of differences arise for different reasons and in different circumstances.

2. Recognize that there are different types of minority groups and that these minority types are associated with the different types of cultural/ language differences.
3. Recognize that all minority children face problems of social adjustment and academic performance in school because of cultural/language differences. *However*, the kinds of problems faced by bearers of primary cultural differences are *different* from the kinds of problems faced by children from backgrounds of secondary cultural/language differences.

Helping Children with Primary Cultural/Language Differences

Most problems caused by primary cultural differences are due to differences in cultural content and practice. One solution is for teachers and others involved with students to learn as much as they can about the cultural backgrounds of the students and to use this knowledge to organize their classrooms; to help students learn what they teach; to help students get along with one another; to communicate with parents and the like. Teachers can learn about the cultural backgrounds of their students through a variety of techniques, including (a) observation of children's behavior in the classroom and on playgrounds; (b) asking children questions about their cultural practices and preferences; (c) talking with parents about the same; and (d) doing research on various ethnic groups with children in school.

Some problems caused by primary cultural differences can also be solved by means of well-designed and implemented multicultural education.

Helping Children with Secondary Cultural/Language Differences

First, school personnel, including teachers, need to study the histories and cultural adaptations of nonimmigrant minorities in order to understand how the children's sense of social identity and cultural frames of reference affect the process of their school, particularly their school orientation or attitudes and behaviors.

Second, special counseling and related programs should be used to help nonimmigrant minorities avoid equating school learning, academic success, and compliancy with school rules and standard practices with either "acting white" or as a threat to their social/cultural identity, language identity, and sense of security.

Third, programs should also be developed to teach nonimmigrant minority students to adopt immigrant minority students' model of schooling. In my comparative research, I have used various concepts to try to describe the immigrants' model, namely, as *alternation model, accommodation without assimilation model*, or simply, *"playing the classroom game."* The essence of the alternation model is that it is possible and safe to participate in two cultural frames of reference for different purposes; that participation in the school cultural frame of reference does not mean a renunciation of minority cultural frame of reference. The principle of accommodation without assimilation practiced by the immigrants is, "Do as the Romans when you are in Rome." My observation from various ethnographic case studies leads me to conclude that many capable nonimmigrant minority students are failing in school because they adopt the attitudes and strategies that are not conducive to school success, and I also conclude from the observation that nonimmigrant minority students adopt such attitudes and strategies that lead to school failure because of secondary cultural differences.

The Role of Minority Communities in Solving the Problems Created by Secondary Cultural/Language Differences.

Minority communities—nonimmigrant minority communities—can play an important part in helping children make a distinction between attitudes and behaviors that lead to academic success from attitudes and behaviors that lead to a loss of ethnic identity and culture or language, that is, to linear accultura-tion. Furthermore, just as society can help reorient minority youths into more academic striving for school credentials for future employment by eliminating the job ceiling and by providing better employment oppor-tunities for the minorities, so also the minority communities themselves can help minority children reorient their time and effort into academic work. At the moment, minority youths tend more or less to divert their time and effort into nonacademic activities. One example of how the minority communities can rechannel the youths' time and effort into academic activities is to provide them with sufficient concrete evidence that the community appreci-ates and honors academic success as much as it does achievement in sports, athletics, and entertainment.

REFERENCES

Acuna, R. (1981). *Occupied America: A history of Chicanos* (2nd ed.). New York: Harper and Row.

Au, K. H. (1981). Participant structure in a reading lesson with Hawaiian children: Analysis of a culturally appropriate instructional event. *Anthropology and Education Quarterly, 10*(2), 91–115.

Baugh, J. (1984). *Black street speech: Its history, structure, and survival*. Austin: University of Texas Press.

Blair, P. M. (1971). *Job discrimination and education: An investment analysis*. New York: Praeger.

Bond, H. M. (1966). *The education of the Negro in the American social order*. New York: Octagon.

Bond, H. M. (1969). *Negro education in Alabama: A study in cotton and steel*. New York: Atheneum.

Boykin, A. W. (1980, November 19–20). *Reading achievement and the sociocultural frame of reference of Afro American children*. Paper presented at NIE Roundtable Discussion on Issues in Urban Reading. Washington, DC: The National Institute of Education.

Byers, P., & Byers, H. (1972). Non-verbal communication and the education of children. In C. B. Cazden, D. Hymes, & V. John (Eds.), *Functions of language in the classroom*. New York: Teachers College Press.

Carter, T. (1970). *Mexican Americans in school: A history of educational neglect*. New York: College Entrance Examination Board.

Carter, T., & Segura, R. (1979). *Mexican Americans in school: A decade of change*. New York: College Entrance Examination Board.

Castile, G. P., & Kushner, G. (Eds.). (1981). *Persistent peoples: Cultural enclaves in perspective*. Tucson: University of Arizona Press.

Coleman, J. S., Camplede, E. R., Hobson, C. J., McPartland, J., Mood, A. M., Wernfield, F. D., & York, R. L. (1966). *Equality of educational opportunity*. Washington, DC: U.S. Government Printing Office.

Cook-Gumperz, J., & Gumperz, J. J. (1979). *From oral to written culture: The transition to literacy*. Unpublished manuscript, Department of Anthropology, University of California, Berkeley, CA.

Davis, C., Haub, C., & Willette, J. (1983). U.S. Hispanics: Changing the face of America. *Population Bulletin, 38*(3).

DeVos, G. A. (1967). Essential elements of caste: Psychological determinants in structural theory. In G. A. DeVos & H. Wagatsuma (Eds.), *Japan's invisible race: Caste in culture and personality* (pp. 332–384). Berkeley: University of California Press.

DeVos, G. A. (1973). Japan's outcastes: The problem of the Burakumin. In B. Whitaker (Ed.), *The Fourth World: Victims of group oppression* (pp. 307–327). New York: Schocken Books.

DeVos, G. A., & Lee, C. (1981). *Koreans in Japan*. Berkeley: University of California Press.

DeVos, G. A. (1984, April 14–16). *Ethnic persistence and role degradation: An illustration from Japan*. Paper presented at the American-Soviet Symposium on Contemporary Ethnic Processes in the USA and the USSR. New Orleans, LA.

Dumont, R. V., Jr. (1972). Learning English and how to be silent: Studies in Sioux and Cherokee classrooms. In C. B. Cazden, D. Hymes, & V. John (Eds.), *Functions of language in the classroom*. New York: Teachers College Press.

Erickson, F., & Mohatt, G. (1982). cultural organization of participant structure in two classrooms of Indian students. In G. D. Spindler (Ed.), *Doing the ethnography of schooling: Educational anthropology in action* (pp. 132–175). New York: Holt.

Fernandez, R. M., & Nielsen, F. (1984). *Bilingualism and Hispanic scholastic achievement: Some baseline results*. Unpublished manuscript, Department of Sociology, University of Arizona, Tucson, AZ.

Fordham, S. (1984, November 14–18). *Ethnography in a black high school: Learning not to be a native.* Paper presented at the 83rd Annual Meeting of the American Anthropological Association, Denver, CO.

Fordham, S., & Ogbu, J. U. (1986). Black students' school success: Coping with the "burden of 'acting white.' " *The Urban Review, 18*(3), 176–206.

Gay, J., & Cole, M. (1967). *The new mathematics and an old culture: A study of learning among the Kpelle of Liberia.* New York: Holt.

Gibson, M. A. (1982). Reputation and respectability: How competing cultural systems affect students' performance in school. *Anthropology and Education Quarterly, 13*(1), 3–27.

Gibson, M. A. (1983). *Home-school-community linkages: A study of educational equity for Punjabi youth.* Final Report. Washington, DC: National Institute of Education.

Grebler, L., Moore, J. W., & Guzman, R. C. (1970). *The Mexican American people.*

Green, V. (1981). Blacks in the United States: The creation of an enduring people? In G. P. Castile & G. Kushner (Eds.), *Persistent peoples: Cultural enclaves in perspective* (pp. 69–77). Tucson: University of Arizona Press.

Gumperz, J. J. (1981). Conversational inference and classroom learning. In J. Green & C. Wallat (Eds.), *Ethnographic and language in educational settings* (pp. 3–23). Norwood, NJ: Ablex.

Guthrie, G. P. (1985). *A school divided: An ethnography of bilingual education in a Chinese community.* Hillsdale, NJ: Lawrence Erlbaum Associates.

Heller, K. A., Holtzman, W. H., & Messick, S. (Eds.). (1982). *Placing children in special education: A strategy for equity.* Washington, DC: National Academy Press.

Hispanic Policy Development Project (HPDP). (1984). *Make something happen: Hispanics and urban high school reform (Vols. 1 & 2).* New York: The Hispanic Policy Development Project.

Holt, G. S. (1972). "Inversion" in Black communication. In T. Kochman (Ed.), *Rappin' and stylin' out: Communication in Urban Black America.* Chicago: University of Illinois Press.

Ito, H. (1967). Japan's outcastes in the United Sates. In G. A. DeVos & H. Wagatasuma (Eds.), *Japan's invisible race: Caste in culture and personality* (pp. 200–221). Berkeley: University of California Press.

Kluger, R. (1977). *Simple justice.* New York: Vintage Book.

Kochman, T. (1982). *Black and White styles in conflict.* Chicago: University of Chicago Press.

Lee, Y. (1984). *Koreans in Japan and United States.* Unpublished manuscript, Department of Anthropology, Northwestern University, Evanston, IL.

LeVine, R. A. (1967). *Dreams and deeds: Achievement motivation in Nigeria.* Chicago: University of Chicago Press.

Mat Nor, H. (1983). *The Malay students problems: Some issues on their poor performance.* Unpublished manuscript, Special Project, Department of Anthropology, University of California, Berkeley, CA.

Matute-Bianchi, M. E. (1986). Ethnic identities and patterns of school success and failure among Mexican-descent and Japanese-American students in a California high school: An ethnographic analysis. *American Journal of Education, 95*(1), 233–255.

Ogbu, J. U. (1974). *The next generation: An ethnography of education in an urban neighborhood*. New York: Academic Press.

Ogbu, J. U. (1977). Racial stratification and education: The case of Stockton, California. *ICRD Bulletin, 12*(3), 1–26.

Ogbu, J. U. (1978). *Minority education and caste: The American system in cross-cultural perspective*. New York: Academic Press.

Ogbu, J. U. (1984). *Understanding community forces affecting minority students' academic effort*. Paper prepared for The Achievement Council of California, Oakland, CA.

Ogbu, J. U. (1986). *Cross-cultural study of minority education: Contributions from Stockton research*. 23rd Annual J. William Harris Lecture, School of Education, University of the Pacific, Stockton, CA.

Ogbu, J. U., & Matute-Bianchi, M. E. (1986). Understanding sociocultural factors in education: Knowledge, identity, and adjustment in schooling. In *Beyond language: Social and cultural factors in schooling language minority students* (pp. 73–142). Sacramento, CA: Bilingual Education Office, California State Department of Education.

Petroni, F. A. (1970). Uncle Toms: White stereotypes in the black movement. *Human Organization, 29*, 260–266.

Philips, S. U. (1972). Participant structure and communicative competence: Warm Springs children in community and classroom. In C. B. Cazden, D. Hymes, & V. John (Eds.), *Functions of language in the classroom*. New York: Teachers College Press.

Philips, S. U. (1976). Commentary: Access to power and maintenance of ethnic identity as goals of multi-cultural education. *Anthropology and Education Quarterly, 7* (4), 30–32.

Philips, S. U. (1983). *The invisible culture: Communication in classroom and community on the Warm Springs Indian Reservation*. New York: Longman.

Ramirez, M., & Castenada, A. (1974). *Cultural democracy, bicognitive development and education*. New York: Academic Press.

Rohlen, T. (1981). Education: Policies and prospects. In C. Lee & G. A. DeVos (Eds.), *Koreans in Japan: Ethnic conflicts and accommodation* (pp. 182–222). Berkeley: University of California Press.

Scherer, J., & Slawski, E. J. (1978). *Hard walls-soft walls: The social ecology of an urban desegregated school* (Final Report of Field Research in Urban Desegregated Schools). Washington, DC: National Institute of Education.

Scribner, S., & Cole, M. (1973). Cognitive consequences of formal and informal education. *Science, 182*, 553–559.

Schmidt, F. H. (1974). *Spanish surnamed American employment in the Southwest: A study prepared for the Colorado Civil Rights Commission under the auspices of the Equal Employment Opportunities Commission*. Washington, DC: U.S. Government Printing Office.

Shade, B. J. (1982). *Afro-American patterns of cognition*. Unpublished manuscript, Wisconsin Center for Educational Research, Madison, WI.

Shimahara, N. K. (1983). *Mobility and education of Buraku: The case of a Japanese minority*. Paper presented at the 82nd Annual Meeting of the American Anthropological Association, Chicago, IL.

Slade, M. (1982, October 24). Aptitude, intelligence or what? *New York Times.*

Skutnabb-Kangas, T., & Toukoma, T. (1976). *Teaching migrant children's mother tongue and learning the language of the host country in the context of the socio-cultural situation of the migrant family.* Helsinki: the Finnish National Commission for UNESCO.

Spicer, E. H. (1966). The process of cultural enslavement in Middle America. *36th Congress of International de Americanistas, Seville, 3,* 267–279.

Spicer, E. H. (1971). Persistent cultural systems: A comparative study of identity systems that can adapt to contrasting environments. *Science, 174,* 795–800.

Stockton Unified School District. (1948). *Community survey: In-school youth.* Unpublished manuscript, Research Department, Stockton Unified School District, Stockton, CA.

Suarez-Orozco, M. M. (1987). Becoming somebody: Central American immigrants in U.S. inner-city schools. *Anthropology & Education Quarterly, 18* (4), 287–299.

Tsang, S., & Wing, L. (1985). *Beyond Angel Island: The education of Asian Americans.* Unpublished manuscript, ARC Associates, Inc., Oakland, CA.

Tomlinson, S. (1982). *A sociology of special education.* London: Routledge & K. Paul.

Wan Zahid, N. M. (1978). *The Malay problem: A case study on the correlates of the educational achievement of the Malays.* Unpublished doctoral dissertation, Graduate School of Education, University of California, Berkeley.

Weinberg, M. (1977). *A chance to learn: A history of race and education in the United States.* New York: Cambridge University Press.

Weis, L. (1985). *Between two worlds: Black students in an urban community college.* Boston: Routledge and K. Paul.

Wigdor, A. K., & Garner, W. R. (Eds.). (1982). *Ability testing: Uses, consequences, and controversies.* Washington, DC: National Academy Press.

Woolard, K. A. (1981). *Ethnicity in education: Some problems of language and identity in Spain and the United States.* Unpublished manuscript, Department of Anthropology, University of California, Berkeley.

3
Apprenticeship in Literacy*

Gordon Wells
Ontario Institute for Studies in Education
Toronto, Ontario

Each year at about this time my students and I grapple once again with the question, "What is literacy?" It is a question to which I am always willing to return, for there are few issues of more importance in the contemporary debate about the goals of education and the nature of the curriculum that will enable those goals to be attained. How one defines literacy affects almost all the other decisions that have to be made.

I have learned a great deal from these annual debates—from listening to the views of my students, all of them professional educators, and from trying to formulate my own views in response. From these discussions has emerged a recognition that there are a number of different conceptions of literacy—or at least of different emphases—each of which is espoused by a significant number of teachers, sometimes to the exclusion of the other alternatives. In the paragraphs which follow, I shall try to set out these alternatives and briefly consider their curricular implications.

LEVELS OF LITERACY

On one thing all the contending parties are agreed: that literacy involves mastery of the written language. However, that is about the extent of the agreement. For precisely what it is that has to be mastered is one of the major issues on which educators differ. Is it merely control of the surface forms of written language that has to be achieved, or is something more involved, and, if so, what? A second issue on which conceptions of literacy differ concerns the extent to which the written mode is itself a focus of attention as opposed to its being treated as a means to other ends.

Before going any further, though, I should make it clear that the account I am going to propose is not a model of literate behavior. Rather it offers a set of distinctions between the processes believed to be involved in such behavior. It it not the processes themselves that are at issue but which processes are

---

* This chapter was presented at Il Jornadas Internacionales de Psicologi Educacion Cultura. Educacion y Desarrollo Humano. I should like to acknowledge the valuable suggestions and criticisms I have received from Gen Ling Chang in its preparation.

emphasized by the different conceptions and, either explicitly or implicitly, accorded value and made the focus of attention. For reasons that will become apparent, I shall refer to these different conceptions of literacy as levels within the overall model of literacy.

The first level of literacy I shall call the *performative*. The emphasis at this level is on the code as code. Becoming literate according to this perspective is simply a matter of acquiring those skills that allow a written message to be decoded into speech in order to ascertain its meaning and those skills that allow a spoken message to be encoded in writing according to the conventions of letter formation, spelling, and punctuation. At the performative level, it is tacitly assumed that written messages differ from spoken messages only in the medium employed for communication.

The second level I shall call the *functional*. This perspective emphasizes the uses that are made of literacy in interpersonal communication. To be literate according to this perspective is to be able, as a member of a particular society, to cope with the demands of everyday life that involve written language. Such demands include being able to read a popular newspaper, write a job application, follow the instructions that explain how to use a household gadget, or complete an official form. From a curricular point of view, a general command of the performative level of literacy is assumed; however, it is recognized that the form of written language varies according to the context of use and, in order to function effectively outside school, students may need to be given specific instruction in handling particular situationally related types of text.

The third level is the *informational*. Those who adopt this perspective are very conscious of the role that literacy plays in the communication of knowledge, particularly what might be called "discipline-based" knowledge. Reading for information is emphasized; writing tends to be treated as less important and is seen largely as a means for recording what one has learned and for demonstrating that learning to others. At this level, the code tends to be treated as transparent, as does the form, since both are considered to be unproblematic. If students have difficulties, these are assumed to be with the content of the text, not with the processes of interpretation or composition. At this level, then, the curricular emphasis on reading and writing—but particularly reading—is on the student's use for accessing the accumulated knowledge that it is seen as the function of schooling to transmit.

The fourth, and final, level in my proposed account is the *epistemic*. At each of the preceding levels, but particularly at the second and third, the concern is with literacy as a mode of communication. However, to focus only on the interpersonal communicative functions of literacy is to fail to recognize the changes that reading and writing can make in the mental lives of individuals and, by extension, of the societies to which those individuals belong. To be literate, according to this fourth perspective, is to have available ways of acting upon and transforming knowledge and experience that are, in general, unavailable to those who have never learned to read and write. From a curricular point of view, literate behavior is seen as simultaneously both a mode of language use and a mode of thinking, and the attitudes to be encouraged are those of creativity, exploration, and critical evaluation.

Of course, in any literacy event involving sustained meaning making, all four levels may be involved, for both composing and interpreting a written text require control of the written code, awareness of the appropriate register for the occasion, accurate and explicit matching of linguistic form to conceptual structure, and a creative and intentional exploration of alternatives within the text. Each of the four perspectives thus has something of importance to contribute to a complete account of what is to be literate. At the same time, it is clear that there is a relationship of inclusiveness as one moves from one to the next, so that it is appropriate to conceive of them as forming a series of levels, with the fourth level representing the most adequate answer to the question, "What is literacy?" (see Figure 3.1).

What is surprising is the very small proportion of educators who spontaneously propose this most inclusive model of literacy. Why this is so can be explained, I believe, by considering the possible relationships between speaking, writing, and thinking.

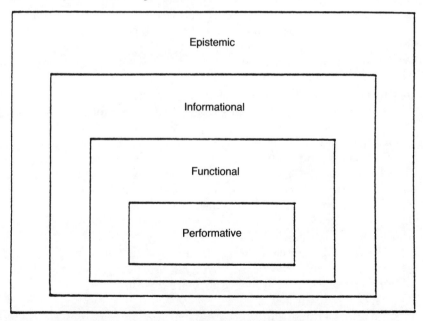

Figure 3.1. Levels in an Inclusive Model of Literacy

RELATIONSHIPS BETWEEN SPEAKING, WRITING, AND THINKING

The failure of the majority of people to recognize the intellectually enabling role of language, and particularly of literacy, was pointed out half a century ago by Sapir (1921) in an oft-quoted analogy:

> It does not follow . . . that the use to which language is put is always, or even mainly, conceptual. We are not in ordinary life so much concerned with concepts as with concrete particularities and specific relations. When I say, for instance, "I had a good breakfast this morning," it is clear that I am not in the throes of laborious thought, that what I have to transmit is hardly more than a pleasurable memory symbolically rendered in the grooves of habitual expression. Each element in the sentence defines a separate concept or conceptual relation, or both combined, but the sentence as a whole has no conceptual significance whatever. It is somewhat as though a dynamo capable of generating enough power to run an elevator were operated almost exclusively to feed an electric doorbell. (p. 14)

As educators, we are all concerned to help children harness the power of language in the service of thought, but in order to do so one must consider the generating process itself and how this differs according to the different purposes that language may be serving. In the above quotation, Sapir does not make a distinction between spoken and written uses of language and, in the last resort, this is surely correct. However, it is not a coincidence that the distinction he makes occurs in a written text, for it is in writing, *par excellence*, that we are most easily able to engage in sustained and creative mental activity.

From research conducted in a variety of disciplines, ranging from the anthropological (Goody, 1977) and sociological (Cook-Gumperz & Gumperz, 1981) to the psychological (Olson, 1977, 1986) and linguistic (Chafe, 1985; Tannen, 1985), it has become apparent that there are a number of dimensions on which spoken and written instances of language use tend to be distinguished. Although these dimensions are partially independent of each other and are differently related to each other in different cultures, all of the above-mentioned researchers are in agreement that, in moving from speech to writing, more is involved than simply a change in the channel (oral/aural, manual/visual) through which the linguistic message is expressed. As a result of the change of mode, the nature of the message itself changes, in response both to the different purposes the two modes usually serve and to the inter- and intrapersonal contexts in which they are typically used. Writing is not simply speech written down.

The nature of these differences can be brought out most clearly by comparing such extremes as casual conversation and sustained imaginative or expository writing. What is most important about conversation, from this point of view, is that it is jointly constructed in a shared social context in which the participants can assume a considerable amount of shared information. Furthermore, in intonation, gesture, and tone of voice, participants have other means in addition to the purely verbal for communicating their meaning intentions. By contrast, sustained prose is written by a writer who is distant in time and space from his or her potential readers; he or she can therefore make far fewer assumptions about shared information and has no immediate feedback from which to check that the reader's interpretation matches his or her own meaning intentions. For these reasons, and because of the nonavailibility of prosodic and nonverbal cues, both writer and reader are forced to rely exclusively on the verbal message, which must therefore be both explicit and independent of knowledge pertaining to the particular context of origin. It is this characteristic of writing that I believe Donaldson (1978) has in mind when she emphasizes the importance of being able to disembed thinking and language from its original context of personal experience.

In addition to differences arising from the distinct interpersonal contexts of speaking and writing, there are also differences arising from the actual processes of production and from the adjustments that the composer must make to take account of the processes involved in the different modes of reception. The most important dimension here is probably that of time. In spontaneous conversational speech, as Chafe (1985) has shown, information is organized in short "idea units" (consisting typically of a single clause, on an average seven words long) which are relatively loosely strung together, often without the relationships between them being made explicit. This mode of organization, he hypothesizes, results from the limits on the amount of information a speaker can handle in a single focus of attention. By contrast, because the act of writing is itself much more time consuming and because there is no pressure to keep a listener's attention, the writer has time to be both more selective in choosing what information to communicate and more deliberate in the arrangement and expression of that information.

As a result of these differences in both context and mode of production, writing involves a relationship between language and thinking that is distinct from the relationship typically obtaining in casual conversation. Whereas conversation is likely to require little more than the selection of familiar ideas "symbolically rendered in the grooves of habitual expression," sustained written prose—and equally poetry—involves processes of composition in which experience is transformed in the attempt to organize and shape it to meet the specific demands of the text. It is in this sense that thoughts and knowledge can, as Scardamalia and Bereiter (1985) put it, be enhanced by writing about them.

The same sorts of benefits can also accrue from reading, of course, if the reader actively interrogates the text and seeks to construct an interpretation that is both meaningful in terms of his or her existing knowledge and values, and also constrained by the semantic structures that are linguistically represented. In comparing spoken and written language, however, I have chosen to emphasize production rather than reception for two important reasons.

First, in discussions of literacy, it is nearly always reading that is made the focus of attention; it seems to be tacitly assumed either that writing is of lesser importance or that anyone who knows how to read will, once he or she has mastered the relatively mechanical skills of handwriting and spelling, be equally able to write. Yet this is very far from being the case. Certainly, to be an effective writer one must also read widely and critically, for it is on these resources that one draws in being one's own first and, ideally, most critical reader. However, there is more to writing than simply generating sentences at random and them making critical decisions as to which ones to retain.

This leads me to the second reason. In emphasizing the production of written language, I have sought to draw attention to the potential intellectual benefits of engaging in the dialectical processes of composing: planning, drafting, rereading, and revising. At its most effective, composing itself "unfolds the truths which the mind then learns. Writing informs the mind, it is not the other way round."

These claims may seem to some to be made too exclusively with respect to written language. Certainly, composing in speech may also be an aid to thought just as one may be led to reorganize one's thinking in listening to the speech of others. However, if the skills of transforming thoughts and knowledge are not dependent on having learned to read and write, they are most effectively extended and developed through engaging in these more reflective modes of language use. Once developed in writing, these same skills then become more readily available in oral discourse: one becomes able to "speak a written language," at least in situations where extended monologue is appropriate. In the fullest sense, therefore, to become literate is to become able to exploit the full symbolic potential of language for thinking in either the written or the spoken mode.

Seen in the light of this discussion, the four proposed levels in the overall model of literacy represent progressively more adequate understandings of the relationship between speaking (and listening), writing (and reading), and thinking. In the remainder of this chapter, I use this account as a perspective from which to address what is known about the preschool experiences that contribute to the development of literacy and to make some suggestions concerning the role of instruction.

THE FOUNDATIONS OF LITERACY

In this section, I consider what children know about written language when they begin to receive systematic instruction in literacy. I also look at what is known about the consequences of different forms of preschool experience for success in acquiring literacy, and more generally, for subsequent school achievement.

First, let us consider what can be called awareness of print: the recognition that certain visual configurations in the environment are of special significance in that they are used for reading. On the basis of her longitudinal study of middle- and lower-class four- to six-year-old children in Argentina, together with subsequent research on other populations (by herself and various colleagues), Ferreiro has shown that "not yet knowing how to read does not prevent [children in a literate society] from having precise ideas about the characteristics a written text must have for reading to take place" (Ferreiro & Teberosky, 1982, p. 27).

Within a Piagetian type of interview situation, Ferreiro and her colleagues used a variety of stimuli—cards with varying numbers of graphic characters, picture storybooks, sentences written down in the presence of the children—to discover just what ideas children have about what can be read and how the graphic display corresponds to the words spoken in reading the text aloud. What they discovered was that, by the beginning of formal instruction, all children, whatever their social class of origin, had developed quite detailed hypotheses in relation to these issues. They also found that there was strong evidence of a common sequence in the progressive development of their understanding about print. A similar approach was adopted to study what the children understood about writing, and here too the results led the researchers to conclude that there is a common sequence of development through recognizable levels of conceptualization, which are not directly dependent on formal instruction.

To me, what is most significant about these findings is their similarity to what has been discovered about the acquisition of spoken language:

1. Children pass through a common sequence of development which is not dependent on deliberate or systematic instruction.
2. The hypotheses they form at various stages in this sequence are often, by adult standards, erroneous and are certainly not based in any direct fashion on imitation of adult models.
3. There is considerable variation in children's rate of development and this is significantly correlated with the range and frequency of the experiences which provide evidence on which to base and modify their hypotheses.

The picture that emerges of the language learner, whether of the spoken or the written form, is one of an active seeker after meaning who is predisposed to construct progressively more complex conceptualizations of linguistic form and to modify them in the light of feedback of various kinds from the environment. Print, that is to say, the systematic organization of the graphic display, like the formal organization of the linguistic system encountered in speech, presents children with a problem space which they explore and attempt to understand.

As with spoken language, the development of effective understanding of print can be facilitated by appropriate behaviors by the people in the child's environment, such as pointing out similarities and differences between particular graphic displays, answering questions about the meaning of such displays or about their internal organization, and so on. But even when such support is lacking or at least is only minimally present, children still progress through the same sequence of development, albeit at a slower rate than those who receive more guidance and encouragement.

If such spontaneous learning is universal, as the findings of Ferreiro and other researchers seem to suggest, what bearing does it have on the progress children make in becoming literate once they embark on the more deliberate learning that is expected of them in school? At the present time, no simple answer can be given to this question. Certainly, the children who are most advanced in their conceptualization of print on entry to school are likely to make satisfactory progress, but the fate of the less advanced is much less predictable. Ferreiro and Teberosky (1982) state the problem as follows:

> Our data reflect a long developmental process from children's initial conceptions of print to their final ones. This process takes place in the preschool period. Some children are at the final levels of development as they enter school. Others reach first grade at the initial levels of hypothesizing about print. The former group has very little to learn in school, since first grade instruction will not challenge their capabilities. The latter group has a great deal to learn. The problem is whether traditionally conceived instruction offers them what they need. (p. 279)

Reviewing the type of instruction offered in Argentinian schools, their conclusion is pessimistic. Teachers, they found, do not take into account what individual children already know in planning the program of instruction. The same is no doubt true of at least some teachers in other parts of the world.

There are other studies which show a strong relationship between level of conceptualization about print on entry to school and subsequent school achievement. In the Bristol Study, for example, a combined test involving "Concepts about Print" (Clay, 1972) and the identification of the letters of the alphabet was administered to two independent cohorts of five-year-old children on entry to school. The aim was to yield a composite measurement of the children's "knowledge of literacy." These scores were subsequently correlated with those obtained on the Neale Analysis of Reading (Neale, 1957–1966) administered two years later. In both cases, a correlation coefficient of 0.79 ($p<$ .001) was obtained, suggesting that the extent of the children's knowledge about print, as measured by this test, was indeed related to their subsequent progress (Wells, 1985b). This interpretation was both confirmed and extended by the results of a follow-up assessment of the younger cohort in the last year of their elementary education. Once again, substantial correlations were found between the children's knowledge of literacy on entry to school and their reading ability ($r = 0.79$, p< .001), their writing ability ($r = 0.73$, $p<$ .001), and their overall school achievement ($r = 0.83$, $p<$ .001) five years later at about the age of 10.

Two different kinds of explanation can be offered to account for these findings. The first is to see the results of the Bristol Study as essentially confirming the arguments of Ferreiro and Teberosky. Children who were advanced in their knowledge of literacy on entry to school made good progress, independently of the sort of instruction they received, while those who were less advanced in their conceptualizations about print did not receive instruction that built upon what they knew or was even at odds with it and, as a result, these children made poor progress. Certainly, our observations of some of the children would tend to confirm such an interpretation as at least a partial explanation of the widely differing levels of literacy and general school achievement.

As a total explanation, however, this seems to me inadequate, as it assumes a view of what is involved in becoming literate that is restricted to the first level in the model—the performative level. If, as was argued earlier, much more is required than learning efficiently to decode print and to encode speech, it is clear that there are more roots to literacy than simply the development of appropriate concepts about print.

Yetta Goodman (1980) suggests that children need to develop understanding about the following:

1. the significance of written language
2. the oral labels used when referring to written language
3. the purposes written language serves for people of different socio-economic status
4. the variety of forms used to construct the meanings communicated by written language (pp. 1–2).

And she adds that it is in "interactions between the learner and his or her world that we must look for the origins of literacy." The second explanation for the ambiguous relationship between early concepts of print and subsequent achievement looks to these other roots of literacy, and to the kinds of interaction with the world from which they grow.

If, for children growing up in literate societies, the development of hypotheses about the organization of print is a universal response to seeing print in their environments, the same universality is not found in the hypotheses they form about the purposes that written language serves, the forms it may take, or the significance it has in the lives of those who use it. These hypotheses are much more dependent on the particular culture to which children belong and on the actual literacy practices of their immediate family and community.

That these practices vary considerably is evidenced by the increasing number of cross-cultural studies which document in detail the literacy events in which members engage and the frequency with which such events occur. See, for example, Scribner and Cole's (1981) study of Vai literacy, Heath's (1983) comparison of the literate practices of three subcultural groups in the Piedmont Carolinas, and Anderson and Stokes's (1984) observations of daily literate events in the homes of three ethnic minority groups in metropolitan San Diego.

Heath's study, based on extensive ethnographic observations in two non-mainstream communities, is particularly relevant to the present argument. What she discovered, and this is supported by the findings of Anderson and Stokes, was that there were quite frequent literacy events in these two communities, and that at least some of them involved children as well as adults. However, there were also important differences between the two communities in the significance that adults attached to the children's encounters with print and the values that they put upon them. Of the black working-class community she writes:

> Just as Trackton parent do not buy special toys for their young children, they do not buy books for them either: adults do not create reading and writing tasks for the young, nor do they consciously model or demonstrate reading and writing behaviors for them. In the home, on the plaza, and in the neighborhood, children are left to find their own reading and writing tasks: distinguishing one television channel from another, knowing the name brand of cars, motor-cycles and bicycles, choosing one or another can of soup or cereal, reading price tags at Mr. Dogan's store to be sure they do not pay more than they would at the supermarket. (p. 190)

Heath goes on to describe how children frequently ask what some piece of print "says," noting that "adults respond to their queries, making their instructions fit the requirements of the tasks." In sum, as she put it, "children in Trackton *read to learn* before they go to school to *learn to read*" (p. 191, original emphases). In terms of the levels of literacy discussed in the first section of the chapter, what these children encounter in their community is essentially limited to the second level—functional literacy.

In Roadville, a nearby white working-class community, a somewhat wider range of uses is made of reading and writing by adults, particularly by the women, who write notes to distant relatives and sometimes read sewing patterns and home decorating magazines. As in Trackton, reading and writing also occur in relation to religious observance. Unlike Trackton parents, however, the parents of Roadville children emphasize the importance of reading and, to a lesser extent, writing. At least in the preschool years, they act on those beliefs:

> Roadville wives and mothers buy books for their children and bring home from church special Sunday School materials supplied for the young. Before their babies are six months old, Roadville mothers read simple books, usually featuring a single object on each page, to their children. Later they choose books which tell simplified bible stories: introduce the alphabet, numbers, or nursery rhymes: or contain "real life" stories about boys and girls, usually taking care of their pets either at home or on a farm. When their children begin to watch "Sesame Street" and "Electric Company" on television, they buy books, games, and toys derived from these shows. They read the advertisements for other games and toys that appear on the boxes the play-things come in and, as their children get older, they advise them to do the same. (pp. 222–223)

In terms of the levels of literacy, Roadville children would appear to be exposed to a wider range than their Trackton peers. In addition to emphasis on the functional value of literacy, children's attention is also drawn to the performative level and, to some extent, to the informational. They might therefore be expected to make satisfactory progress at school. However, this is not the case. The major reason, Heath suggests, is to be found in the attitude Roadville parents adopt to text:

> In Roadville, the absoluteness of ways of talking about what is written fits church ways of talking about what is written. Behind the written word is an authority, and the text is a message which can be taken apart only insofar as its analysis does not extend too far beyond the text and commonly agreed upon experiences. New syntheses and multiple interpretations create alternatives which challenge fixed roles, rules, and "rightness." (pp. 234–235)

Significantly, Roadville children also have very restricted opportunities for writing and little choice over the occasion or the content. Although the literacy events they engage in are different from those of Trackton children, in the end they are hardly more beneficial as a preparation for schooling. "Neither community's ways with the written word prepares it for the school's ways" (p. 235).

By contrast, the third of Heath's communities—the mainstreamers of the nearby urban center—were much more successful in providing an environment that prepared their children to succeed in school. Some of the features of this environment are planning and keeping to a schedule, training children to act as conversational partners, question-answerers, and information givers, and providing a general orientation to literate sources. From an early age, children are expected to take an interest in books and information derived from books. They also see their parents using reading and writing in relation to their work and leisure activities in ways that emphasize the importance of written sources of information.

Storyreading is an important part of the children's experience, both at home and at Sunday School or playschool. This is how Heath describes such occasions:

> Teachers and mothers expect the children to sit quietly and listen until the reader indicates the children may participate in discussion about the story. . . . The teacher usually acts as narrator for the text, and she models and questions. She asks questions about the story which directly relate to the story's content most of the time. . . . Often teachers follow up with "How do you know?" questions, in which they ask the children to identify points in the story or, more often, portions of the pictures, which let them know the location, weather, pending action, or other unexplained events of the story. (p. 254)

Not surprisingly, children who have had such experiences fit easily into the routines and expectations of classrooms in which activities tend to be highly structured and teacher-dominated. Most of these children also learn to read and write with little difficulty, for the ways of relating to written language in school are similar to those they have encountered at home. Very clearly, the model of literacy that is paramount in these homes is the informational (third level), supported by some emphasis on both the performative and the functional.

But what of the fourth level—the epistemic? Are there homes in which children observe or engage in literate practices that might lead them to form, however embryonically, a model of literacy that emphasizes the use of language to develop and facilitate thinking? Despite the impression Heath gives of a way of life that is largely pre-scripted, probably some of the mainstream children had experiences of literacy which were of this kind. Certainly, we observed such events in some of the homes in the Bristol Study. Significantly, they were most likely to occur in the context of stories, either during or just after a reading, or on some later occasion when a story was recalled in relation to an ongoing or anticipated event.

The importance of storyreading in the preschool years has been strongly advanced by a number of researchers, including Teale (1984) and Doake (1981). The Bristol Study found it to be, of all the literacy-related activities investigated, the strongest predictor of later school achievement (Wells, 1985b). The reason for this, I believe, is that the experience of sharing a story with an adult has the potential for introducing the child to all four levels of the model of literacy simultaneously. In listening to a story and attending, however globally, to the printed text from which it is read, children are beginning to gain experience of the sustained meaning-building organization of written language as well as of its characteristic rhythms and structures. The are also beginning to make the connection between print and speech (first level). From some stories, too, they will gain a sense of the functional value of literacy (second level), though this is perhaps the least emphasized of the proposed levels. As listeners, they are also learning to pay attention to the linguistic message as the major source of information and, at the same time, to extend their experience vicariously and to develop their general knowledge as they achieve an understanding of the content of the story (third level). One indirect form of evidence for this benefit is the substantially larger vocabularies of children who are frequently read to.

However, the most important benefit to children from having stories read to them is that it leads them to construct an interpretation on the basis of the text alone and in this way to begin to come to grips with the symbolic potential of language—its power to represent experience in symbols which are independent of the objects, events, and relationships that are symbolized and which can thus be interpreted with reference to contexts other than those in which the experience originally occurred. Where this interpretative activity is accompanied by exploratory talk, in which the events of the story are related to the child's own experience and conjectures and reactions are developed and encouraged, it is also the beginning of the child's discovery of the power of language for sustaining and developing thinking (fourth level).

Not all shared storyreading is of this kind, however. Sometimes the child is content simply to listen to the story. Sometimes the adult has other concerns and does not have time to talk. But the most frequent reason, I believe, is that many adults—like the Roadville parents described by Heath—treat the text as fixed and authoritative, not as the basis for the consideration of alternative interpretations and for the explorations of other possible worlds.

Having considered some of the ways in which children's experiences of literacy events vary according to the practices and values emphasized in their communities, we are now in a better position to explain the observed relationships between the extent of school entrants' understanding about print and their subsequent school achievement. As has already been emphasized, all children spontaneously develop hypotheses about written language, its form, functions, and value, on the basis of their experiences of literacy events. However, the forms these hypotheses take depend very much on the particular nature of their experiences. All children develop hypotheses at the performative level, but whether they will develop hypotheses at higher levels will depend on the actual events they witness and participate in, and on the value that is apparently put on different types of literacy events by their parents and other members of the community.

To some extent, their subsequent success in school will depend upon how well the instruction they receive in reading and writing is matched to the understanding they have already developed about print. But more important, in my view, is the inclusiveness of the model of literacy they have constructed on the basis of their experience of literacy events in their community. The more inclusive is their model, the better they will be able to meet the expectations of the school that they will use literacy as a symbol system that allows them to access information and operate upon and transform it.

In practice, however, the children who have the most advanced conceptualization of print on entry to school tend also to be those who have constructed the most inclusive model of literacy. They succeed in school not only because they have well developed concepts about print, but also because they have begun to discover the power that language, and particularly written language, has as an instrument of thought (Wells, 1986).

FACILITATING THE DEVELOPMENT OF LITERACY

Against this background it is easy to see what the role of the school should be—though not so easy perhaps to realize it in practice! From studies of children in the preschool years, the evidence is overwhelming that children are active creators of their own understanding. They can and do attempt to gain control over written language so that they can use it to achieve their own purposes. From the moment of entry to school, therefore, there are achievements to celebrate and a foundation to build on. Children also already have strategies of meaning-making that should be recognized and encouraged.

At the same time, it is important to recognize that the differences between children in their preschool experiences may have led them to construct quite varied models of literacy. This is not to say that the processes children engage in when attempting to make sense of written language are necessarily different from one group to another, but rather that the conceptions of what they are doing that are reflected back to them by adult members of their communities may vary according to the particular models of literacy that are emphasized in different communities. As a result, some children may come to school with initial conceptions of literacy that fail to match the implicit assumptions embodied in the curriculum. They may have only part of the model described by the four levels presented above. Whatever the conceptions, however, they represent a valuable achievement. It is important, therefore, that teachers endeavor to find out what each child already knows and can do with respect to written language so that when planning further experiences they can build on the child's existing knowledge as opposed to ignoring it, or still worse, undermining it. This is very clearly the message to be taken from the conclusions reached by all the researchers referred to above.

However, the overall curriculum itself may need to be subjected to critical scrutiny. What sort of model of literacy does it presuppose? As the differing perspectives described in the first part of this paper make clear, many teachers and administrators have very narrow conceptions of the nature of literacy and its role in facilitating children's intellectual, social, and affective development. The external pressures on schools to go "back to the basics" may further entrench these views. The inadequacy of a model confined to the performative level has now come to be recognized (although it is still all too prevalent as a guide for practice in the early grades). However, an emphasis on the functional level is now being widely proposed as a solution to the problems encountered in school by many children from minority and low social class groups. The grounds are that such am emphasis is in the children's best interests in preparing them to cope with the demands which they are expected to meet in the wider community outside the school. On the basis of the arguments set out earlier, however, I believe that such a proposal is misguided, for in denying these children the opportunity to become fully literate, it can only serve to perpetuate the existing disadvantages experienced by these groups.

It is not sufficient, therefore, when setting the educational goals of literacy to look only to the functions that reading and writing typically serve in the lives of community members. Nor is it sufficient to see literacy as an additional means of accessing information through the use of textbooks, works of reference, or even original sources, important though this function of literacy undoubtedly is. If the goal of education generally is to enable individuals to become creative and critical thinkers and communicators, only a model of literacy that recognizes the importance of the epistemic level can be accepted as adequate, and this is so whatever the cultural background from which the students come.

Such a model should inform the curriculum from the very beginning. From an analytical point of view, it may appear that the four levels form a developmental progression: that being able to form or recognize letters, for example, is a prerequisite for comprehending and composing continuous text. However, in practice this is not the case. Children encounter written language in complete, contextualized events and employ processes related to all four levels simultaneously in attempting to make sense of these encounters. Such a multidimensional mode of learning has been amply demonstrated in research on the initial acquisition of spoken language: form, meaning, and function are all attended to at once as the child, simultaneously and progressively, gains mastery over the language system and uses that system to construct a representation of social reality (Bruner, 1983; Halliday, 1975; Wells, 1985a). The evidence so far available suggests that literacy is based on analogous learning strategies. If this is so, the four proposed levels should not be seen as forming a pedagogical progression. Instead, teachers should attempt from the beginning to provide learning opportunities that give emphasis to all four levels and to the relationships among them.

There is not space in this chapter to spell out the form that a curriculum based on these principles should take or the sorts of activities through which it might be realized. In any case, to attempt such a task in the abstract would be inappropriate because it is in the detailed working-out of the curriculum that each school and each teacher needs to be responsive to the experiences of individual children. There are, however, a number of guiding principles that are, I believe, of universal validity.

1. Children should be treated as active constructors of their own knowledge and understanding. They should be encouraged to share the responsibility for selecting the tasks in which they engage, for deciding on the means for attaining their goals, and for evaluating the outcomes of their attempts.
2. Language should be seen, in general, as a means to achieving other goals: even when attention needs to be focused on the code, this should be in the context of an intrinsically meaningful activity.
3. Writing, reading, speaking, and listening should be seen as complementary processes, each building on and feeding the others in an integrated approach to the exploration of ideas and feelings, the consideration of alternatives, and, finally, the formulation and communication of conclusions.
4. An important place should be accorded, at all stages, to the sharing of stories, both those in the literature of the culture and those that children themselves construct on the basis of their own experiences. As well as being valuable in their own right, stories provide an important bridge from the particularized example to the general principle and from the basic narrative mode in which we all make sense of our individual experience to the more abstract logical modes of exposition and argument.

But perhaps most important of all is the need for teachers to see their role as that of collaborating with their pupils in the making of meaning. Literacy, fully understood, is the most useful and versatile tool for the pursuit of this craft. Teachers should be, and be seen by their pupils to be, masters of this craft. By working as apprentices with their teachers, pupils will have the opportunity to become masters in their turn who are able to create new meanings appropriate to the needs of the communities to which they belong.

REFERENCES

Anderson, A. B., & Stokes, S. J. (1984). Social and institutional influences on the development and practices of literacy. In H. Goelman, A. A. Oberg, & F. Smith (Eds.), *Awakening to literacy*. Portsmouth, NH: Heinemann.

Bruner, J. S. (1983), *Child's talk*. New York: Norton.

Chafe, W. L. (1985). Linguistic differences produced by differences between speaking and writing. In D. R. Olson, N. Torrance, & A. Hildyard (Eds.), *Literacy, language and learning* (pp. 105–123). Cambridge: Cambridge University Press.

Clay, M. M. (1972). *The early detection of reading difficulties: A diagnostic survey*. London: Heinemann.

Cook-Gumperz, J., & Gumperz, J. J. (1981). From oral to written culture: The transition to literacy. In W. F. Whiteman (Ed.). *Writing, Vol. I: Variation in writing* (pp. 89–109). Hillsdale, NJ: Lawrence Erlbaum.

Doake, D. (1981). *Book experience and emergent reading in preschool children*. Unpublished doctoral dissertation. University of Alberta, Edmonton, Canada.

Donaldson, M. (1978). *Children's minds*. London: Fontana.

Ferreiro, E., & Teberosky, A. (1982). *Literacy before schooling*. Portsmouth, NH: Heinemann Educational Books.

Goodman, Y. (1980). The roots of literacy. In M. P. Douglas (Ed.), *Claremont reading conference forty-fourth yearbook* (pp. 1–32). Claremont, CA: Claremont Graduate School.

Goody, J. (1977). *The domestication of the savage mind*. Cambridge: Cambridge University Press.

Halliday, M. A. K. (1975). *Learning how to mean*. London: Arnold.

Heath, S. B. (1983). *Ways with words*. Cambridge: Cambridge University Press.

Neale, M. D. (1957–1966). *Neale analysis of reading ability*. London: Macmillan.

Olson, D. R. (1977). From utterance to text: The bias of language in speech and writing. *Harvard Educational Review, 47*, 257–281.

Olson, D. R. (1986). The cognitive consequences of literacy. *Canadian Psychology, 27*(2), 109–121.

Sapir, E. (1921). *Language*. New York: Harcourt Brace.

Scardamalia, M., & Bereiter, C. (1985). Development of dialectical processes in composition. In D. R. Olson, N. Torrance, & A. Hildyard (Eds.), *Literacy, language and learning* (pp. 307–329). Cambridge: Cambridge University Press.

Scribner, S., & Cole, M. (1981). *The psychology of literacy*. Cambridge, MA: Harvard University Press.

Tannen, D. (1985). Relative focus on involvement in oral and written discourse. In D. R. Olson, N. Torrance, & A. Hildyard (Eds.), *Literacy, language and learning* (pp. 124–147). Cambridge: Cambridge University Press.

Teale, W. H. (1984). Reading to young children: Its significance for literacy development. In H. Goelman, A. A. Oberg, & F. Smith (Eds.), *Awakening to literacy* (pp. 110–121). Portsmouth, NH: Heinemann.

Wells, C. G. (1985a). *Language development in the pre-school years*. Cambridge: Cambridge University Press.

Wells, C. G. (1985b). Pre-school literacy-related activities and success in school. In D. R. Olson, N. Torrance, & A. Hildyard (Eds.), *Literacy, language and learning* (pp. 229–255). Cambridge: Cambridge University Press.

Wells, C. G. (1986). *The meaning makers: Children learning language and using language to learn*. Portsmouth, NH: Heinemann.

4

Responsibilities and Expectations: Interactive Home/School Factors in Literacy Development Among Portuguese First Graders

Adeline Becker
Brown University

INTRODUCTION

Over half a million Portuguese people live in the New England area, 90 percent of whom are from the Azores Islands. The Azores, an archipelago of nine volcanic Portuguese islands, are located in the Atlantic Ocean approximately 900 miles from Lisbon and 2,100 miles from New York.

The Portuguese have among the lowest literacy rates in Europe, a phenomenon that has been partially recreated in New England where Portuguese students have one of the highest dropout rates in the region. Until the early 1970s, education in the Azores rarely exceeded four years of schooling for the majority of the population. Consequently, many of the Azoreans in New England who emigrated before the mid-1970s are not able to read their native language beyond second-grade level. While Portuguese immigration in the 1980s has declined considerably and education levels have continued to climb, the majority of adult immigrants in New England still tend to have minimal literacy skills and little formal education.

This chapter examines family responsibilities and expectations in the Portuguese immigrant home and explores their differential impact on the reading performance of first-grade students.

While a significant body of literature has focused on the parents' role in the development of their children's early literacy skills, little is known about the impact of nonliterate aspects of the home environment on success in beginning reading. Researchers, for example, have investigated various home factors affecting reading achievement, such as family income (Armor, 1972; Coleman, 1972; DeLone, 1979), parental education levels (Kennett, 1975), family size, position in the birth order (Douglas, 1968), and household structure (Whiting & Whiting, 1975). The relationship of early reading success and parental responsiveness to print has also been well documented as impacting on the success of early readers (Heath, 1982; Teale, 1978; Yaden & McGee, 1984). But, as Hiebert (1986) notes: "There is a need to look at the contributions of both parents and children in creating print-related experiences in the home" (p. 149). In this regard, research also points to informal home experiences as relevant to a child's acquisition of literacy (Goodman & Goodman, 1978; Harste, Burke, & Woodward, 1982; Smith, 1976).

Tobin (1981), for instance, has compared personal and home characteristics of early readers, nonearly readers, and preschool readers, concluding that parents of the most fluent readers involved their children in informal gamelike phonics activities and directed their children's attention to relationships between spoken and written words. Dunn (1981) has also shown that parents who viewed the teaching of letters and numbers as their responsibility had children who performed better in early reading.[1]

Metalinguistic influences on literacy have generated much interest in current research by Olson, the Goodmans, S. B. Heath and Kontos and Huba among others. These researchers have all supported the causal relationships between cognitive stimulation through verbal interplay at home and independent early reading success.

Heath (1986), in fact, relates the differential uses of home language as relevant to literacy attainment. She states, however, that "for many language and culture groups, there is little fit between the kinds of language uses chosen by the school and those developed in the family and community" (p. 151).

In *Becoming a Nation of Readers: The Report of the Commission on Reading* (1985), reading aloud to children is presented as the single most important parental activity for building the knowledge required for eventual success in reading. The report recommends that parents not only read to preschoolers but informally teach them about reading and writing and support their continued growth as readers throughout school.

While this is a laudable goal, for many parents it is also an unrealistic expectation given that literacy has become not just a pedagogical phenome-

---

[1] While this literature supports a much criticized skill-based approach to literacy and encourages parental participation in this process, it is noteworthy since it mirrors the reality of a great many classrooms, including the first-grade Portuguese class observed in this study. Neither the research cited nor the Portuguese classroom practices reflects my own whole language orientation, a methodology which I find considerably more compatible with the life experiences of minority learners. Labov (1985), for example, notes that many minority students come from backgrounds where cooperation and sharing are the norm. Group interaction, and learning from one's peers rather than individualistic teacher dominated environments, represent a more productive atmosphere for learning to read. He concludes that because the skills developed in vernacular cultures depend on a different strategy, that is, noncompetitive interactions, the repression of these strategies continues to result in massive educational failure.

non, but one of equity as well. While 45 percent of 17-year-old non-minority students have reading proficiency scores that indicate an ability to comprehend, analyze, and summarize complex written information, less than 20 percent of minority students are able to do this (National Assessment of Educational Progress, 1985). The disparities are even greater among the parents of these students.

Alma Flor Ada (1988) reports on a unique literature project for children and parents that "grew out of an awareness of the importance of parent's involvement in their children's education (while recognizing that) many of them had never read a book before" (p. 16). Similarly, in a comprehensive study of reading collaboration between teachers and parents, Tizard, Schofield, and Hewison (1982) document the benefits to children of parental involvement in the reading process. A 1986 study by Lapp also recognizes that "both the popular press and education journals abound with articles suggesting that students enjoy more success in school when their parents are actively involved in the learning process" (p. 18).

Yet, the criteria for what constitutes literacy and its value within society varies greatly. Disparate groups experience literacy in disparate ways. Anderson and Stokes (1984), for example, show how literacy is differentially socialized by blacks, Mexicans, and Anglos, while McDermott (1985) sees the literacy acquisition process for blacks as a regeneration of their pariah status where the inability to read becomes one way of achieving high status among one's black peers while rejecting the values of the white majority.

Cazden (1985) agrees, noting that the social context of learning to read is a critical factor in analyzing the mismatch between minority students and their teachers. Children in the top reading group of her study, most of whom were white, spent three times as much time on task as the students in the lower groups, most of whom were black. The structure of the reading task resulted in lower group children waiting for more direction, reading less, and becoming more dependent on the teacher. A self-fulfilling prophecy of dependency, withdrawal, and lack of confidence was perpetuated.

In *Silencing in Public Schools* Michele Fine (1987) further questions the educational treatment of minorities. "If the process of education is to allow children, adolescents, and adults their voices—to read, write, create, critique, and transform—how can we justify the institutionalizing of silence at the level of policies which obscure systematic problems . . . . . , a curriculum bereft of the lived experience of students themselves, a pedagogy organized around control and not conversation, and a thorough-going psychologizing of social issues which enables (a student) to bury himself in silence and not be noticed?" (p. 172).

Similarly, Paulo Freire's approach to literacy links knowledge to power and emancipates individuals by enabling them to participate in "the unveiling of reality" (Freire & Macedo, 1987, p. 66). As described by Giroux (1988), literacy is "inherently a political project in which men and women assert their right and responsibility not only to read, understand and transform their own experiences, but also to reconstitute their relationship within the wider society. In this sense, literacy is fundamental to aggressively constructing one's voice as part of a wider project of possibility and empowerment" (p. 64).

It is clear that "in addition to examining the process of learning to read as a problem of human cognition, it is also of value to study it within its social matrix" (Seitz, 1977, p. 30). While researchers are generally aware that "successful learning . . . depends on the support of the family as well as the school" (Peterson & Kellam, 1977, p. 17) "there remains considerable evidence that non-school factors may be more important determinants of educational outcomes than are 'school' factors" (Averch, Carroll, Donaldson, Kiesling, & Pincus, 1971, p. XII).

What has dramatically emerged, in fact, is our need to look not only at families able to provide literate home environments, but increasingly at those elements operating in nonliterate households which also serve to support and reinforce the reading process in school. While no one would deny the educational advantages of parental engagement in early print-related activities, the reality of contemporary urban America is that large numbers of parents have neither the skills nor the ability to create a literate home environment. With so many students from homes where parents have limited education and where no reading matter is available, the question arises as to what other forms of knowledge and experience gained in the home may be contributing to early success in the literacy acquisition process.

THE STUDY

My own investigations indicate that various factors operate in nonliterate homes which contribute to differential success in early reading. Research that I conducted among eight Portuguese first-graders in urban New England showed that despite similar intellectual capabilities and lack of parental literacy involvements, that the children were, in fact, performing differentially with respect to their progress in reading. All eight youngsters were enrolled in a Portuguese bilingual first-grade class where reading instruction was provided in Portuguese by a native Portuguese-speaking teacher. All were non-English speaking. Their similar cognitive capability was confirmed by their Portuguese-speaking teachers (both kindergarten and first grade), their bilingual aides, and guidance counselor. However, at the end of first grade, three students were considered by their teacher as performing badly in Portuguese reading, that is, they were in the lowest reading group or reading readiness; of the remaining students, two were in the middle reading group where they were just beginning the first-grade reader, and three were doing well, that is, in the top reading group where they had finished the first-grade reader.[2]

Patterns of family interactions were used as clues in understanding why students were performing differentially given equal ability. Extensive family observation conducted over a four-month period from June to September, during various times of the day and different days of the week, with durations ranging from 50 minutes to two-and-a-half hours, yielded fruitful data. Without knowing the individual reading ability of any of the eight students, I was able to construct, with 100 percent accuracy, a hierarchy reflecting their relative reading performance.

This was accomplished primarily by investigating various possible causative factors, including family income (DeLone 1979), parental occupation, (Goldberg, 1971; Wolf, 1966), and metalinguistic influences (Hoffmann, 1971; Kifer, 1975a, 1975b; Kontos & Huba, 1983; Mason & McCormick, 1983; Olson, 1984). Intelligence and reading success (Burt 1966, Herrenstein, 1971) was ruled out as an area of initial exploration since students in the study were selected on the basis of similar intellectual ability. Differential performance due to kindergarten experiences (Morrison & Harris, 1968) was similarly eliminated since all of the children attended the same kindergarten class.

Of interest also was Hess' (1969) work with environmental influences on the development of reading readiness and Grayum's studies (1958) of parental attitudes and beginning reading achievement. Kennett's (1975) research on parental educational levels and the impact of motivation on performance (Kagan, 1974) were especially useful.

Following are brief descriptions of the eight students and their families.

FAMILY PROFILES

The Top Group: Gloria Quadros—Student #1

The Quadros family emigrated from a small village in São Miguel, the Azores, three years ago. The six family members include a nonemployed maternal grandmother, a mother who works second shift in a wire factory, a father who was a farmer in Portugal and is now a part-time janitor in a

---

[2] Teacher judgment and terminology were used in characterizing the top, middle, and lowest reading groups. Since the teacher was responsible for grouping students and grading their performance, her criteria for student evaluation were unquestioned within the school system. A native of the Azores, the Portuguese first-grade teacher had sole responsibility for providing reading instruction in the native language to all the students in the study.

clothing store, a 17-year-old brother who quit high school two years earlier, a three-year-old brother, Joaquim, and seven-year-old Gloria who is the top performing reader in the Portuguese first grade.

The family lives in a two-room basement apartment with a curtain in the kitchen hiding a fold-out cot that serves as a bed, which Gloria shares with Joaquim. The family speaks no English. Although Gloria claims to be fluent, her English language skills are virtually nonexistent. Gloria's mother had three years of schooling; her father had none. Both are illiterate. There is no reading matter in their home.

Gloria maintains major responsibility for Joaquim, caring for him after school while her mother works, even though her grandmother and father are at home. She also assists with the housework.

As her mother says, "I work. My husband can't help. Gloria has to help." Although her mother is pleased that Gloria does well in school, she says, "It doesn't matter if Gloria completes high school." Her father concurs. He says, "She's a good girl. She'll get a good job. João [the oldest son] didn't go." Gloria, on the other hand, says "I'm going to college."

One hot summer afternoon, without being asked, Gloria begins hosing down the courtyard leading to the apartment, saying that it will cool off the house. Her parents smile appreciatively to her while her father says "She's a smart girl; she knows what to do."

Gloria often initiates cleaning and child-care projects, receiving praise or nods of appreciation after each event. During one conversation with the family, Joaquim begins crying. Gloria's mother looks at her. She picks up her brother and engages him in play while her family nods.

The Top Group: Rosa Brandão—Student #2

Rosa's parents are the only ones in this study to have completed sixth grade. They moved to New England from Graciosa, one of the smaller Azorean Islands. They are both literate in Portuguese, being able to read material at approximately a fourth-grade level.

Mrs. Brandaõ works in a jewelry factory. Her husband has been laid off from his job in a rubber factory and is now working part-time in a store selling Portuguese religious artifacts. They have just bought the store, located next door to their five-room duplex apartment. When he goes back to work in the factory, they will continue to operate the store part-time with six-year-old Rosa and her eight-year-old brother helping.

Rosa has her own bedroom which she cleans and cares for. Her mother has very high blood pressure and shouldn't be working full time. She has to, she says, because "he's laid off." Of Rosa, she comments, "She's extremely helpful. They (Roberto and Rosa) do all the vacuuming and cleaning."

One afternoon Rosa is working in the store, unpacking boxes and putting things on shelves. Later that day she sits at the kitchen table eating a piece of cake. She offers me some and then washes her plate and puts it away. Her mother begins preparing dinner and Rosa sets the table without being told. As they pass each other in the kitchen, her mother pats Rosa on the head and smiles.

There is no reading material in the house, other than the children's school books. Mrs. Brandão used to help with homework but stopped. "The doctor says I'm doing too much and they don't really need my help anymore." Both Rosa and her parents agree that she will graduate from high school and maybe even continue her education beyond that.

The Top Group: Sara Costa—Student #3

The Costas are a family of three who emigrated from Madeira almost two years ago. Both parents work the first shift in a lighting factory leaving seven-year-old Sara alone during the summer and holidays from 6:15 a.m. to 4:30 p.m. They lock her in the apartment before leaving for work.

Sara usually watches television, plays records, reads her school books, or colors. She prepares her own breakfast and lunch, cleans the dishes and puts them away. When school is in session, she goes off by herself but comes home to a neighbor's apartment in the afternoon.

Sara often helps in the preparation of dinner. She cleans her own room, runs the vacuum, dusts, and helps with the bathroom. She accompanies her mother shopping and occasionally does the shopping alone. "She has to take care of these things." her mother says. "We both work."

Neither of Sara's parents speaks English. Sara's English is very limited but well constructed and almost accent-free. Both parents completed fourth grade; both can read Portuguese at about a second-grade level. There is no adult reading material in their four-room apartment.

Sara's room is filled with lots of books from a summer library program, most of which she can't read. She wants to be a teacher and, in her play with other children, she assigns reading and writing work. When her play is finished, she puts all the toys away. She never needs to be told to tidy her things.

Her parents are proud of Sara's language and literacy skills but are indifferent to her school grades and performance. "She reads to me in English" her father relates, "even though I don't know what she's saying." Her mother listens attentively while Sara teachers her new vocabulary and corrects her grammar much the same way as she conducted her play-school class.

Sara says she wants to go to college and be a teacher. Her parents say they don't care if she completes high school. "It's up to her."

The Middle Group: Maria Santos—Student #4

After being in the United States a year-and-a-half, Maria Santos' father died, leaving his wife, Maria, aged seven, and Emilia, her nine-year-old sister, and fifteen-year-old son and a sixteen-year-old daughter from a previous marriage, both of whom live with their natural mother. Emilia is learning-disabled and attends a special school. Maria's half-brother and sister have both dropped out of school.

Mrs. Santos and her former husband, a farmer in Povoação, São Miguel, never attended school. They worked together in a textile factory before his death. Mrs. Santos is on welfare, unable to work because she "has to take care of the children."

Maria has assumed much of the responsibility for Emilia's care. She reads to her in Portuguese, calms her after a tantrum, and sits with her as she watches television. Mrs. Santos thanks Maria for taking care of Emilia. She is very gentle with both daughters. She says, "Maria is smart. It's good to know how to read and write." Maria says she wants to work in an office. She doesn't want to go to college because it's too much work. Mrs. Santos agrees.

When an ice cream truck goes by, Maria runs to her mother's purse and tosses it on the floor after finding it empty. Variations of the scene are repeated as the girls ask their mother for different things and are unable to get them because "it all depends on the welfare checks."

Mrs. Santos is illiterate. There are no newspapers or other adult reading material in the home. Maria and Emilia's school books and a number of coloring pictures with captions constitute the only reading matter.

Maria is considered the best reader in the Middle Group. Her teacher says that she is doing as well as Sara Costa and should be moving to the Top Group shortly.[3]

The Middle Group: Carolina Cordeiro—Student #5

The Cordeiro family emigrated from a small village in continental Portugal almost three years ago. Carolina, seven, is a middle child with a 10-year-old sister, Dora, and a two-and-a-half-year-old brother, Tony. Her mother works a double shift (from 3 p.m. to 3 a.m.) in a textile factory, and her father works on a car bumper assembly line from 7 a.m. to 6:30 p.m. Dora babysits while her parents are gone. Her father says, "She has to help out a

---

[3] It is interesting to note that both the Portuguese bilingual teacher and her Portuguese aide readily compared student performance in the class. This was done aloud in front of all the students as well as privately to individual students and to me. An example of this is the comment made aloud to Maria that she is "doing just about as well as Sara," and that if she "kept up the good work" she would be "moved to the top group."

lot in the house." Of Carolina, Mrs. Cordeiro adds, "She doesn't have too much to do."

Carolina herself claims to do "a lot in the house." Dora comments, "She does nothing but watch TV and play with Tony." Carolina tends to ignore her sister, interrupting most conversations. On one occasion, Dora calls to Carolina to put her things away before dinner. Carolina ignores her and watches television. Dora eventually cleans up herself.

Other than the girls' school books, there is no reading material in the house. Mr. Cordeiro completed four years of school in Portugal and can read the Portuguese newspaper although he seldom buys it. His wife has three years of schooling and is barely literate. When Carolina needs help with school work, she asks Dora.

One afternoon Mrs. Cordeiro asks Carolina to take Tony outside and stay with him. Carolina carries him into their fenced-in yard and returns within five minutes. Dora yells, "You're not supposed to leave Tony alone." Carolina shrugs and Dora rushes out to her brother. Mrs. Cordeiro doesn't seem to notice.

Her parents "don't care" if Carolina graduates from high school. They discuss plans for returning to Portugal. Her teacher notes that Carolina "talks too much" and "doesn't pay much attention in class. She's somewhat irresponsible."

The Low Reading Group: João Tavares—Student #6

João Tavares, seven, was the only male in the study. The youngest of 18 children (14 of whom were from his father's first marriage and live elsewhere), João is also the only male in his father's second family of four children. Mr. Tavares is 15 years older than his second wife. They've been in the United States almost two years and are non-English speaking.

The six members of the Tavares family live in three rooms. During the summer months, the girls, ages 5, 11, and 12 spend all day at home sewing, crocheting, cooking, and cleaning. João is outside playing from 10 a.m. on. At night he goes out with his father to chat with friends around the neighborhood. The father is a retired rubber factory worker, and the mother works days in a jewelry factory. Mr. and Mrs. Tavares are from Ribeira Grande in São Miguel, the Azores. He completed fourth grade and she finished second grade. There is no reading material in the house for either the children or their parents.

The older girls missed over 60 days of school between them in order to babysit for their five-year-old sister. João says, "I never have to watch anyone." He tells me, rather proudly, that he smokes. His older sister says, "He thinks he's such a big shot."

When the family goes to church on Sunday, João doesn't accompany them. He's too prideful and fidgety, his mother claims. The girls wait on João, bringing him food, making his bed, picking up after him. On one occasion, Mrs. Tavares wants him to remove his muddy shoes. She takes them off while he screams. He runs out of the house without them. His mother laughs.

João grabs the tricycle from his five-year-old sister. She cries. Mrs. Tavares says to her husband, "Do something." He pretends to take off his belt while both he and João smile. His mother laughs and walks away.

While Mrs. Tavares and the older girls do the major food shopping, João is sent out almost daily to the local market to buy rolls, cheese, and other small items. "That is his responsibility," says his mother. He enjoys the attention and independence.

The first-grade teacher calls João "lazy. All he wants to do is play." His mother says, "He won't finish school." His father shrugs his shoulders. "I don't want to," João brags. "School is dumb."

The Low Reading Group: Olga Medeiros—Student #7

An extended Medeiros family occupies all four apartments in their building. The children, Luis, 13 years old, Emma, 10, and 7-year-old Olga all sleep in different apartments. Luis sleeps upstairs with Mrs. Medeiros' sister's family, Emma with Mrs. Medeiros' parents, and Olga with Mrs. Medeiros' brother's family. They all return to their one-and-a-half room apartment for meals, clothes, and television watching.

Arriving from Arrifes, a small village in São Miguel two years ago, Mr. Medeiros now works in a junkyard while his wife stays home. He completed fourth grade while Mrs. Medeiros only went to school for one year. "She's not too smart," Mr. Medeiros says of his wife. She smiles and nods in agreement.

Mrs. Medeiros and her mother do all the cooking and cleaning for the four families. The other adults are all working. Olga helps clear the dishes at her grandparents' apartment. Her father says, "See what she does. She's a good little girl." He pats her head. Olga is wearing a big white bow in her hair. "We had a baby last year, but it died at birth. Olga is our baby." Olga dances around the room and sits on her father's lap.

Emma stayed in third grade for two years. "She's like her mother," says Mr. Medeiros. "Not smart. Olga's smart. She does her work in school." Olga is the youngest of all the children in the extended family. She twirls herself around the kitchen and speaks in a baby voice. "Look at me." Her parents laugh at all her antics. "She's my cute little girl," her mother says.

There is no reading material evident in any of the four apartments. Olga keeps the extended family entertained by crawling on the floor, making baby noises, and dressing in other people's clothes. "I don't like to go to school," she says. "It's too much work."

The Low Reading Group: Armanda Videiros—Student #8

The Videiros family arrived from Ribeira Quente, a small fishing village in São Miguel, almost a year ago. Mr. and Mrs. Videiros each had three years of schooling. Both are illiterate. Mr. Videiros works days in a belt buckle factory. His wife works the night shift in a textile factory. Their four daughters, ages four, five, seven, and eight are tended to by Mrs. Videiros' sister and brother whose families occupy two other apartments in the building.

Mrs. Videiros' sister visits frequently. Her seven-month-old and two-year-old boys are among the ten children, all under eight years old, who are running around the three-room apartment at any given moment. Some are having cheese puffs and soda for breakfast. Armanda is feeding her seven-month-old nephew some hot cereal. He is sitting on her lap as she puts tablespoon after tablespoon of food into his mouth. He chokes on the large portions several times, but neither Armanda or the adults pay any attention. When Armanda is done, her aunt yells at her "Why don't you change him? He smells."

The two-year-old is wandering around the kitchen. Twice he tries to stick his finger in the oscillating fan. No one pays attention to him. When he later reaches for some popcorn with his left hand, Mrs. Videiros slaps him. "Don't use your left hand," she yells.

Armanda rinses out the dirty diaper and takes two of the young children downstairs to play. She leaves her naked nephew on the bed. When he falls off, Armanda's aunt calls her. When Armanda enters, she is slapped across the face by her aunt. "Why do you leave the baby alone?" Armanda starts to respond when her mother slaps her, too. "Shut up when someone talks to you."

Armanda and her older sister's responsibilities are concentrated on child care. Neither helps with cleaning, shopping, or cooking. "That's my work," Mrs. Videiros says. "All they can do is help with the babies." It does not seem to be considered an important task.

"Armanda is very slow," says her teacher. "She never seems to know what she is supposed to do. She doesn't trust anybody." Armanda's parents don't care if she does well in school. Neither does Armanda.

DISCUSSION

Within these eight families, all of the parents except for the Brandãos, parents of the second best reader, had fewer than six years of schooling.[4] Rosa Brandão's parents had both completed six years of education in Portu-

---

[4] For greater understanding, the students are matched with numbers hierarchically signifying their reading achievement, for example, Student #1 = the best reader.

gal and were able to read at a fourth-grade level. The father of the highest reader, Gloria Quadros (Student #1), had no schooling at all. Gloria's mother had completed three years. Both parents, however, were illiterate. Maria Santos (Student #4), Olga Medeiros (#7), and Armanda Videiros (#8) all had at least one illiterate parent and one parent able to read at a second grade level or below. The rest of the parents all read at approximately a second-grade level. All of the parents were monolingual in Portuguese.

There was no adult reading matter in any of the eight homes and only in the case of Sara Costa (Student #3) were there some children's books. These were English library books from a summer day care program. Since no one could speak or read English, these were never used.

Rosa Brandão and Maria Santos (Students #2 and #4) had parents who, several times in the course of the academic year, helped their children with homework. While this occurred less than once every two months, with considerable variation in time and intensity, it is noteworthy. Overall, however, there was much similarity among the eight families with respect to the level of education, socioeconomic status, and literacy backgrounds. Because these often cited factors which impact on early reading performance were not operational in this research, other factors began to emerge. The single most significant one was parental expectations for performance of household chores.

The variation in home responsibility among the eight first graders was substantial. Home responsibility was defined as babysitting for younger siblings, house cleaning, and neighborhood grocery shopping, all chores that the eight first graders shared to varying degrees. Five of the eight children had major cleaning responsibility. If responsibility was looked at in isolation, the correlation between reading achievement and home responsibility was high in many instances for both the better readers and the poorer ones.

For example, a student in the top reading group (Gloria Quadros, Student #1) and in the lowest reading group (Armanda Videiros, student #8) each had considerable babysitting responsibilities. Similarly, Rosa Brandão (Student #2) and Olga Medeiros (Student #7) both had major housecleaning responsibilities, and Sara Costa (Student #3) and João Tavares (Student #6) assumed large roles in the family's grocery shopping. In this regard, there was no relationship between the amount of the student's responsibilities at home and the students' reading achievement level in school. However, when these same home responsibilities were analyzed along with parental expectations for their successful fulfillment, the relationship between responsibilities and reading achievement became more discriminatory.

Parental expectations were studied in three major areas—expectations for the execution of home responsibilities, expectations for school performance, and expectations for future education. Expectations were defined as either high or low. High expectations included criteria for the evaluation of the successful completion of the task using the term "successful" in whatever manner was defined by the family. Expectations were considered low when there was no interest in whether the task was ever performed, much less the quality of the performance.

Gloria Quadros' parents (Reader #1) had high expectations for her home responsibility and low expectations for both her school performance and future education. That is, they expected their daughter to complete her home tasks successfully but did not care if she did well in her school studies or whether she would ever graduate from high school. The child's own expectations for all three areas including school performance and high school graduation, however, were high. Similarly, Rosa Brandão, Sara Costa, and Maria Santos (Students #2, #3, and #4) and their parents shared high expectations for home responsibilities but only Rosa Brandão's parents (Student #2) shared their child's high expectations for both school performance and future education. Gloria, Rosa, and Sara (Students # 1–3) all in the top reading group, in fact, had high expectations for all three areas, home responsibilities, school performance and future education even though Gloria's and Sara's parents had high expectations for home responsibility only.

In the families where parental expectations for home responsibility were low, the student's expectations for home responsibility were similarly low, as were their expectations for school performance and future education. This was consistently found among the readers in the lowest group, João Tavares, Olga Medeiros, and Armanda Videiros (Students #6, 7 and 8).[5]

While there was no distinction among the eight children in reading performance and their parents' expectations for that performance, there was a clear relationship between their parents' expectations for home responsibility and their reading achievement. In some cases, high responsibility was assumed for one major chore, for example, babysitting for Armanda (Student #8) and cleaning for Olga (Student #7). In these instances, however, their parents did not regard the responsibility as important and did not take the children performing the tasks seriously. In the Medeiros family, for example, Olga was looked upon as a "cute" but essentially noncontributing family member in the fulfillment of family responsibilities. In the Videiros family,

---

[5] As previously noted, João (Student #6) was the only male in the sample. While this was not deliberate, its bearing may be significant since sex roles in Portugal have been seen as highly differentiated. "The different fates of the sexes are stressed from birth" (Cutleiro, 1971, p. 111). It is not unusual for male children to have no responsibility for housecleaning or babysitting since these are activities commonly associated with females (Cutleiro, 1971). The other factors which contribute to segregation of roles and responsibilities comprise a complex network, the explication of which is not within the scope of this study. It is important to recognize, however, that these factors were not taken into consideration when analyzing the raw data for João. The same general criteria were applied to him as were used for evaluating responsibilities for the other seven female children. Because use of a single standard may affect interpretation of the findings for João, his story should be viewed with the above information in mind and interpreted accordingly.

babysitting activities were not valued, nor was the child's performance of these activities. The parents' continued lack of appreciation of the performance of household tasks by Olga and Armanda contributed to both children's low self-expectations and reinforced the contention that merely having a great deal of home responsibility was not, in and of itself, a significant factor correlating with high reading achievement. It is only when viewed in connection with high parent expectations for fulfilling that responsibility that the responsibility assumes significance.

Parent expectations for performance of home responsibilities, in fact, was the key factor in understanding the differential achievement levels among the eight students. There are many possible explanations for this. One is the ability of an individual to generalize expectations, in this case from the home to the school. Another is the existence of a positive relationship between expectations for achievement and actual achievement.

A third is the way in which the responsibilities and expectations engendered in the home work to support or negate a student's school success. Related to this are the criteria applied by the teacher in determining membership in the various reading groups, "top," "middle," and "low."

In the case of the Portuguese teacher, students were grouped according to her perceptions of what constitutes a good or poor reader, including the student's ability to work independently, quietly, and obediently. These traits, supported by the families of the top readers, reveal as much about cultural values as they do about reading performance.

In much the same way as Cazden's (1985) characterization of ability groupings reflected a mechanism for reinforcing desired behaviors, so too is the Portuguese teacher's use of a combination of skill mastery (which in itself reflects a desciplined, and highly structured teacher-directed orientation) and independent learning supportive of the achievement of those students whose home environment conforms to these expectations for success.

The readers in the top group, in effect, were receiving the same message in their home and in their school, providing a clear signal for how they were expected to perform.

CONCLUSION

Gearing notes that people bring their own mappings or "implied agendas" to different situations. These are "expectation(s) as to how the encounter promises or threatens to unfold" (1976, p. 184). So, too, do children bring expectations learned at home to the school environment. By having the ability to successfully perform a given task reinforced at home, children acquired greater confidence of their ability to perform other tasks and to perform them in other places. A parent's recognition of the satisfactory completion of a chore valued in the home provided that necessary mapping from which the child's expectations for school performance were later generalized. The result was a self-fulfilling prophesy with those children who expected to perform well, actually doing so and those who did not have these expectations, experiencing increased failures (Entwistle & Webster, 1972; Rist, 1970; Zigler, 1971).

The children whose efforts at home were positively reinforced by their parents demonstrated a generalized set of higher expectations for their school performance and their future education even when their parents' expectations did not include good grades or high school completion. Their parents' high expectations for home responsibility became for the children a combination of motivation and reward, encouraging the successful completion of home tasks and the confidence to undertake school-related ones. As Hess (1969) and Hess and Shipman (1965) have shown, this congruence between home expectations and rewards and school expectations and rewards can lead to improved school performance.

These findings are based on a very small sample. If confirmed through larger studies with varied populations, their significance would dramatize the potential consequences which result from discrepancies in home/school expectations for student performance.

There are, undoubtedly, many other nonschool factors which impact on student performance. These, too, need to be explored through ethnographic research which focuses on family and community as one basis for understanding differential school achievement. The cost of low achievement levels and high illiteracy rates are a price too high to pay for inattentiveness to the critical relationship that exists between students' lives at home and their performance in school.

A first step in acknowledging this relationship must be "confirming and legitimating the knowledge and experience through which children give meaning to their lives" (Giroux, 1988, p. 71). It is through this recognition that the education process truly begins.

REFERENCES

Ada, A. F. (1988, May/June). The Pajaro Valley experience. *Rethinking schools, 2*(4), 16–17.

Anderson, A. B., & Stokes, S. J. (1984). Social and institutional influences on the development and practice of literacy. In H. Goelman, A. Oberg, & F. Smith (Eds.), *Awakening to literacy* (pp. 24–37). London: Heinemann.

Armor, D. J. (1972). School and family effects on black and white achievement. In F. Mosteller & D. P. Moynihan (Eds.), *On equality of educational opportunity* (pp. 32–50). New York: Random House.

Averch, H. A., Carroll, S. J., Donaldson, T. S., Kiesling, H. J., & Pincus, J. (1971).

How effective is schooling? A critical review and synthesis of research findings. Santa Monica, CA: Rand Corporation.

Burt, C. (1966). The genetic determination of differences in intelligence: A study of monozygotic twins reared together and apart. *British Journal of Psychology, 57,* 137–153.

Cazden, C. B. (1985). Social context of learning to read. In H. Singer & R. B. Ruddell (Eds.), *Theoretical models and processes of reading* (3rd ed., pp. 595–610). Newark, DE: International Reading Association.

Coleman, J. S. (1972). The evaluation of equality of educational opportunity. In F. Mosteller & D. P. Moynihan (Eds.), *On equality of educational opportunity* (pp. 86–104) New York: Random House.

Cutleiro, J. (1971). *A Portuguese rural society.* London: Oxford University Press.

deLone, R. H. (1979). *Small futures. Children, inequality and the limits of liberal reform.* New York: Hartcourt, Brace, Jovanovich.

Douglas, J. W. B. (1968). *All our future: A longitudinal study of secondary education.* London: P. Davies Co.

Dunn, N. E. (1981). Children's achievement at school entry age as a function of mothers' and fathers' teaching sets. *Elementary School Journal, 81,* 245–253.

Entwhistle, D. R., & Webster, M. (1972). Raising children's performance expectations: A classroom demonstration. *Social Science Research, I,* 147–158.

Fine, M. (1985). *Literacy profile of America's young adults.* The National Assessment of Educational Progress (the National Report Card).

Fine, M. (1987). Silencing in public schools. *Language Arts, 64*(2), 157–174.

Freire, P., & Macedo, D. (1987). *Literacy: Reading the word and the world.* South Hadley, MA: Bergin and Garver Publishers.

Gearing, F. O. (1976). Steps toward a general theory of cultural transmission. In J. Roberts & S. Akisanya (Eds.), *Educational patterns and cultural configurations: The anthropology of education* (pp. 183–193). New York: David McKay.

Giroux, H. A. (1988, Winter). Literacy and the pedagogy of voice and political empowerment. *Education Theory, 38*(1), 61–75.

Goldberg, M. L. (1971). Socio-psychological issues in the education of the disadvantaged. In H. A. Passow (Ed.), *Urban education in the 1970s* (pp. 57–68). New York: Teachers College Press.

Goodman, K., & Goodman, Y. M. (1978). Learning to read is natural. In L. B. Resnik & P. Weaver (Eds.), *Theory and practice of early reading* (Vol. 1, pp. 137–154). Hillsdale, NJ: Lawrence Erlbaum Associates.

Grayum, H. S. (1958). How parents' attitudes affect children's reading. *The Reading Teacher, 7*(4), 195–199.

Harste, J. C., Burke, C. L., & Woodward, V. A. (1982). Children's language and world: Initial encounters with print. In J. Langer & M. Smith-Burke (Eds.), *Bridging the gap: Reader meets author* (pp. 105–127). Newark, DE: International Reading Association.

Heath, S. B. (1982). Protean shapes in literacy events: Ever-shifting oral and literate traditions. In D. Tannen (Ed.), *Spoken and written language: Exploring orality and literacy* (pp. 91–117). Norwood, NJ: Ablex.

Heath, S. B. (1986). Sociocultural contexts of language development. In *Beyond language: Social & cultural factors in schooling language minority students* (pp. 143–

186). Los Angeles, CA: Evaluation, Dissemination and Assessment Center, California State University.

Herrenstein, R. (1971, September). I. Q. *The Atlantic Month, No. 228*, pp. 43–64.

Hess, R. D. (1969). *Maternal behavior and the development of reading readiness in urban negro children.* Washington, DC: DHEW, Division of Educational Laboratories, National Laboratory of Early Childhood Education.

Hess, R. D., & Shipman, V. (1965). Early experience and the socialization of cognitive modes in children. *Child Development, 36*, 869–886.

Hiebert, E. H. (1986). Issues related to home influences on young children's print-related development. In D. B. Yaden, Jr., & S. Templeton (Eds.), *Metalinguistic awareness and beginning literacy: Conceptualizing what it means to write.* Portsmouth, NH: Heinemann.

Hoffman, E. (1971). Pre-kindergarten experiences and their relationships to reading achievement. *Illinois School Research, 8*, 6–12.

Kagan, J. (1974). Motivation and attitudinal factors in receptivity to learning. In H. F. Clarizio, R. C. Craig, & W. A. Mehrens (Eds.), *Contemporary issues in educational psychology* (pp. 34–58). Boston: Allyn and Bacon.

Kennett, K. F. (1975). Family environment, family size and measured intelligence. *Interchange, 6*, 16–21.

Kifer, E. (1975a). Relationships between academic achievement and personality characteristics: A quasi-longitudinal study. *American Educational Research Journal, No. 12*, 191–210.

Kifer, E. (1975b, November). *The relationship between the home and school in influencing the learning of children.* (ERIC Document Reproductive Service No. 133073).

Kontos, S., & Huba, M. (1983, April). *The development and function of print awareness.* Paper presented at the biennial meeting of the Society for Research in Child Development, Detroit, MI.

Labov, W. (1985). Cited in Cazden: Social context of learning to read. In H. Singer & R. B. Ruddell (Eds.), *Theoretical models and processes of reading* (3rd ed., pp. 595–610). Newark, DE: International Reading Association.

Lapp, D. K. (1986, August/September). Parental involvement in learning: The critical link. *Reading Today, 4*(1), 18–25.

Mason, J. M., & McCormick, C. (1983, April). *Intervention procedures for increasing preschool children's interest in and knowledge about reading.* Paper presented at the annual meeting of the American Educational Research Association, Montreal, Canada.

McDermott, R. P. (1985). Achieving school failure: An anthropological approach to illiteracy and social stratification. In H. Singer & R. R. Ruddell (Eds.), *Theoretical models and processes of reading* (3rd ed., pp. 558–594). Newark, DE: International Reading Association.

Morrison, C., & Harris, A. J. (1968). Effect of kindergarten on the reading of disadvantaged. *The Reading Teacher, 22*, 4–9.

National Academy of Education. (1985). *Becoming a nation of readers: The report of the Commission on Reading.* Washington, DC: National Academy of Education, Commission on Reading. U.S. Government Printing Office.

Olson, D. R. (1984). See! Jumping! Some oral language antecedents of literacy. In H. Goelman, A. Oberg, & F. Smith (Eds.), *Awakening to literacy* (pp. 185–192). London: Heinemann Educational Books.

Peterson, A. C., & Kellam, S. G. (1977). *Longitudinal predictors of achievement: Achievement history, family environment and mental health.* (ERIC Document Reproduction Service # 139866).

Rist, R. C. (1970). Student social class and teacher expectations: The self-fulfilling prophecy in ghetto education. *Harvard Educational Review, 40,* 411–451.

Seitz, V. (1977). *Social class and ethnic group differences in learning to read.* Newark, DE: International Reading Association.

Smith, F. (1976). Learning to read by reading. *Language Arts, 53,* 297–299.

Teale, W. H. (1978). Positive environments for learning to read: What studies of early readers tell us. *Language Arts, 55,* 922–932.

Tizard, J., Schofield, W. N., & Hewison, J. (1982, February). Collaboration between teachers and parents in assisting children's reading. *The British Journal of Educational Psychology, 52,* 1–15.

Tobin, A. W. (1981). *A multiple discriminant cross-validation of the factors associated with the development of precocious reading achievement.* Unpublished doctoral dissertation, University of Delaware. Newark, DE.

Whiting, B., & Whiting, J. (1975). *Children of six cultures.* Cambridge: Harvard University Press.

Wolf, R. (1966). The measurement of environment. In A. Anastisi (Ed.), *Testing problems in perspective* (25th annual volume of topical readings from the Invitational Conference on Testing). Washington, DC: American Council on Education.

Yaden, D. B., Jr., & McGee, L. M. (1984). Reading as a meaning-seeking activity: What children's questions reveal. In J. A. Niles & L. A. Harris (Eds.), *Thirty-third yearbook of the national reading conference* (pp. 101–109). Rochester, NY: National Reading Conference.

Ziglar, E. (1971). The retarded child as a whole person. In H. E. Adam & W. E. Boardman, III (Eds.), *Advances in experimental clinical psychology* (Vol. I). New York: Pergamon Press.

Part II
Towards the Development of Language, Reading, and Writing

5

Creative Reading: A Relevant Methodology for Language Minority Children

Alma Flor Ada
Director of Doctoral Studies
Multicultural Program, School of Education
University of San Francisco

The use of language—and, through it, the possibility of communicating thoughts and feelings, sharing past experiences, and planning for the future—is an attribute of human beings. The better we can understand, recall, analyze, share, and shape the world around us, the more fully human we are.

In normal community life, all individuals, unless they are physiologically or mentally impaired, learn the language of their group, using it with ease and efficiency. And that language, acquired readily and naturally, is the basis for all social activities, for enlarging any field of learning, and for acquiring and preserving useful knowledge. In communities where the use of written language is widespread, the process of acquiring reading and writing skills follows and complements that of oral language acquisition. In other words, where family and community interaction takes place, it is natural for all children to learn to use their language effectively. And if the group to which the children belong reads and writes a great deal, learning to read and write comes easily to the children as well. The entire process can and should occur spontaneously, with little difficulty.

In contrast, learning to read and write is not always spontaneous or easy for language minority children. Inappropriate or irrelevant methods, and a focus on English rather than the native language, prohibit or inhibit a natural acquisition process.

Contemporary applied linguistics distinguishes clearly between learning a second language and acquiring it (Krashen, 1981). In a learning process, the emphasis is on knowing the rules and norms of the language, whereas in an acquisition process, the emphasis is on communication. Thus, while those who have "acquired" a language may know very little about its grammatical rules, they have no difficulty in using that language system effectively for self-expression and communication. On the other hand, it is unfortunately true that those who "learn" a foreign language by familiarizing themselves with its rules and norms may find themselves unable to communicate in it easily and effectively (Krashen & Terrell, 1983).

This concept can be applied to reading as well, since reading is a part of the process of communicating through language. By learning the mechanics of reading, one does not necessarily become a good reader. Indeed, many good readers acquire the skill not because they have been taught, but because they have been exposed to the joy of reading. Yet many of the approaches to teaching reading are extremely tedious and meaningless to children. Instead of encouraging the youngsters to read, those methods instill a fear of or aversion to reading, which is perceived as a potential source of frustration and failure. The difficulties are compounded when the stress is for the children to become literate in their second language, rather than their mother tongue. In the process of deriving meaning and significance from the text, anticipation and intelligent guessing play a very important role (Smith, 1985; Goodman, 1986), yet it becomes very difficult to make adequate predictions, or even to confirm one's hypotheses, in a language one does not yet master (Thonis, 1976, 1983).

There is no doubt that children who are read to frequently, who have access to attractive books, and to whom reading is presented as an enjoyable discovery process, will learn to read. That is, they will acquire reading skills and habits with virtually no effort. But, although reading is indeed an acquired skill—the logical extension of the process of learning to speak—the present-day reality of literacy in the United States is far different from what might be expected in a highly developed society (see Walsh's Introduction, this volume).

A racist self-proclaimed sage has tried to explain away the failure of ethnic minorities in school by expounding the notion that certain minority groups are culturally deficient or either genetically inferior to or mismatched with the mainstream society. The reality is far more complex, involving the dynamic interaction of many societal forces, among them the effects of colonization, exploitation, and discrimination (Sue & Padilla, 1986).

Historically, reading has been an ability restricted to the elite. It has been a source of power, jealously guarded until very recently. Indeed, slaves who learned to read and write were subject to the death penalty. Yet, the great promise of American democracy has been that everyone would have equal opportunities to excel and to actively participate in the decision-making process that shapes his or her social reality (Aronowitz & Giroux, 1985). Such participation requires communicative and critical thinking skills. And, the exercise of freedom requires critical reflection. A population that cannot read, that does not read, and that is not used to analyzing information critically cannot participate in a democratic process. Failing to educate the population is indeed a negation of the exercise of freedom (Freire, 1982b).

People are free not because a constitution or a series of laws guarantees freedom, but because freedom is in fact exercised. Freedom is action. Unless one acts freely, one is not free. When we are discussing, then, the teaching of reading and the development of critical thinking skills through creative reading, we are really talking about preparing youth to exercise democracy, to preserve freedom; that is, to take action.

The ability to act upon one's own life to change it, entails a particular understanding of social reality. Formal education, however, can reflect one or the other of two opposing outlooks. At one end of the spectrum, social reality is narrowly defined as a linear succession of events that inevitably occur as the result of certain causes: "Things are as they are." This viewpoint attempts to justify any present situation as "natural." The mere fact of its existence justifies any condition. "If things are as they are, it is because they are meant to be that way." It is paradoxical that the advocates of this approach tend to view physical reality, which was not created by human beings in the first place, as something that can easily be changed—tunnels are drilled, mountains are blasted, dams are built, forests are destroyed—while at the same time showing great reluctance to change social reality, which after all, is a recent human creation. The education based on this viewpoint is geared toward creating followers, individuals capable of carrying out instructions; of accepting existing codes, norms and rules; of spending most of their lives doing menial tasks that require very little intellectual growth—in short, individuals who, through schooling, have been programmed to be passive and contently bored. Needless to say, most of the education taking place in a typical classroom falls into this category.

At the other end of the spectrum we find a more dynamic interpretation of social reality, conceived as an endless process in constant change, the product of our actions and choices, a dissatisfaction with *what is* and a search for *what ought to be*. The education based on this perspective leads to the creation of leaders, individuals with critical minds, capable of analyzing reality and shaping their own environment. It is this educational route that may allow ethnic minority children to elude the present statistical predictions that assign them the highest rates of dropouts—"pushouts" is probably a better term—drug addicts, juvenile delinquents, psychiatric cases, suicides, unemployed, and poor.

Approaches to reading tend to parallel these two perspectives on reality. Common in most schools are practices which support the former. The reading process is divided into a number of isolated skills placed along a continuum, a scope, and sequence. The assumption is that the various skills must be mastered sequentially, so not until the first are mastered will the subsequent ones be introduced. Thus, students are moved from readiness, or prereading, skills to word attack skills, and then on to literal comprehension skills. Only when these are mastered will inferential skills be introduced. Critical thinking, problem solving, and creative skills are restricted to those children who have managed to reach the upper-reading levels.

Unfortunately, many language minority children do not make it. True, their bodies are in the classroom and, year after year, move from grade to grade, but their imagination, their initiative, their interest, were killed early on. Some by boredom; others by fear. By kindergarten, many are failing; they "fall below the norm" in first grade. They are condemned as not sufficiently good, bright, or capable by a system that imposes external norms, that presupposes to know what every child should learn or do at a given time. Yet the reading they are allegedly being taught is not reading at all, it is discreet prereadiness skills or exercises in phonics.

An alternative approach to reading is grounded in a dynamic view of reality. Here the goal is to have children read with pleasure, ease, assurance, freedom, and enthusiasm. Such an approach has these five essentials.

1. The materials are interesting, to awaken the children's desire to read
2. The children's oral language development is continuously fostered through the reading process.
3. The method selected for teaching initial reading is geared to success, instilling in the children confidence in their ability to learn.
4. The reading process is immediately meaningful to the children in that it is relevant both to their real world and to the process of effecting positive changes in that world.
5. Parents are actively involved in the process.

What follows is an analysis of each of those five elements, within the context of the Creative Reading Method (Ada, 1980, 1988; Ada & Olave, 1986).

THE QUALITY OF THE READING MATERIALS

Materials of the highest quality are essential to a successful reading process. The materials must be well written, handsomely illustrated, and engaging. Every child has a right to the best. Because children reared in poverty are often deprived of aesthetic, uplifting experiences, our minority children have an even greater need for beautiful materials.

One of the charges that might be leveled against today's American schools is that they have given up on aesthetics as a common good to which all children are entitled. Precisely now, when technology has made it possible for everyone to appreciate works of art and, through recordings, slides, videocassettes, and reproductions, to have access to the best examples of beauty in all cultures, these are being denied school children who have no other opportunity of being exposed to them. Schools have become bleak and ugly. There is an elitist belief that most children would not be interested in, would not accept, or would even be repelled by the fine arts.

We know that a positive attitude and a feeling of well-being are highly conducive to learning. We also know, as has been demonstrated in the suggestopedia studies (Pollack, 1979), that some classical music helps foster that feeling of well-being, that receptiveness to learning. Yet, very little, if anything, is being done to take advantage of fine art and good music as a means of creating a more pleasant, more learning-receptive environment in our schools.

In the teaching of reading, we have the opportunity to select the best of children's literature—books that combine an attractive format and handsome illustrations with good writing, that make effective use of humor, that, in sum, are designed to make reading a joy.

ORAL LANGUAGE DEVELOPMENT AND READING

The ample and varied research in reading has produced few conclusive statements. Yet, there does seem to be agreement on two variables as having a significant correlation with success in reading. These variables are that the children who tend to achieve greater success in reading are those who have good oral language development and those to whom parents read aloud frequently. And, of course, in most cases, these happen to be precisely the same children.

These findings pose a very special challenge. Schools that are in place only to perpetuate existing inequalities will use the findings to support the thesis that minority children fail because of their inherent limitations. Those who believe that the underlying reason for education is to provide that which otherwise would not be available will recognize the need to develop the children's oral language as a basis for success in reading, as well as for its own sake. They will also see the need to establish reading aloud to children as an essential part of the reading process.

Traditionally, institutionalized education has a domesticating role, as clearly described by Paulo Freire (1982b). Students are taught to obey, to passively follow rules, without ever questioning the source of authority or the reasonableness of the tasks. Schools may often fail in providing students with useful knowledge, but they seldom fail in getting them used to obeying, to performing boring, dehumanizing tasks, without complaint. Schools have a good record, too, in convincing students that if they fail in the established value system, there is no hope for them in society, and that full responsibility for the failure is theirs. Recognizing this situation should in no way negate the possibility of a very different kind of dynamics within the school, as very lucidly expressed by Henry Giroux in his call to radical educators "to join together in a collective voice as part of a wider social movement dedicated to restructuring the ideological and material conditions that work both within and outside of schooling" (Giroux, 1986, p. 39).

For a teacher to assist students in the process of developing the totality of their human potential, in becoming truly active agents of their own lives, capable of determining their future and of transforming their reality, it is necessary, first of all, to analyze the orientation of classroom activities and attitudes.

If the children are to develop the skills that will prepare them for leadership roles, they need opportunities to talk, to question, to debate, to share experiences, and to express their opinions. And they need opportunities to write. As the great Latin American thinker José Martí (1979) said, "Aprender a leer es aprender a andar; aprender a escribir es aprender a ascender" ("To learn to read is to take a step forward; to learn to write is to take a step upward").

There is a correlation between children's oral language development and their reading ability. The greater their store of oral language, the more likely they will come to grips with a book, to understand it, and to make the predictions necessary for smooth reading. It is therefore extremely important to work toward the development of children's oral language skills.

In light of the above-mentioned linguistic principles, such development is achieved mainly through the meaningful use of language. Every time the occasion arises, children should be spoken to and encouraged to speak. They need language development models. Just as babies only a few months old begin to learn their language because their parents speak to them, regardless of whether or not they can understand what is said, school-age children need models that include unfamiliar words, for this is how they will learn those words. And just as a mother does not explain to her baby every word she utters but, instead, uses words in a meaningful manner, children should be spoken and read to in a rich and abundant language that provides true context, from within meaning can be garnered. It is in this way that children add unfamiliar words to their reading vocabulary.

Children's literature and folklore can be of enormous help. The simple poems, tongue twisters, riddles, and cumulative tales found in folklore are easy to remember because of their frequent use of rhythm and rhyme. Songs are an excellent means of developing vocabulary and syntax, for adding music to rhythm and rhyme fosters retention. What better language development exercise than a song a day! Besides, songs help allay anxiety, which works against learning, and create a cheerful classroom atmosphere, which is conducive to any learning task.

THE INTRODUCTION TO THE READING PROCESS

There has been a very long feud over reading methods. Traditionally, educators have joined one of two opposing camps: that of advocating phonetic methods or that of defending sight-reading approaches.

In itself, the feud reflects one of the serious problems facing American schooling—the pendulum effect. That is, for the most part, schools entirely abandon one method in favor of a new one, which eventually will also be replaced, sometimes returning to a modified version of the previous one. Teachers resent this process, because they often find themselves forced into adopting a method they do not necessarily feel comfortable with, only to have to abandon it when they are beginning to master it. In the interest of progress, the pendulum might be better replaced by a spiral, for this allows advancement to be made by carrying the best of a given process to a new level, with a new twist.

At first glance, the two opposing methods have both good and bad points. The phonetic method is economical: after mastering a limited number of sounds and sound combinations, children are able to decode an almost unlimited number of words. It can also be said in favor of this method that it recognizes the basic structures of the language. Its disadvantages are that it works with artificial language; children are drilled in producing and recognizing sounds in isolation, quite apart from their language experience; and the process of learning something that has little to do with actual reading often leads to frustration.

The sight-reading approaches, on the other hand, utilize more natural language and therefore can awaken more interest on the part of the children. Unfortunately, this process is slower, depending on the memorization of whole words, and some children are unable to make the transition to decoding new words.

Outside these two mainstream approaches, the language experience method, in which the children dictate and read their own productions, has perhaps been the best possible individual approach to reading available in some classrooms. Unfortunately, it does not have the widespread application it deserves.

Now, more and more, the whole language approach to reading, pioneered in New Zealand by Sylvia Ashton-Warner, supported by the research of Frank Smith and Kenneth and Yetta Goodman, is becoming increasingly popular in Canada and the United States. It parallels the natural acquisition approach to second language teaching and offers a very sound possibility to developing communicative competencies in spoken and written language.

Another method, proposed by Paulo Freire (1982a), has been used very successfully for adult literacy. It utilizes a whole word, or a whole phrase, that will be remembered because of its implications to the group, as a generative word—a word to be broken down in syllables which, in turn, will be used to create new words. This approach suggests the possibility of a syncretic method, that is, a method which takes the best from the phonetic and the sight-reading approaches.

The development of a syncretic reading method in Spanish is aided by the correlation between sound and symbol in Spanish syllables. Producing highly motivating and engaging readings with a limited number of syllables requires a good deal of creativity, but it is possible. The syncretic method has the advantage of becoming economical: After mastering each new set of five syllabic combinations, the children incorporate a large number of words to their reading vocabulary. More important, it is a method geared to success. The children have the opportunity to constantly reinforce that which they already know (sets of syllabic combinations)—not by reading the same words (which would be monotonous), but rather by encountering the same syllables in new words. By never presenting the syllables in isolation, by always basing the text on natural, everyday language, and by creating high-interest stores enhanced by good art, it is possible to offer the children a syncretic approach to Spanish reading.

It is important not to confuse the syncretic method with the "eclectic" approaches, which incorporate at random elements from the phonetic and the sight-reading approaches and which seem to abound in recent reading programs. The syncretic method is systematic. It carefully controls the introduction of new words formed by known syllabic combinations. Moreover, because it is inspired by Freire's methodology, it uses dialogue to make those words highly significant to the children and to guarantee their retention. The use of rhyme, rhythm, and humor helps facilitate the decoding and remembering of words.

THE READING PROCESS, MEANINGFUL HERE AND NOW

Burdened with economic and social problems, insecure about their ethnic identity, and insufficiently equipped with oral language skills, minority students continue to fail in reading when this is presented mechanistically, as a passive, receptive process.

Many language minority children come from homes where reading is not a daily practice. It is thus imperative to provide a meaning for the reading process as such, a meaning that the children can readily perceive. And because these children are immersed in a world of poverty and dissatisfaction, it is imperative that they perceive reading not only as relevant to their present reality, but as a means of effecting positive changes in that reality.

The Creative Reading Method proposes that reading be introduced, from the start, as a holistic process, the relevance of which goes beyond the transmission of the information provided by the text. A true reading act is an interactive dialogue with the information set forth in the text. In the Creative Reading Method, children are exposed to the complexity of this dialogue, even before they are able to recognize words or letters. That is, the reading process is initiated through either the reading of picture stories, with no words, or the listening to read-to stories. The story then becomes the basis for the dialogue, but it is not the end: only the beginning.

This dialogue contains four phases. For the sake of exposition, the four phases have been given names and will be discussed separately, although in a creative reading act they may happen concurrently and be interwoven.

Descriptive Phase

In this initial phase the children receive information, that is, they learn what the text (or an illustration) says. Traditionally, this is where reading begins and ends. In this methodology it is only the beginning. Appropriate questions might be along these lines: What happened? Where, when, and how did it happen? Who did it? Why?

These are the usual reading comprehension questions and, for the most part, the only ones asked of beginning readers. They are questions whose answers can be found in the text, are known by the teacher, and indicate whether or not the children have understood and can repeat the information given them. Some questions are undoubtedly important, but they are not enough. A discussion that stays at this level suggests that reading is a passive, receptive, and, in a sense, domesticating process.

Personal Interpretive Phase

Once the information has been presented, the children are encouraged to weigh it against their own experiences, feelings, and emotions. This step is extremely important. It fosters the reading process by bringing it within the children's grasp and thus making it more meaningful. It helps develop the children's self-esteem by showing that their experiences and feeling are valued by the teacher and by their classmates. What is more important, it helps the children understand that true learning occurs only when the information received is analyzed in the light of one's own experiences and emotions.

Much has been said about the need for affective instruction that recognizes the emotional needs of minority children. Unfortunately, the affective component is often considered peripheral, not truly essential to the learning process. The Creative Reading Method, on the other hand, stresses recognition of each child's individuality as an integral part of that process. Clearly, as the children's own experiences are being validated, so too are those of their family and community. Cultural validation is not something that is superimposed or added on, but part of the very core of the process.

Questions appropriate to this second phase might be: Do you know of (or have you seen, felt, experienced) something like this? Have you ever (done, felt, thought, wanted) something similar? How is what you saw (did . . .) different from what happened in the story? What would you have done (said, thought)? What about your family? Friends? How did what you read make you feel? Did you like it? Dislike it? Did it worry you? Make you happy? Frighten you?

A better understanding of one's self, and of others, is an added benefit of this part of the dialogue. The respect shown by others for one's personal experiences helps increase one's self-esteem.

Critical Phase

Once the children have compared and contrasted what is presented in the reading with their personal experiences, they are ready to move on to a critical analysis, to the level of generalized reflection.

The questions asked at this level will help the children draw inferences about the information presented: Is what happened valid? Always? When? Is it always necessary? Does it benefit everyone alike? Or does it favor some at the expense of others? Does everyone accept it? Are there any alternatives to this situation? What are these alternatives? What do they depend on? Would people of a different culture (class, sex) have acted differently? How? Why?

The analysis is, of course, determined by the children's level of maturity and previous experience. Yet, let no one think that young children cannot adopt a critical attitude. On the contrary, critical thinking is a process that can and should get underway very early, though naturally it should be grounded in that which is familiar to the children.

Creative Phase

The goal of the Creative Phase is to awaken the children's critical awareness. This is not a mere intellectual exercise, but rather, a process by which children draw on both the text and their experiences in order to make decisions regarding the world around them. That is, in receiving the information, comparing and contrasting it with their own feelings and experiences, and arriving at a critical analysis, the children make a sort of self-affirmation; they are in a position to make decisions for improving and enriching their lives.

The dialogue at this phase is aimed at helping children discover aspects of their lives that they can improve upon and at encouraging them to make decisions with that purpose in mind. Of course, it is not a question of the children changing the entire world, but of changing their own world by beginning to assume responsibility for their own lives and for their relations with others.

PARENTAL INVOLVEMENT

The reasons why language minority children in the United States may be somewhat slow to acquire oral language skills are generally thought to include the following:

- The displacement of the nuclear family (parents and children) and the separation from the extended family (grandparents, uncles, and aunts), thus lessening child/adult interaction.
- The absence of one parent from the home, or the need for both parents to work outside the home, thus reducing not only the time, but also the quality of the attention that parents can make available to their children.
- The relatively low levels of literacy and schooling of many parents.

Yet, there is another reason for the lag in the acquisition of oral language skills, even more prevalent and detrimental than those given above:

- Parents and children alike perceive the home language as being less important than English and have the mistaken notion that the best way to learn English is to give up the mother tongue.

Parents who hold to that idea reflect the natural desire of all parents to have their children use language well. Their very human attitude is deeply rooted in the unconscious. Their mistake lies not in wanting their children to become good English speakers, but in thinking that turning away from one's first language makes it easier to acquire a second. Yet, all the evidence indicates that the opposite is true. Surprising as it may be to some, the best way for a language minority child to truly master English is to fully develop the home language (Cummins, 1981). (On the issue of the transferability of reading skills from Spanish into English, see also Ada, 1987.)

Of course, aside from serving as the basis for children's cognitive growth and for their acquisition of a second language, there are other equally important reasons for first language development.

Some of these reasons are sociocultural:

- Only by using their home language will children be able to relate fully to their culture and come into possession of the cultural heritage that is theirs.

- Mastery of two languages is useful and valuable in its own right.
- The society of the United States needs bilingual people in order to maintain relations with the Spanish-speaking countries of this hemisphere.

There are also psychological reasons:

- A person's psychological strength is derived from his or her self-concept. One's home language is a part of one's personal identity. Renouncing that language is tantamount to renouncing a part of oneself, and this is harmful to a positive self-image.
- Emotional well-being is linked to interpersonal communication, to family relationships, and to the degree of integration within the nuclear family and the community.
- Giving up one's first language diminishes the interaction between children and their family and community.

Parents can offer the most effective collaboration in oral language development and in the acquisition of reading and writing skills. So that they may better fulfill that role, it is sometimes necessary to help them understand the meaning and importance of those processes.

A good way to attract parents to the school is to offer a program in which their children participate. Better yet, involve them in organizing such a program. The occasion might be a play staged by the children or an evening in which the children sing, recite, and read some of their own stories. Storytelling sessions followed by book displays that would give the parents the opportunity to see models of how they can interact with their children and a book are also excellent. For a detailed description of successful parent involvement based on the use of children's literature see Ada (1988).

Once the parents are at the school, they might be told how important it is for their children to have a good command of the mother tongue:

- In order to develop as well-rounded human beings.
- In order to do well in school.
- In order to make it easier to learn English.

Any doubt the parents may have in this regard should be discussed and dispelled. Then, ways in which they can best help their children might be suggested to them.

To encourage their children's oral language development, parents might:

- Ask their children to tell them what they have done in school every day.
- Encourage their children to share their thoughts and feelings with them. The parents should not feel compelled to offer solutions, but they should

know that it is important for their children to have someone with whom they can feel close.

- Talk with their children about their own experiences, both current ones and those of their childhood and youth. These experiences will not only enrich their children's lives, they will give the children confidence to share their experiences as well.
- Ask their children for suggestions when there is something to be done, bought, or repaired. Once the children have expressed their opinions and suggestions, they should be asked to explain their reasons. Their opinions deserve respect.
- Encourage their children to reflect on everyday experiences, including what they see on television, through questions such as: Why did that happen? Could it has turned out differently? What possible solution can you think of?
- Teach their children songs, sayings, games, and riddles; tell them stories or legends they remember, and, if possible, read their children stories.

If our language minority children are to find a role in a highly technological, information-oriented society, if they are to be able to escape from the present statistical predictions, they need to master the art of communication, to become truly literate, and to develop critical thinking skills.

The purpose of the Creative Reading Method is not to place the burden of our responsibility on children, but rather to liberate them from the feeling of being trapped by unmalleable, self-defeating circumstances. Through actual demonstration and experience, teachers need to give students the confidence that they can improve their present environment, their human relationships, and their emotional responsiveness. If teachers succeed in giving this much to language minority children, they will have succeeded in validating the learning experience for those who might otherwise have found little relevance in the classroom.

REFERENCES

Ada, A. F. (1988). The Pajaro Valley experience: Working with Spanish-speaking parents to develop children's reading and writing skills in the home through the use of children's literature. In T. Skutnabb-Kangas & J. Cummins (Eds.), *Minority education: From shame to struggle*. Clevedon, England: Multilingual Matters.

Ada, A. F. (1987). *Teaching for transfer: Spanish to English. Tranferencia del español al inglés*. Reading, MA: Addison-Wesley.

Ada, A. F. (1980). Creative Reading: A new approach to teaching ethnic minority students to read. *Aids to Bilingual Communication Report, 1*(2), 1–8.

Ada, A. F., & Olave, M. P. (1986). *Hagamos caminos*. Reading, MA: Addison-Wesley.

Aronowitz, S., & Giroux, H. (1985). *Education under siege*. South Hadley, MA: Bergin and Garvey.

Ashton-Warner, S. (1963). *Teacher*. New York: Bantam Books.

Cummins, J. (1981). The role of primary language development in promoting educational success for language minority students. In Office of Bilingual Bicultural Education (Ed.), *Schooling and language minority students: A theoretical framework*. Los Angeles: California State University.

Freire, P. (1982a). *Education for critical consciousness*. New York: Continuum.

Freire, P. (1982b). *Pedagogy of the oppressed*. New York: Continuum.

Freire, P., & Macedo, D. (1987). *Literacy: Reading the word and the world*. South Hadley, MA: Bergin and Garvey Publishers.

Giroux, H. (1986). *Radical pedagogy and the politics of student voice*. Unpublished paper.

Goodman, K. (1986). *What's whole in whole language*. Portsmouth, NH: Heinemann Educational Books.

Kozol, J. (1985). *Illiterate America*. Garden City, NY: Anchor Press/Doubleday.

Krashen, S. D. (1981). Bilingual education and second language acquisition theory. In Office of Bilingual Bicultural Education (Ed.), *Schooling and language minority students: A theoretical framework*. Los Angeles: California State University.

Krashen, S. D., & Terrell, T. D. (1983). *The natural approach*. Hayward, CA: The Alemany Press.

McCracken, M., & McCracken, R. (1979). *Reading, writing & language: A practical guide for primary teachers*. Winnipeg, Canada: Peguis Publishers Limited.

Martí, J. (1979). *Obras escogidas*. La Habana, Cuba: Editora Política.

Pollack, C. (1979). Suggestology and suggestopedia revisited. *Journal of Suggestive-Accelerative Learning and Teaching*, *4*(1), 16–31.

Sue, S., & Padilla, A. (1986). Ethnic minority issues in the United States: Challenges for the educational system. In Bilingual Education Office (Ed.), *Beyond language: Social and cultural factors in schooling language minority students*. Los Angeles: California State University.

Smith, F. (1985). *Reading without nonsense* (2nd ed.). New York: Teachers College Press.

Thonis, E. (1976). *Literacy for America's Spanish speaking children*. Newark, DE: International Reading Association.

Thonis, E. (1983). *The English-Spanish connection: Excellence in English for Hispanic children through Spanish language and literacy development*. Northvale, NJ: Santillana.

6
Contexts for Literacy Development for ESL Children

Sarah Hudelson
Division of Curriculum and Instruction
Arizona State University

INTRODUCTION

Second language learners are present in our elementary schools in ever increasing numbers. As language educators one of our major tasks is to assist these children to grow as readers and writer of English, since such abilities are critical to success in school. Given this responsibility, a question logically posed is how to achieve this goal most effectively. One possible answer to that question would be that we would act on information we have about the processes of reading and writing (both in English as a native language and ESL) and translate that research and theory into classroom practice.

In my own struggles to translate theory and research into classroom practice, I have set up what I have called a continuum of ESL literacy experiences or a continuum of contexts for ESL literacy, represented here in the chart below (see Figure 6.1, p. 104). The continuum includes both reading and writing. In terms of reading, the continuum begins more globally, with the environment in general and becomes more narrow, focusing on more specific aspects of the environment. The continuum includes varied purposes for reading and moves from instructional strategies that rely on reader-created texts to strategies that facilitate learning from a variety of texts created by authors who are not the children themselves. In the area of writing the continuum places initial stress on writing for self-expressive purposes which leads gradually to both literary and informational aims. The continuum emphasizes early fluency and first draft comfort followed by reader response and continued drafting (revising and editing) in varied kinds of writing. The audience for writing include self and others.

ENVIRONMENTAL PRINT STRATEGIES

Using this continuum of contexts and current information we have about ESL children's reading and writing development, it is then possible to make specific suggestions for classroom literacy activities. Beginning with reading

103

Figure 6.1. ESL Literacy Experiences Continuum.

Reading

Print in the Environment	Literary forms	Print in content areas	Print in daily life
Print attached to experiences			
environmental print: signs, goods, tv	predictable, patterned books, poems, songs, literature	texts, reference materials	newspapers, maps, references, phone books, etc.
key words, language experience			
reading to survive	read to enjoy, expand oneself, understand self and others	read to learn and apply new information, apply information to real situations, react, make decisions, get things done, etc.	
create texts, read for self expression			

Writing

Self expressive	Literary or Poetic	Informational or Transactional
write to give personal thoughts, ideas, reactions	write to create some kind of piece (genre)	write to present information clearly, write to persuade
primary audience often self as well as others	audience of others as well as self—write to entertain	audience of others as well as self-clarity is vital
journals, diaries, personal narratives	stories, poems, songs, jokes, advertisements, etc.	announcements, signs, notes, reports, directions, summaries, explanations, informational books and stories, opinions, arguments

initial drafting—share with audience—audience response, revising—final edited form

Copyright © 1985 by Sarah Hudelson.

and with the context of the physical environment, there is information available that child ESL learners in the United States frequently find themselves in environments in which English print surrounds them (Goodman, Goodman, & Flores, 1979; Rigg, 1987). Examples of English environmental print include such signs and labels as McDonald's, K-Mart, Crest, Cheerios, Cocoa Puffs, Masters of the Universe, Yield and Stop signs, street signs, print around the school and so on. The prevalence of print in the environment means that the first experiences ESL children have with English reading may be the English in the world around them. ESL learners make guesses about the contents of the print; they try to make sense of the print in the world around them. Some ESL children may begin to read by struggling with environmental print. Therefore, environmental print provides a logical area in which to plan and carry out literacy activities (Hudelson, 1984; Rigg, 1987).

Environmental print instructional strategies may include walking field trips around schools and neighborhoods so that children may examine and write down examples of print around them. As a homework assignment, children may be asked to bring in examples of environmental print in their homes. Children may divide their examples into print they are sure that they can read and print that they have questions about. In-class categorizations of the print and logical guesses about certain examples may take place in the class. Teachers may work with children to refine their hypotheses about certain signs and labels. In-class activities such as constructing a grocery store and role-playing customers and store clerks or creating a fast food restaurant and assuming the roles of customers and servers will give children the opportunity to use both oral and written English, focusing on English environmental print. On a more sophisticated note, children might examine the written language of advertising and spend time creating their own products and commercials. Or as part of a social studies unit on communities, children might construct an ideal community and decide on the kind of signs that they would have in their Utopia.

Bringing environmental print into the classroom activates children's interest and inquisitiveness about the print that surrounds them. It helps children see that there is some English that they can read. It also provides children with the opportunity to bring confusing print into school and ask about it, which facilitates vocabulary development in English. And using environmental print demonstrates a practical use of English reading: to get along in the world. For all of these reasons the context of the environment as one for reading and writing should be explored.

LANGUAGE EXPERIENCE AND EXPRESSIVE WRITING

From the broadest context of the physical environment the continuum moves into a slightly narrower context, that of the life experiences that ESL learners have. Considerable evidence has demonstrated that a second language develops much as does a first language, in a language-rich environment where learners are participating in interesting experiences to which comprehensible language input is attached (Allen, 1986; Lindfors, 1987). Research also has shown that ESL readers' comprehension of text is affected by their familiarity with its contents (Barnitz, 1986; Rigg, 1986). This means that ESL children will understand material that is experentially familiar to them better than they understand unfamiliar material. Therefore it seems logical consciously to connect some of the experiences children are having first to their oral expression and subsequently to text that they will read.

One way to do this is to allow learners to create their own texts based on their own experiences to which language has been attached. Language experience stories provide for this learner creation of comprehensible text, as children dictate to the teacher what the contents of a story will be (Dixon & Nessel, 1983; Rigg, 1981). The experiences children narrate may come from their lives outside school—for example, a television program watched, a movie seen, a neighborhood party attended, a refugee camp experience survived. Additionally, teachers may organize in-class activities to which first talk and then writing is attached. These activities may be based on child interests—for example, creating and playing a game or they may focus on cultural awareness, for example, preparing a Thanksgiving dinner.

Content area curricula provide a logical place from which to structure content learning experiences that also form the basis for language experience stories. In other words, language experience work becomes an integral part of content curriculum (Dixon & Nessel, 1983). If, for example, children are studying the concepts of light and shadow in science, the teacher could organize an activity in which learners would measure and record the lengths of their shadows at various times of the day and/or measure and contrast their body heights to the length of their shadows. Following the activities, children discuss what they have learned about shadows and then narrate what they have learned. From the experiences that they have, learners dictate a narrative to the teacher, who writes down what the children have said. This dictation becomes one of the children's reading texts.

Moving from the reading to the writing area of the continuum, teacher demonstration of the talking-writing connection in language experience may connect logically and naturally to ESL learners writing their own experiences rather than dictating them to another person. Such self-expressive writing may take the form of diaries or journals, including dialogue journals where children write to their teachers and their teachers respond to them (Kreeft, Shuy, Staton, Reed, & Morroy, 1984). Personal narratives that consider individual life experiences may also be encouraged through the employment of the writing workshop strategy, where children create first drafts, share what they have written with others, and engage in revision of their pieces.

This approach to writing, documented originally with native speakers of English (Graves, 1983), has been found to be an effective strategy for ESL writers as well (Hudelson, 1989; Urzua, 1987). As learners attach English to their life experiences both inside and outside school, they should be encouraged both to describe and to reflect upon these experiences through writing as well as through talking.

READING AND WRITING EXPERIENCES WITH LITERATURE

While language experience stories and personal narratives may play an important role in ESL children's literacy development, they should not be used to the exclusion of other kinds of reading and writing. In order for children to become proficient users of English, they must experience the many forms of text material available in our highly literate society. One of the most important kinds of text material is what the continuum refers to as literary forms, meaning such pieces as stories, fables, tall tales, poems, limericks, nursery rhymes, jokes, songs and so on. Children learning ESL need frequent and continued experiences with these literary forms.

An excellent place to begin children's experiences with literary forms is with what some call predictable reading materials (Genishi & Dyson, 1984; Heald-Taylor, 1987; Rhodes 1981). In some works, factors within the texts contribute to predictability. These elements include repetition of both language and incident, in, for example, stories such as *The Little Red Hen*, and *The Three Bears*, and *The Three Little Pigs*. In addition these stories illustrate the basic Western story structure of setting, characters, initiating event, conflict, resolution of conflict. Other stories are predictable because of redundancy of rhythm and rhyme, as in *May I Bring a Friend?* (De Regniers, 1965). In this tale, as the main character brings a succession of wild animals to a fancy party he repeats, "I told the queen and the queen told the king that I had a friend I wanted to bring. The king told the queen, 'My dear, my dear. Any friend of our friend is welcome here.'" Children's songs and poems such as "Old McDonald Had a Farm" and "I Know an Old Lady Who Swallowed a Fly" and "This is the House that Jack Built" also fall into this category. Finally, many children's books such as *The Carrot Seed* (Krauss, 1945) and *The Very Hungry Caterpillar* (Carle, 1969) are predictable for readers who take advantage of real world knowledge, in these two cases of how plants grow and how caterpillars turn into butterflies.

The stories, songs, poems, and so on, should be used repeatedly as learners listen to them, follow along while someone else reads, read them in pairs or independently, read them chorally or in parts, create skits or dramas and act them out, and read them to others (older children reading to younger children, for example). Instead of basal reader stories, children may read the same story or book and then meet in a literature study group to discuss their reactions to the work (Bird & Alvarez, 1987). Children may also respond to their reading through the use of literature logs, a special kind of journal in which readers react in writing to what they have read (Flores et al., 1985). Using stories and books within content area work should also be undertaken, as the examples of plant and animal life cycles illustrate. In addition, children and teacher may want to compare and contrast stories and other literary forms from their own cultures with stories from this culture. (A Vietnamese tale, "The Brocade Slipper," for example, is quite similar to "Cinderella.") Using predictable materials exposes ESL learners to elements of literary language. ESL children learn how the elements or parts of a story fit together, how verses in a story connect, how a chorus functions and so on as they hear, read, and act out stories. As children are able, teachers will expand the variety of literary pieces being shared with children, for example, from stories that are read in one sitting to books shared chapter by chapter.

Listening to and reading literary forms extends naturally into children creating their own literary forms, whether these be stories, poems, songs, jokes and so on. This is what is referred to as literary or poetic writing on the writing side of the continuum. ESL children have demonstrated that they are able to create literary pieces, based on their familiarity with particular genres (Flores et al., 1985; Hudelson, 1989; Johnson, 1985). Therefore, writing individually or with others, ESL children should be asked to create drafts of stories, songs, poems, and so on. And, using the writer's workshop approach previously mentioned, learners should read what they have written to others, attend to the comments of listeners who respond to what has been written, and make substantive changes in what they have created. Through writing, as well as through reading, ESL children develop as story readers and writers.

CONTENT AREA LITERACY

From the context of literary pieces it is necessary to consider another kind of reading that ESL children will have to do, the reading in content areas that they are or will be studying. Subject area textbooks comprise a lot of this kind of reading. The aim of content area texts is to present information in an expository fashion. Frequently significant amounts of information are presented in a few pages, resulting in density in text and a heavy concept/content load, with little or no thought given to the readability of the material, even for native speakers of the language. Authors usually convey at least part of their information through additions to the print such as illustrations, diagrams, charts, graphs, boldfaced headings, subheadings and the like. This kind of academic text (and academic language) may present particular comprehension difficulties for ESL learners (Chamot & O'Malley, 1987; Mohan,

1986). Yet second language learners must be able to construct meaning from these kinds of materials if they are to achieve academically in United States classrooms. So educators working with ESL learners must address this issue.

Teachers working with second language learners can make use of what native language reading educators refer to as content area reading strategies. Educators working in reading in the content areas have reached some conclusions about reading instruction that have direct relevance to ESL learners. The first conclusion is one related directly to an assertion already made about ESL reading comprehension: A person's comprehension of material being read is affected by the knowledge the person already has about the topic. When readers are asked to read something for which they have prior knowledge or background, they will understand it better than material for which they have little or no prior knowledge or background (Readence, Bean, & Baldwin, 1985). Applying this to classroom instruction means that teachers must activate children's background knowledge before children read content area material.

The easiest and most direct way to do this is to ask children what they know about a topic before they read about that topic. In ESL settings, as well as in native language contexts, this would most effectively be done in groups, so that children could benefit from the knowledge and language input of other learners. If children are going to read about insects, for example, they could be asked to generate a list of everything they know or think they know about insects (the teacher could serve as transcriber). Then reading could follow, one purpose of which would be to compare prior information with information in the text selection. What new information did they learn? Was there any information in the text that contradicted what they said they knew? Children could also be asked to generate questions that they wanted answers to, answers that might be found in the selection. If the answers were not found, children could consult other sources of information (Goodman & Burke, 1980).

A version of the Directed Reading Thinking Activity (DRTA) often used with basal reader stories might also be utilized. In a DRTA the learners begin by predicting the contents of a story based on the title, any subtitles and the pictures. The children then read through the story section by section, using what they are reading to confirm or disconfirm their initial predictions and to make revised predictions. Applying this to content area reading (Readence, Bean, & Baldwin, 1985), children could use such textual features as titles and subtitles, diagrams, illustrations, underscored words and so on both to predict the contents of the selection and to create questions that they wanted answered. Such activation of prior knowledge and/or consideration of contents is crucial to making ESL children active participants in the process of constructing meaning from text.

What happens if ESL learners have no prior knowledge of a particular topic or area of study? In that case the teacher must work with the children to build their background knowledge before they read. From the point of view of second language learning this is especially important, because background building will provide ESL students with additional English input. The most effective way to build background knowledge is to engage the learners in an activity or activities that will involve them considering some of the major content or concepts that they will later read about. Using the example of the topic of insects may help to clarify this point.

If children are going to read about the physical characteristics and habits of insects, what kinds of activities might be undertaken to develop their background knowledge in these areas? The teacher might start by brainstorming with the students the kinds of insects (bugs) they see around them. After a list has been developed, groups of children could be assigned to make observations of certain of these insects—one group, for example, observing ants, another flies, another ladybugs, another grasshoppers, and so on. Perhaps with a set of questions, children could be asked to record what they observe and to bring back their observations to share with others. If possible, habitats such as an ant farm might be set up in the classroom. Or children could capture and bring in insects to the room for observation. Other activities might include giving groups of children cards with pictures of insects on them and asking the children to put the insects or groups or categories. How would the children categorize them? How do they think certain bugs are alike and different? Comparisons could be made across groups. Films, filmstrips, videotapes, outside experts, and written sources of information other than the textbook could also be brought into the classroom to give the children a broad experience with bugs. All of these (prereading) activities would give ESL learners content and language experiences which should serve to facilitate their interaction with the science textbook.

Moving once again to the writing half of the continuum, many content area reading experts suggest that learners be asked to do something with what they have learned beside memorizing facts to be given back on a test (Smith, Carey, & Harste, 1982). Stress is given to asking learners to use information from reading, reacting to, and reflecting upon what they read and sharing their reflections and understandings with others. One way to do this would be an adaptation of the dialogue journal called the learning log. In learning logs, children use writing as one way of thinking about and perhaps drawing conclusions about what they have learned. After engaging in the classification of insect cards, for example, learners could be asked to write about what they had learned about insects from carrying out the activity and seeing the ways insects could be classified. Again after reading about insects, learners could be asked to write down the most important things they learned.

In addition to using learning logs, other kinds of writing could also be done, either individually or in groups. Stress is given to collaborative group work, both by content area reading experts (Langer, 1982; Smith-Burke,

1982; Smith, Carey, & Harste, 1982) and by second language educators (Enright & McCloskey, 1985, 1988; Gaies, 1985; Rigg & Enright, 1986; Urzua, 1980). Collaborative writing projects might include children creating dramatizations or scripts of something that they had read, for example, an account of Alexander Graham Bell's discovery that his telephone worked, Thomas Edison's invention of the electric light bulb, Marie Curie's discovery of radium. Groups might collaborate on the creation of a report about something being studied by the class, for example, different groups researching and reporting (orally and in writing) on various insects. In such reporting the aim would be the clear presentation of information in transactional or informational writing. Such variations on the Jigsaw (DeBerkeley-Wykes, 1983) focus on children working together, on each group developing its own expertise and then sharing its knowledge with others. The processes of children working together, talking, reading, making notes, creating written drafts, sharing those drafts and making revisions all intertwine content area learning and language (including literacy) development.

REAL WORLD LITERACY

A final context for literacy development is that of print in daily life or real world reading and writing. What this means is that people spend a great deal of time reading and writing text that is not of the school or textbook variety. People read and write different kinds of materials for varying purposes. In one day, for example, I read the local newspaper, the yellow pages in the telephone book, recipe directions from a cookbook, part of a murder mystery, the price on cosmetics in a drug store, a menu in a restaurant, a wedding invitation, a city map, and a map in a shopping mall. I did the following kinds of writing: part of this article, a shopping list for the grocery store, appointments in my calendar, a list of names a friend called to give me, call numbers for some library books, a proposed travel itinerary from a travel agent.

This variety, I would suggest, is not unusual and suggests that elementary school educators would do well to acknowledge real world reading and writing and develop classroom activities that incorporate this context in the classroom. With the caveat that activities involve children actively in making sense of print and creating text, there are a multitude of possibilities for involving ESL children in authentic real world reading and writing. Examples would include using maps and atlases in social studies work and then asking children to create maps of their own neighborhoods. At another time children could read recipes in order to create some dishes as part of a unit on nutrition. Then learners could collect recipes from their home cultures and bring them to school to be compiled into a class book of recipes. A social studies activity could involve children in examining the newspaper to report on stories of particular interest to them. Reading the newspaper could lead to children becoming interested in producing their own class or school newspaper. Penpals could be organized between classes at different schools, so that children would both receive and write letters. In these and many other activities both reading for varied purposes and writing in expressive and transactional ways would be promoted.

CONCLUSION

These, then, are some of the literacy contexts and purposes that should be recognized as educators consider the literacy development of ESL learners in elementary schools. Certainly these contexts apply to native speakers of the language as well, which means that many of the activities suggested for ESL children would also be appropriate for English language children. A reality for all learners in our society is the multiplicity of literacy contexts, a multiplicity which demands creative responses by educators. It is my hope that the literacy continuum presented here will facilitate educators consideration of how most effectively to provide for second language learners' achievement of multiple aspects of English literacy.

REFERENCES

Allen, V. (1986). Developing contexts to support second language acquisition. *Language Arts, 63*, 61–66.

Barnitz, J. *Reading development of nonnative speakers of English.* (1986). Orlando, FL: Harcourt, Brace Jovanovich and the Center for Applied Linguistics.

Bird, L., & Alvarez, L. (1987). Beyond comprehension: The power of literature study for language minority students. *ESOL in Elementary Education Newsletter, 10*, 1–2.

Carle, E. (1969). *The very hungry caterpillar.* New York: World Publishing.

Chamot, A., & O'Malley, M. (1987). The cognitive academic language learning approach: A bridge to the mainstream. *TESOL Quarterly, 21*, 227–250.

De Berkeley-Wykes, J. (1983). Jigsaw reading. In J. W. Oller & P. A. Richard-Amato (Eds.), *Methods that work* (pp. 313–319). Rowley, MA: Newbury House.

De Regniers, B. (1965). *May I bring a friend?* New York: Athenaeum.

Dixon, C., & Nessel, D. (1983). *Language experience approach to reading (and writing).* Haywood, CA: Alemany Press.

Enright, D. S., & McCloskey, M. (1985). Yes talking!: Organizing the classroom to promote second language acquisition. *TESOL Quarterly, 19*, 431–453.

Enright, D. S., & McCloskey, M. (1988). *Integrating English: Developing English language and literacy in multilingual classrooms.* Reading, MA: Addison-Wesley.

Flores, B., Garcia, E., Gonzalez, S., Hidalgo, G., Kaczmarek, K., & Romero, T. (1985). *Holistic bilingual instructional strategies.* Phoenix, AZ: Exito.

Gaies, S. (1985). *Peer involvement in language learning.* Orlando, FL: Harcourt, Brace, Jovanovich and the Center for Applied Linguistics.

Genishi, C., & Dyson, A. (1984). *Language assessment in the early years.* Norwood, NJ: Ablex.

Goodman, K., Goodman, Y., & Flores, B. (1979). *Reading in the bilingual classroom: Literacy and biliteracy.* Rosslyn, VA: National Clearinghouse for Bilingual Education.

Goodman, Y., & Burke, C. (1980). *Reading strategies: Focus on comprehension.* New York: Holt, Rinehart and Winston.

Graves, D. (1983). *Writing: Teachers and children at work.* Portsmouth, NH: Heinemann Educational Books.

Heald-Taylor, G. (1987). Predictable literature selections and activities for language arts instruction. *The Reading Teacher, 41,* 6–13.

Hudelson, S. (1984). Kan yu ret an rayt en ingles: Children become literate in English as a second language. *TESOL Quarterly, 18,* 221–238.

Hudelson, S. (1989). *Write on: Children writing in ESL.* Englewood Cliffs, NJ: Prentice-Hall.

Johnson, C. (1985). What do you know about witches? *ESOL in Elementary Education News, 7,* 11.

Krauss, R. (1945). *The carrot seed.* New York: Harper and Row.

Kreeft, J., Shuy, R., Staton, J., Reed, L., & Morroy, R. (1984). *Dialogue writing: analysis of student-teacher interactive writing in the learning of English as a second language.* (National Institute of Education Final Report NIE-G-83-0030). Washington, DC: Center for Applied Linguistics.

Langer, J. (1982). Facilitating text processing: The elaboration of prior knowledge. In J. Langer & M. T. Smith-Burke (Eds.), *Reader meets author/Bridging the gap* (pp. 163–179). Newark, DE: International Reading Association.

Lindfors, J. (1987). *Children's language and learning* (2nd ed.). Englewood Cliffs, NJ: Prentice-Hall.

Mohan, B. (1986). *Language and content.* Reading, MA: Addison-Wesley.

Readence, J., Bean, T., & Baldwin, S. (1985). *Content area reading: An integrated approach* (2nd ed.). Dubuque, IA: Kendall-Hunt.

Rhodes, L. (1981). I can read: Predictable books as resources for reading and writing instruction. *The Reading Teacher, 34,* 511–518.

Rigg, P. (1981). Learning to read the LEA way. In C. W. Twyford, W. Diehl, & K. Feathers (Eds.), *Reading English as a second language: Moving from theory* (pp. 81–90). Bloomington, IN: Indiana University.

Rigg, P. (1986). Reading in ESL: learning from kids. In P. Rigg & D. S. Enright (Eds.), *Children and ESL: Integrating perspectives* (pp. 55–91). Washington, DC: Teachers of English to Speakers of Other Languages.

Rigg, P., (1987, April). *Using environmental print.* Presentation at convention of TESOL, Miami Beach, FL.

Rigg, P., & Enright, D. S. (Eds.). (1986). *Children and ESL: Integrating perspectives.* Washington, DC: Teachers of English to Speakers of Other Languages.

Smith-Burke, T. (1982). Extending concepts through language activities. In J. Langer

& M. T. Smith-Burke (Eds.), *Reader meets author/Bridging the gap* (pp. 163–179). Newark, DE: International Reading Association.

Smith, S., Carey, R., & Harste, J. (1982). The contexts of reading. In A. Berger & H. A. Robinson (Eds.), *Secondary school reading: what research reveals about classroom practice* (pp. 21–38). Urbana, IL: ERIC Clearinghouse on Reading and Communication Skills.

Urzua, C. (1980). A language learning environment for all children. *Language Arts, 57,* 38–44.

Urzua, C. (1987). "You stopped too soon": Second language children composing and revising. *TESOL Quarterly, 21,* 279–304.

7
Integrating Computerized Speech and Whole Language in the Early Elementary School

Roser Salavert
Educational Consultant
Citywide Office/District 75
New York City

Access to computers is clearly an issue for limited English proficient (LEP) children. The 1987 document released by the U.S. Congress (Roberts & OTA staff, 1987) reports that the percentage of teachers who use computers in teaching their LEP students is less than one-half the percentage of teachers who use computers in teaching other students.

The question of access is compounded by the issue of quality; the type of programs and activities that language-minority children are engaged when they have access to computers tend to be compensatory in nature. It has been documented that the exclusive use of computer-assisted instruction for reme-dial purposes may diminish student's self-image (The Thomas Rivera Cen-ter, 1986). The use of computers, on the other hand, can be an empowering learning tool for LEP students particularly if their use is based on current second language acquisition theories (Cummins, 1986; Hakuta & Gould, 1987; Johnson, 1985; Roberts & OTA Staff, 1987). The few attempts that have been made to introduce the child to literacy through word processing in the native language first, and then in English, have been acclaimed as successful (Johnson, 1985; Roberts & OTA staff, 1987). However, little is known about the process of acquisition of literacy in this context, and limited research has been conducted on how the utilization of synthesized speech with LEP students can contribute to this process (Salavert, 1988). This chapter addresses the above issue, and describes my recent investigation on the effects of whole language and speech output on development of literacy in the young LEP child.

THE IMPACT OF COMPUTERS IN THE DEVELOPMENT OF LITERACY SKILLS

To acquire literacy is more than to psychologically and mechanically dominate reading and writing techniques. It is to dominate these techniques in terms of consciousness; to understand what one reads and to write what one understands; it is to *communicate* graphically. (Freire, 1974, p. 48)

The type of literacy advocated by Freire is the one advocated herein. Literacy in Freire's statement does not only imply the ability to read facts, but the ability to understand them, which brings up the genuine concept of literacy. Reading is more than a perceptual and sensory-motor process; it is a cognitive process in which the reader supplies the context; and this tacit knowledge is fundamental to literacy (Freire, 1974; Hirsh, 1987; Thonis, 1981). Reading is not a skill easily transferable from one language to another. The mechanical aspects of reading as well as writing, such as eye movements and the understanding of speech-print connections, are transferable, but the background knowledge that is necessary to interpret text is specific to subject matter and to the child's (reader's) experience, and thus it cannot be automatically transferred (Thonis, 1981). Therefore, the critical understanding of reading and writing occurs only when the child is exposed to material which is meaningful to her and creates a need for communication that transcends the present situation (Forester, 1977; Goodman & Goodman, 1976; Heath, 1986; Walsh, 1987).

The use of computers to promote the development of literacy skills emphasizes the use of child-centered programs that are characterized by giving the students control over their own learning. Among them, there is programming, simulations, and word processing. From a pedagogical perspective, child-centered programs appear to conform with a reciprocal interaction model of instruction in that the role of the teacher (computer) is that of facilitating student learning in a collaborative context. By contrast, the emphasis of computer-Assisted Instruction (CAI) is on drill-and-practice type activities and conforms with traditional schooling. In Cummins' view (1986) CAI would follow a transmission model of instruction given that it is the teacher (computer) who initiates and controls the learning interaction, and who imparts knowledge and skills to students.

The use of computers in the process of reading, writing, and composing is widely recommended for both first and second language learners (Daiute, 1984; Johnson, 1985; Perkins, 1985; Robinson & Versluis, 1985; Tucker, 1985; Underwood, 1984). Robinson and Versluis (1985) view the computer as "a liberating influence and a powerful tool" that facilitates writing production. Some of the positive aspects highlighted in their work are: (a) text appearance is enhanced from textbook to TVE screen, (b) errors are amenable to correction in a motivating and nonembarrassing form, and (c) children become book-producers rather than book-consumers. Thurber (1986) adds that the interactive capability of word processing facilitates focusing the attention on the act of writing and thus the development of a sense of audience. Seltzer (1986) reports significant changes in the attitude of five-year-old children towards writing as a result of using word processing. Seltzer suggests that the main reason for this change lies in that the computer eliminates the limitation imposed by the lack of manual dexterity typical of young children, and helps concentrate on the creation of stories. In her study, Seltzer encouraged the children "to rehearse an idea for a topic by drawing a picture or conferring with their classmates prior to writing in the computer" (p. 51). This process helped develop the children's awareness of writing as a process. Seltzer also reports a marked contrast between the way in which children accepted the rehearsal, drafting and revising of stories as natural stages of the writing process, and their reluctance to rewriting a handwritten assignment prior to the introduction of the computer.

The use of word processor with LEP students is just beginning. "The LEP student is put at the back of the line" (Roberts & OTA Staff, 1987), despite the evolving and growing use of technology in schools. Between 1981 and 1986, the percentage of schools with computers grew from about 18 percent to 96 percent, according to the 1987 report prepared by the Office of Technology Assessment of the U.S. Congress. Johnson (1985) claims that linguistic-minority students face a social as well as a language barrier in their access to computer education:

> patterns of use observed in white schools versus minority schools represent *two very different philosophies* regarding the appropriate role of computers in teaching. The low SES predominantly minority schools used computers in a *compensatory* manner, to raise achievement levels through drill and practice for low achievers. (pp. 2–3)

In the same report to the Carnegie Corporation, Johnson (1985) reports that there are a few word processing projects under progress which preliminary data are very encouraging. Among them, The Title VII demonstration project in the Temple Elementary School District in Arizona. Using Magic Slate, a word processor published by Sunburst, Maez and his colleagues designed and implemented individualized computer summer programs for over 300 students. Students wrote daily journal entries, stored the text on a diskette, and teachers responded daily to each student. Preliminary results of this project indicated increased quantity and quality in writing as well as increased use of peer editing.

Another valuable example of this effort to use computers in the process of writing and composing with second language learners is the international writing networks, initially developed by the Laboratory of Comparative Human Cognition at the University of California at San Diego. Results of the research conducted by Rosa and Moll (1985) on the use of this microcomputer communication network between children from California and students from Madrid (Spain) indicates the potential of such system in developing children's writing and composing in their first and second languages, and in enhancing their sensitivity to the values of their own culture and that of other cultures.

ADDING SYNTHESIZED SPEECH OUTPUT TO COMPUTER-BASED INSTRUCTION

Another technological innovation of great potential in the classroom, and in the development of second language literacy is the use of synthesized speech. The addition of voice to a computer-based environment has been in existence for some time, but its has been primarily used by visually-impaired students (American Printing House for the Blind, 1987), and by other speech-impaired individuals (Fishman, 1987). However, the number of educational programs that incorporate some type of synthesized speech is growing every day.

According to Fishman (1987), there are two basic types of voice or speech output aids—text-to-speech synthesizers and digitized speech. A text-to-speech synthesizer or simply called "synthesizer" is a machine that creates the speech output based on programmed instructions. Digitized speech uses human speech as its basis. The speech is stored in the computer memory as a sequence of numbers. At a signal, these numbers are sent through another circuit which reconverts them into speech signals. Despite the high quality of the voice and its intelligibility, digitized speech is not widely used for educational purposes because it takes a large amount of computer memory, and the vocabulary of the system is limited to prestored words. In contrast, synthesizers create the speech output, thus enabling the machine to say anything that one can spell just by instructing the machine how to read it aloud. They do not require a large computer memory; cost can thus be minimized. Despite their mechanical sounding voice, speech synthesizers are extensively used in educational software programs.

Using the Echo IIb speech synthesizer, Rosegrant conducted several studies on the effectiveness of the use of speech output with handicapped youngsters (in Trachtman, 1984), and more recently with young children (Trachtman, 1986). She found that the youngsters' opportunity to have control over the electronic voice helped them to unlock their own abilities to speak, read, and write. Similarly, beginning readers found the immediate aural feedback provided by the speech output motivating, and effective in facilitating the learning process. In combining word processing and speech output, Rosegrant proposes a new approach—editorial approach—to writing. The main thrust of the editorial approach is the need to develop a writer's ability to read and hear internally what he or she has written. Rosegrant (1986a, 1986b) emphasizes that a good writer is also a good editor, and as a good editor this writer must able to carry out internal discourse. This internal discourse involves:

1. An "inner voice" for reading the text aloud and subvocally.
2. A "critical ear" to hear and judge how the text sounds.
3. A sense of the requirements of the text which goes beyond the needs of the writer and involves a concern for the audience.
4. A careful eye for meeting the conventions required of text for public presentation in print.
5. A repertoire of skills and categories for writing which are used for deciding how to improve a written text. (p. 3)

The uniqueness of the editorial approach when comparing it to process writing or product writing is its use of speech output as an external voice which fulfills the functions of the internal discourse while helping the child to develop it. While Rosegrant acknowledges the benefits of process writing or the emphasis on the child's self-expression, and the advantages of product writing with its emphasis on form, she proposes the editorial approach as a unique approach to the development of editorial skills, a critical aspect of good writing. Rosegrant's investigation showed that there exists a positive association between the development of a "critical editor's ear" and the use of speech output. Because of the potential of Rosegrant's editorial approach, I adapted a word processor program with talking capabilities (Appendix A) to the Spanish language, and studied the effects of speech output in the child's first language and in English in his development of literacy skills, as detailed in the following section of this chapter.

THE EFFECTS OF COMPUTER-GENERATED SPEECH OUTPUT ON THE DEVELOPMENT OF LITERACY IN YOUNG LEP CHILDREN

The purpose of this investigation was to study the effects of whole language and speech output on literacy development. To that purpose, the study linked the knowledge gained from studies of second language literacy to the knowledge in the use of computer technology. This knowledge was then combined into an "integrated language" approach that encompassed student experience, literature, and word processing.

The method utilized to study the acquisition of literacy within an experimental computer learning environment reflects the rationale of a whole language approach to literacy. That is, first, that a learning environment must foster a child's overall development and facilitate the acquisition of literacy as a form of self-expression and communication graphically and, second, that LEP children can learn best to read and write when integrating the four language domains (oral, auditory, reading, and writing) in meaningful tasks. The integration of computerized speech with whole language permitted the establishment of a computer learning environment whereby children were encouraged to explore language from all perspectives using their own computer generated materials. Moreover, the accommodation of the speech synthesizer to the Spanish language provided the children participating in the study with a unique opportunity. They were able to work in their preferred language, "teach" Spanish to the computer (that is to fix the pronunciation of the program to produce right Spanish sounds), and begin exploring literacy in a second language.

Subjects, procedures, and treatment. The sample consisted of twelve Puerto Rican children from grades pre-1 to 3, who represented four levels of English proficiency. All of them were enrolled in a transitional bilingual education (TBE) program at the time of the study. These children were introduced to picture story making (Appendix B) and talking word processing (Appendix A) programs. They used these programs to create, narrate, listen to, read, and write stories in Spanish and in English. Children worked in groups of two or independently, with the researcher and/or a teacher from 15 to 20 minutes three times a week over a period of 10 weeks. Data collected included information gathered through children's work samples, teacher's feedback, students' records, and observations.

Analysis of data, main findings and conclusions. Data were analyzed in a holistic and integrative manner. It was holistic in that I looked for individual and group trends, as well as major highlights in the progress of each individual child and the group in general. It was integrative in that I analyzed each set of data separately, cross-referencing the findings obtained, and eventually reported them as they related to the primary research questions and in the form of case studies. It was thought that the case studies would substantiate the findings of the study and also would facilitate the application of this approach in other classroom settings.

The following examples of individual children serve to illustrate the impact of this integration of whole language and speech output. Wendy, a seven-year-old girl, was in a bilingual first grade classroom at the time of the study, but working below grade level. Wendy's initial performance appeared to indicate that she did not see the relationship between words, their forms, and their meaning. The story making program gave Wendy an opportunity to express herself through pictures. In creating a story, Wendy had to explore relational, temporal, and spatial concepts, which provided her with language experiences relevant to the development of metalinguistic awareness. The more she mastered the use of the control and command program keys the easier it was for her to modify icons, create a context for a story, and choose appropriate objects. One of her stories is illustrated below (Story 1).

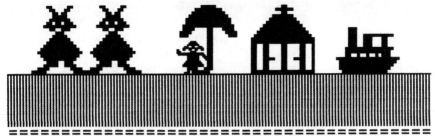

LA NENA TACUSBJ MA ME MO MU

Story 1.

From a developmental perspective (Ferreiro & Teberoski, 1979), the story reflects a child's perception of the written code as a representation of sound segments of speech. In this particular example, Wendy writes "la nena tiene una sombrilla" (the girl has an umbrella), making one word out of three. She writes /TACUSBJ/ for "tiene una sombrilla" (has an umbrella):—"T" stands for "tiene" (has); "A" is "una" (an);—"SBJ" means "sombrija," that is "sombrilla" (umbrella);—"CU" can either be a connector or a part of one of the words for which a sound has not been clearly identified.

This example also shows that Wendy is in a transitional stage between what Ferreiro and Teberoski (1979) refer to as the syllabic and the alphabetic hypothesis. The first referring to the child's attempts at assigning a sound value to each letter, each letter standing for one syllable, and the alphabetical hypothesis to the child's ability to apply the alphabetical principles to reading and writing. In the case of Wendy, she analyzes familiar names and writes them alphabetically, for example, "la nena" (the girl), but she resolves the problem posed by new words through the syllabic hypothesis. At this stage of writing development, the speech output was not used in free composing since it may have been a frustrating experience for Wendy. Speech output, on the other hand, was very helpful in the listening to of oral stories which had been narrated by Wendy, and typed in the computer by the teacher. Eventually, she used speech output in free writing activities. Thus, in Wendy's case, the computer learning environment facilitated the development of metalinguistic awareness, and the acquisition of literacy.

The case of Benito, a bilingual third grader, illustrates a different use of the speech output. For him, the use of speech output was instrumental in enhancing his writing skills in Spanish as well as in English. As the stories reproduced below indicate, there are significant differences between the work done with speech output (Story 2), and the work done without it (Story 3). The contribution of the computerized speech is evident in spacing (8.3% errors with speech output vs. 25% without it), and spelling (1 mispelling error with speech output vs. 8 without it).

```
EL HOMBRE ESTAVA COJIENDO  UNAS FLORES

PARA LA MAMA UN NINO DIJO NO NOLAS

COJAS OSI TE PASA UN TREN POR ENSIMA.
```

Story 2.

While experimenting with the talking word processor, Benito discovered that the speech output was helpful in composing. He also discovered that this aural feedback worked best for him if used according to the characteristics of the language.

Therefore, working in Spanish Benito did not use the speech mode while typing, since the pronunciation of many of the words had to be fixed to ensure an acceptable Spanish sound. He preferred to correct complete paragraphs. After writing a paragraph, Benito would listen to the machine read the entire text—one or more times—identify the words which did not sound right, and fix them. Initially, the teacher helped Benito in fixing the pronunciation but by the tenth week of the project, Benito had learned how to fix the pronunciation by himself. When composing in English, Benito used the speech output to check the sounds of a word one by one, to verify the meaning of each statement and to determine the wholeness of a paragraph. Afterwards, he would work on the paragraph in the same manner as he had done with a Spanish text.

The utilization of speech output and a whole language approach also provides some evidence of transferability of skills. This is particularly evident in the case of Cesar where composing activities at the computer had an immediate impact on his handwritten work. Cesar exhibited an apparent proficiency in English (Lau D). At the time of the study, however, he was

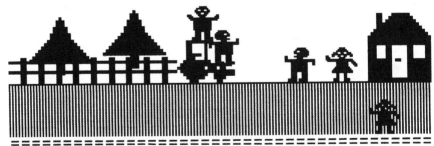

```
LLE GO MAMI  LLE GO MAMI VASMOS AVERLA.
NOS TRAJO ALGO SI SI MIRA IO QUE ME
TROJO UN  CARITO  HIAMI UN PELUCHE
PAPA YAVOI BOI HAORA
VAMOSHADENTRO.
```

Story 3.

receiving special education speech services geared at improving his pronunciation and fluency in English. When he was introduced to computers he was also experiencing difficulties in Spanish reading. He did not have any reading or writing abilities in English.

Cesar approached the computer with enthusiasm and interest. He worked diligently at his stories and soon he and his classmate, Francisco, an advanced student, formed an excellent working team. The talking word processor was introduced at a point when Cesar had already mastered the story-making program, and was ready for a new challenge. His increased focused attention and behavioral control allowed him to work at the computer for longer periods of time and to produce complete stories. Cesar, who according to his teacher had not written anything in class, suddenly appeared extremely interested in developing literacy skills. He produced his first written work on October 22nd (Story 4), four weeks after the study had begun.

Cesar and I "taught" Spanish to the computer. He soon developed good discriminatory skills and was capable of discriminating between the sound of a Spanish word read in English, a pseudo-Spanish sound, and an acceptable sound for a Spanish word. By late December, Cesar had learned how to fix the pronunciation of a word by himself and enjoyed doing so. He was then introduced to English reading.

The speech output was particularly effective in modeling the pronunciation of some blends and sounds that Cesar could not read. The use of his picture stories as well as his Spanish stories, as the basis for his written work in English was very motivating. By January his handwritten work and his typed texts expressed complete thoughts and showed a good understanding of the rules of the grammar (Stories 5 and 6).

As illustrated in their examples, children's feeling of competence and interest in literacy are closely related to their awareness of having control over the computer. The integration of speech output and whole language promoted the child's natural reading process. The language experience stories created by the children themselves made reading and writing much more meaningful, and eventually they constituted the basis for these children's own learning. While the study showed that stories—the making, telling, reading, and writing of stories—do facilitate the learning process, it also demonstrated that to be effective, stories as well as the use of speech output should be used in a variety of ways depending upon the age, language proficiency, learning style, and degree of literacy skills.

IMPLICATIONS

The combination of speech output and a whole language approach appears to hold promise to enhance the intrinsic motivation of students towards learning and consequently for improving their achievement in school. One immediate

A

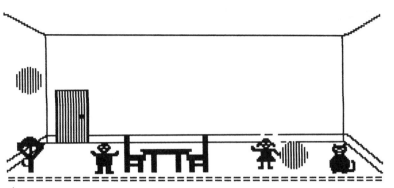

Los nenes esTabanjugandocon
la bola y se Pasa Va la bola
y abia un goto y un esPejo
y abia una bentana.

B

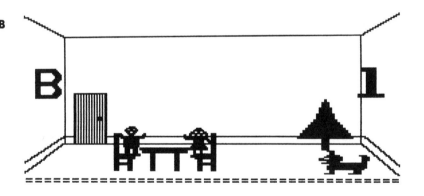

abia una vez dos nenes jugando
con una Pitola y se muria
de jugando ymino un animal
entro en la casa.

Story 4.

A

La tormenta de nieve
Un dia hizo una tormenta
de nieve.

Fueron afuera los niños
a jugar con la nieve.
Las niñas y los niños tirando
nieve

B

Mama llamó a las niñas y los
Niños y fueron a dormir.

Story 5.

ME AND MY FRIEND PLAY FOOTBALL AND WE GO IN SCHOOL AND WE GO TO OUR HOUSE

Story 6.

implication of the study is the obligation of educators and school administrators to replace the widely spread use of deficits models, that is, remedial and compensatory programs, for an open model that fosters the linguistic, emotional, and cognitive growth of the LEP child. A model that empowers children, and utilizes their linguistic strengths and cultural knowledge as the basis for literacy development.

A second important implication is the perception of the computer as a tool that the child can utilize to enhance his learning, rather than the perception of the computer as a teaching aid. This distinction has implications at both the teacher and the student levels. At the teacher's level it implies the active involvement of the teacher in the computer activities, that is, planning, formulation of goals, modification of behaviors, clarification of objectives, and so forth. The teacher can no longer expect the child to work on her own, unless he has actively prepared the child to do so. At the child's level, the computer needs to be perceived as an empowering tool. The child must perceive himself as "the expert" who has control over the computer, rather than perceiving of the computer as a intelligent machine who teaches him.

Another implication to be drawn from the study is the contribution of computerized speech. First, the uniqueness of speech output makes possible the use of whole language within the computer environment. Secondly, it facilitates the child's understanding of the interrelationships that exist between oral, listening, reading, and writing skills. Finally, and despite the technical limitations imposed by the program adopted for this study (the fact that it was designed to be used with English only), the use of speech output helped the beginner writer of the present study in acquiring the ability to carry out the internal discourse that is critical for a good writer. In the preliterate LEP child, the speech output facilitated the development of behaviors and skills that are associated with learning to read and write, for example, increased focused participation, hypothesis testing, space and temporal orientation.

Despite the relevance of these findings, continued research is deemed necessary in order to make broad generalizations. Further research on the design of a *bilingual* word processor with speech output, and on the use of whole language and computerized speech with older preliterate students is also considered of particular interest.

APPENDIX A TALKING TEXT WRITER

Manufacturer: Scholastic, 1986

Cost: $100 (approximately)

Availability: Apple IIe with 128K or Apple IIGS and Echo+ Speech Synthesizer or IIc with Cricket Speech Synthesizer.

Printer Options: The program's custom option can configure Talking Text Writer to almost any printer.

Program Description: Talking text Writer combines word processing with synthesized speech to help children learn to read and write. The program allows students to type any text and hear it spoken back to them. Using a developmental approach to learning that places an emphasis on motivating the students and providing support to early readers and writers, the Talking Text Writer fosters a sense of competence in the student and a feeling that he or she is in control of the learning process.

APPENDIX B KIDWRITER

Manufacturer: Spinakker Corporation Co., 1984

Cost: $45 (approximately)

Availability: Commodore 64, Commodore 128, Apple IIe, Apple IIc.

Printer Options: Black and white only, Apple Scribe, Imagewriter, Imagewriter II, EPSON and IBM.

Program Description: Provides an original format for story writing and illustration. It lets the child choose from 99 different characters and objects, and a variety of picture settings thus encouraging them to create their own stories. Children are also encouraged to write their stories using the program's word processing capabilities.

REFERENCES

American Printing House for the Blind. (1987). Current Status: Winter 1987. *Micro Materials Update Leaflet.*

Cummins, J. (1986). Empowering minority students: A framework for Intervention. *Harvard Educational Review, 56,* 18–36.

Daiute, C. A. (1984). Can the computer stimulate writers' inner dialogues?. In W. Wresch (Ed.), *The computer in composition instruction.* Urbana, IL: National Council of Teachers of English.

Ferreiro, E., & Teberoski, A. (1979). *Literacy before schooling.* London: Heinemann Educational Books.

Fishman, I. (1987). *Electronic communication aids.* Boston: College Hill.

Forester, A. D. (1977, November). What teachers can learn from natural readers. *The Reading Teacher,* pp. 160–166.

Freire, P. (1974). *Education: The practice of freedom.* Writers and Readers Publishing Cooperative.

Goodman, K., & Goodman, Y. M. (1976). *Learning to read is natural.* Paper presented at the Conference on Theory and Practice of Beginning Reading Instruction, Pittsburgh, PA.

Hakuta, K., & Gould, L. J. (1987). Synthesis of research on bilingual education. *Educational Leadership, 44,* 38–46.

Heath, S. B. (1986). Sociocultural contexts of language development. In *Beyond language: Social and cultural factors in schooling language minority students* (pp. 143–187). Los Angeles, CA: Evaluation, Dissemination and Assessment Center.

Hermann, A. (1987). Teaching ESL students writing using word processing. *TESOL Newsletter, 15,* 8–11.

Hirsch, E. D., Jr. (1987). *Cultural literacy.* Boston: Houghton Mifflin.

Johnson, D. M. (1985). *Using computers to promote the development of English as a second language.* A report for the Carnegie Corporation, Pittsburgh, Pa. Unpublished manuscript.

Perkins, D. N. (1985). The fingertip effect: How information-processing technology shapes thinking. *Educational Researcher, 14,* 11–17.

Roberts, L., & OTA Staff. (1987). *Trends and status of computers in schools: Use in chapter I programs and use with limited English proficient students.* Washington, DC: U.S. Congress Office of Technology Assessment.

Robinson, B., & Versluis, E. (1985). Electric text: A choice medium for reading?. In D. Chandler & S. Marcus (Eds.), *Computers and literacy* (pp. 125–139). Philadelphia: Open University Press.

Rosegrant, T. (1986a). *Talking Text Writer.* New York: Scholastic Inc.

Rosegrant, T. (1986b). *It doesn't sound right: The role of speech output as a primary form of feedback for beginning text revision.* Paper presented at the Annual Meeting of the American Educational Research Association, San Francisco, CA.

Salavert, R. (1988). *Integrating computerized speech and whole language in the elementary school: A study with limited English proficient students.* Unpublished doctoral dissertation, University of Massachusetts, Amherst, MA.

Seltzer, C. (1986, January). The word processor. A magic tool for kindergarten writers. *Early Years/K-8,* pp. 51–52.

Thonis, E. W. (1981). Reading instruction for language minority students. In *Schooling and language minority students: A theoretical framework* (pp. 147–183). Los Angeles: Evaluation, Dissemination and Assessment Center, California State University.

Thurber, B. (1986). *Computers, language and literacy.* Paper presented at the Symposium on Language and the World of Work in the Twenty-First Century, North Dartmouth, MA.

The Thomas Rivera Center. (1986). The new information technology and the education of Hispanics: The promise and the dilemma. *Policy Pamphlet Series 1.* Claremont, CA: Claremont Graduate School.

Trachtman, P. (1984, February). Putting computers into the hands of children without language. *Smithsonian World*, pp. 42–50.

Underwood, J. H. (1984). *Linguistics, computers and the language teacher: A communicative approach.* Rowley, MA: Newbury House.

Walsh, C. (1987). Language, meaning and voice: Puerto Rican students' struggle for a speaking consciousness. *Language Arts*, *64*, 196–206.

Part III
Pedagogy, Empowerment, and Social Change

8

Community Literature in the Multi-Cultural Classroom: The Mothers' Reading Program

**Maritza Arrastia with Sara Schwabacher,
Ana Betancourt, and the Students of the Mothers'
Reading Program, American Reading Council**
American Reading Council, New York, NY

The collective voice of a community that does not read has not yet been cast into literature. The Mothers' Reading Program was created to demonstrate that a community becomes literate through the process of making a literature of its own. The program's curriculum is built on the dual process of allowing the community's voice to be spoken, and then transforming the spoken voice to text.

When the Mothers' Reading Program was designed by the American Reading Council in 1983 it was conceived as an application in an urban setting of the model Paulo Freire had originated in underdeveloped sections of Brasil (Freire, 1970). Because we would be working with a diverse, urban community rather than the rural, homogeneous groups Freire had worked with, we decided to define our community as a "community of interest." Our target population, our community, was originally conceived as women with small children who already spoke English or were native English speakers. The first lesson we learned in implementing the program was flexibility. The women who came to us were older than we had originally expected, and the population in our classes reflected the ethnic diversity of the communities in which we were based—first New York City's East Harlem and later the Lower East Side. The Latin, North American black, African, Chinese, Vietnamese, and Bengali women did not always have full command of spoken English and used their native language as their primary mode of communication and, therefore, had difficulty communicating with fellow students with a different ethnic origin. At various times, our classes have included native English speakers from the South, and women from other nations including Sierra Leone, Puerto Rico, Santo Domingo, El Salvador, Mexico, Bangladesh, China, and Vietnam. This unexpected diversity gave us the opportunity to truly test the effectiveness of our learner-centered concept. We discovered that to be women, mothers and adult learners made a community that transcended ethnic differences. We found that, indeed, the group exploration of this community's shared world through dialogue was the source of a rich and varied community literature.

Dialogue, defined in the Freirean sense, is a form of discourse that gradually sharpens the natural ability to converse and communicate through spoken language beyond sharing ideas, beliefs, opinions, impressions, prejudice, and bias. Participants in dialogue discover their own widely held knowledge and widely held error and begin to peel the layers of the language itself to find the source of their ideas and the relation of those ideas to the surrounding world. This process encourages the participants to think critically about their ideas and their realities so that they can begin to change them.

Despite the diversity in the program, the overriding community of interest has made powerful bonds. The group is all women, most are mothers or have shared the mother role with other women in their families of origin, most live in the same neighborhood, and all share the goal of owning mainstream English.

We found that the common exploration of our shared world through dialogue began to generate a shared, common, spoken language. Those who spoke English and were focused primarily on reading and writing mainstream English could use the language and texts we developed together to that end. Those whose goal was to acquire speaking, reading, and writing skills in English could work with the same materials and learning tools. We found that mainstream English was, to some extent, a second language for all of us including the native English speakers in the class who had emigrated to New York from the South or spoke a variant of English that was not identical to written, "mainstream" English, and for the teachers whose original languages are Spanish and Chinese.

The mix also allowed for a wider pooling and exchange of skills. Some of the women who spoke little English had some literacy in their native language which, after they began to learn more English, enabled them to transfer skills that at times came more slowly to the native English speakers who had no literacy at all. At the same time, the native English speakers brought their greater command of spoken English and their greater experience negotiating and surviving life in a North American city. When the group first came together, communication between members who spoke little English was mediated through the teachers and through those members of each group with more English. After a few months of dialogue, making texts together, and reading those texts together, individually and in small groups, the group had built a pool of shared language, and more of the dialogue could take place in English. Each woman developed an appreciation for her strength and contribution to our common project and for those of her fellow students.

As we have become more skilled at turning our natural ability to communicate through conversation into that more directed form of shared verbal exploration of our world that is dialogue, our ability to think critically about this world has grown. This has enabled us to "bring in" to the process the very difficulties presented by working with a diverse group. Our dialogues have covered, at different times, such topics as funeral customs in our various cultures, recipes, child-rearing practices, different standards of hygiene and feelings and stereotypes about self-ornamentation and body odor, and decisions about how much of the teacher's time was to be spent speaking one or the other language.

While we have worked together, finding great richness in our cultural diversity and creating literature together that reflects this diversity, we have also found that each of the groups has enough particular interests to merit, if possible, the creation of a class specifically for that group. After two years of a mixed Spanish and Chinese group we began a class specifically for Chinese-speaking women. The Latin and Chinese classes participate in activities such as field trips together, however, and some of the women in the Chinese class attend both classes.

We have dealt with the cultural diversity in much the same way as we have dealt with other diversities we have encountered, such as differences in levels of reading and writing. Our principle has been to maintain the group as a community, a common matrix, and to provide specialized attention to specific needs as resources allow. While it would be ideal to have each of the special interest groups work together with its own teacher and/or facilitator for a portion of the class, it is not necessary to wait until there are sufficient resources to have a class for each specialized group in order to begin the work of dialogue and the creation of community literature. In fact, there always need to be moments when the overall community comes together, reflective as it is of the neighborhood itself.

The following philosophical premises formed the basis of our program:

- An illiterate community is one for whom written language has no use and which does not experience written language as a living life element.
- A community, and its individual members, while they may be illiterate, has a full life, culture and inner world and a rich, functioning, whole language system.
- The task for the literacy teacher is to create literature, together with the community of learners, from that rich whole language; together the group grows the wing of written language onto the spoken word.

- This literature is about the issues—internal, experiential, existential, and social, that are vital to the group. It is therefore easier to achieve when a group has at least some major interests in common.
- The themes of the literature are discovered collectively through a dialogue in which the teacher plays an active, but varyingly explicit, role. She must pay attention to the group's concerns and feelings as well as to her own within the group. At times the themes are largely teacher-initiated (always based on respectful, careful, serious attention to the group's reality); at other times they appear to emerge almost spontaneously from the concerns of one or another member or of the whole group and at yet other times they arise from a pressing community issue.
- By making literature out of experience collectively the group has a living experience of the usefulness of literature. It begins to become a literate community, one for which written language has a vital use.
- The living literature and the literacy grow together.
- The teacher is a member of the learning community with one predominant job: Learning the community and paying attention to its concerns so that together teacher and learner discover the generative theme for their shared literature.

THE ROLE OF THE TEACHER

The teacher's major teaching tool is her self; the major piece of work is the insertion of that self into the community. Yet, it can be a terrifying experience to approach a group of learners without the distancing props of the teacher: the workbook, the textbook, the predetermined "content" to be poured into the "emptiness" of the would-be learner's "ignorance." In contrast to the traditional transmission or "banking" model (Freire, 1970) of schooling, the teacher who uses the community literacy approach is not looking for the learners' emptiness, but for the learners' fullness, is not looking for what the learner has yet to learn, but is exploring what the learner already knows. She does this from her own fullness and life experience. Rather than coming in with exercises on phonics, or verb drills, or plans for a role-playing skit because she has decided this is the hole she must fill in the students, she comes with open eyes and ears and a series of methodological options to pursue. (These options, at certain times, might include any of the teaching activities named above, and an infinity of others, because the issue is not so much what is being done, but who owns it.)

The community literature approach is decidedly learner-centered, owned by the learner. The texts created flow from the learner community's concerns, experience, and inner world. This is not to say that the teacher abdicates an active role. For instance, what if the learners as a group decide they want to do only verb drills, or only phonics work, because they believe this is "real learning"? A lifetime of experience with traditional education teaches many that mechanical drillwork is the horse that pulls the cart of learning whole language. Does the teacher then do only drills? Perhaps for a time the teacher does. It is important to give learners what they want. But she also engages in a dialogue about the process of learning itself. She remains an active member of the group, and promotes dialogue to explore the process of learning itself, the why of this approach. She states clearly that whole language is the horse that pulls the cart of the individual skills. Yes, skill work has a decided purpose and use, but it must follow whole language, not the other way around.

WHOSE CLASSROOM IS THIS?

Many urban-based learners have expectations of how learning is supposed to occur (a passive process in which the learner is an empty vessel to be filled), although it is that very process which failed them before and served to alienate them from language and literature. Therefore a tug-of-war ensues in which the teacher urges the learners to believe they indeed are full of knowledge from which they can build to learn more, while the learners demand that the teacher act like a "real teacher" and "fill them up." Only explicitly taking on this issue through dialogue can break the impasse. Many rich discussions can be held, and many electrifyingly vital texts developed, upon the question, "Whose classroom is this?"

Power has both societal and personal dimensions. On a societal plane, illiterate communities are far from the society's centers of political and economic power; on a personal plane, members of poor communities often experience themselves as devoid of personal power, disempowered. When reading is taught to members of a disempowered community using the texts—the written voice—of the powerful, reading becomes an experience of personal disempowerment, of self-alienation. The world presented in the texts is not resonant with the world of the would-be reader. By taking the simple step of using the learners' own voices in print as the reading material, and validating the learners' own reading of their own world, reading can be reclaimed as an experience of personal power rather than its opposite.

Ultimately, learning is always a matter of power because people only learn from that part of the self that feels powerful. Learning is a striving for mastery of the self and of the environment. There is simply no learning without this, and most good teachers have either rationally or intuitively always relied on empowering the learner.

A sense of power is basic to hope, and learning occurs in that part of the self that hopes. This is why the Freirean approach has been effective in places in which enormous social changes were going on and the possibility of change and the usefulness of literacy were evident—places where there was hope. In these emergent societies, change became the horse that pulled the cart of learning, of enormous whole language transformation.

But does the Freirean approach work in the absence of such enormous social change? Or is the challenge in an urban, advanced industrial setting, where hopelessness and alienation reign, different? In our setting, is the process reversed? Can the collective, community acquisition of literacy be one of the horses that pull social change?

EMPHASIS ON "COMMUNITY"

The approach we are describing has many similarities to other approaches based on whole language, language experience, and the writing process. Many approaches affirm the richness of the individual learners' experience and build on it to teach. Our emphasis, however, is on the collective, community aspect of the process.

Reading Is Individual, Literacy Is Collective

Because reading is a private act and always involves a one-on-one encounter between an individual and a piece of text, it is possible for nonreaders to learn the mechanics of reading using any text. But the acquisition of reading by individuals from illiterate communities using the texts of the powerful is not the same as community literacy.

The philosophical premise of the Mothers' Reading Program is that a community is illiterate because it does not have a living literature of its own. Illiteracy is not only an inability to read written texts; it is the silence of a community's voice in print. This is why the Mothers' Reading Program begins by first reading the community's world through dialogue, and then transforming that spoken, shared voice into texts.

These texts are vital. If they were to be peeled off, the living reality that created them would be underneath. The texts of any social class have a vitality for that class. A social class that is validated by its own literature can approach the texts produced by another class. A social class that is not validated by its literature, however, often experiences the texts of another, more powerful class as invalidating, invasive, self-alienating.

Members of illiterate communities who become readers as individuals using the texts of a more powerful social class often do it by taking on the culture of that class and losing their connection to their class of origin. Learning through the community literature approach makes learners conversant in the language and culture of the more powerful class while remaining connected to their own class and culture.

Speech Is Individual, Language Is Collective

The casting into literature of a community's shared language, its shared spoken exploration of its world, is also collective. Language is learned socially. It is one of the principal connectors of a group. The language spoken by each individual is a particular manifestation of the language of her group. Each speaker's tools are words, syntax, values, myths that are shared by her group. It has been the Mothers' Reading Program experience that stories with conflict, beginning, middle, end, and resolution almost always emerge as the group reads the world. This pattern, in our experience, appears to be the way language orders reality. Most of the Mothers' Reading Programs texts are crafted collectively with students and teachers speaking and the teacher scribing; some combined individual writings using invented spelling with teacher-scribed texts; some are written individually. They are all reflective of the same core reality the women share. Whether or not the women in the class read print, regardless of how much print they read, they are always reading their world through the mediation of a language of words, rules, and patterns.

LEARNING THE COMMUNITY

The approach we are describing requires that the teacher pay attention to the individual student, to the immediate community she shares with them—the class—and to relevant aspects of the larger community.

It is important to learn and understand what the key conflicts, issues, and concerns are in the overall community and to have a general knowledge of what the citywide, national, and international issues are that have a bearing on the community. Something as distant as a war in Bangladesh, for instance, can lead to emigration that completely alters the population of a neighborhood in the Lower East Side of New York City, can place demands on a host agency, and on the composition of a literacy class. In addition, the language, culture, and politics of distinct communities each bring different histories and realities to the form and content of the literature and literacy it creates.

THE TEACHER AS A MEMBER OF THE COMMUNITY

In traditional education, the teacher is, by definition an outsider, an authority, one who has what the learner lacks. The teacher commands. In our class, the teacher is a member of the learning community. She does not command, she leads. She directs a process of which she is an integral member.

In the first place, the teacher has a very material connection to the group.

There is a need for her services because this group needs to learn to read. She has a job because of the need. She has as much of a survival interest in the literacy project as the learner does.

Most often, the teacher—who frequently is a woman (or a man who has eschewed more traditionally "male" forms of work), and who frequently shares the same ethnic and/or class background as the learners—is one of those people who by choice or birthright, comes from the same disempowered sectors of the population as the learner, but has learned the language and culture of the ruling class. The teacher, then, is both a material and objective part of the learning community. It is this material connection, this real bond, that the teacher draws from and builds on to apply the community literature approach to literacy.

A NOTE ON "HOW TO"

By necessity, the community literature approach is not an exact recipe. It is a method that requires the teacher to adapt, change, and insure that the class reflects its participants. The core of the method is the discovery of the group's individual voices, and its shared voice, and the casting of that voice into literature. The teacher's primary skill needs to be her ability and willingness to pay attention and to listen, to be both active—indeed one of the voices of the chorus—and detached; she must be willing to respect the idiosyncrasy of the group.

Elements of the process we, teachers and students together, developed include:

- Use of a generating image (and later, use of themes discovered through exploring this image, abstract scenarios, controversies exposed by the themes) to explore our shared life and experience through dialogue, and create written language that is vital, quickened by this living experience.
- Writing as a group, through dialogue and consensus.
- Use of the teacher as dialogue "leader," raising questions, bringing up new angles, selecting which among the various strands of the dialogue to pursue. The questions the teacher uses to generate the story, again, are reflective of the teacher's ability to pay attention to the group and are different for each teacher and each group. They can include: What is going on in this picture? Who is this woman? What is her name? How old is she? What did she dream last night? What was the first thing that came to her head when she woke up today? The avenues are infinite but choosing among them is not capricious or arbitrary. Rather, the selection is based on a sense of what's true and appropriate for the moment and the group, a sense that can only come from two sources. One is faith—faith

that the group does share a reality and that this reality can be explored through dialogue. The other is attention. If the teacher is paying attention, she will know where to take the dialogue, and where to follow it, in the same way that a teacher using a different approach knows it is time to handout the ditto sheet.

- Incorporation of all the voices that emerge in the dialogue into the text, even the most varying and discrepant statements, sometimes as a way of acknowledging the character's many inner voices, or, other times by giving the discrepant voice to a new character.
- Use of the text primarily for reading (to be read out loud, read in chorus, and individually) and secondarily, for skill work.

While the process detailed above technically resulted in the increase of a sight vocabulary and the building of phonic skills, it existentially created the vital experience, the one whereby written language is apprehended as another dimension of the same whole language we speak, the one whereby written language is appropriated. We also began developing tools to further the appropriation of this new written language by the students: for example, the personal dictionary, in which participants collected their chosen words and the personal diary, in which they freely wrote (without concern for spelling).

Much of the text we created was simply transcripts of class conversations. Statements were selected that carried visceral emotional content. We read back quotes from the conversations and built more thoughtful dialogues around them, digging for the depth and breadth contained in the statements. The examples which follow illuminate the power, fluidity, and personal significance of the spoken word.

CLASS CONVERSATIONS
(Dialogue among African-American students)

- If I think about the things that they (slaves) went through I would hate everybody.
- My family didn't tell me to hate whites. It's what I went through myself.
- My father, I loved him so much. He never hollered. Anytime I get attached to someone it seems they die. I don't want to get attached to people because they die. My father died. My mother died. My daughter died.
- I don't want to feel that way. I stay as far as possible.
- This is the way they (my children) were raised up. I didn't let them out of my sight. The youngest one had to listen to the oldest one. This is the way they are today. They have their differences but not that much.

Willie says, later for girls. He's not interested. He's interested in sports. He says, girls cost money. I tease him sometimes. A mother has to say something. My ten-year-old Anthony loves girls. He and his father joke about the sexy parts in movies. Willie gets embarrassed and goes away.

One day Anthony's little girlfriend came to the house to meet me. I can't get over the things kids do.

(Dialogue between African-American and Latin women)

- Yesterday we went to La Guardia Community College to hear a man from Nicaragua talk about the literacy campaign there.

It was great. I loved it. The whole country is learning to read the same way we're learning.

I met a woman there who went to school for 10 years to learn to read. Now she's writing a book like I want to do.

I was surprised, I guess because she was white. But anybody can have problems reading.

It's amazing how many people don't read.

- In the old days children had to work and couldn't learn. Now they go to school and don't learn.

After the conference I started thinking about poverty in Honduras. I had a terrible dream about starving children, all skinny and naked. Someone in the dream slaughtered a pig. There was a lot of meat.

DEATH RITUALS
(Latin, African-American, Chinese, and Vietnamese student participants)

- I saw my friend. She was wearing a blue yarn flower in her hair and looked upset. I asked her what happened. She said her husband died. In China we put flowers in our hair when someone dies.

When someone dies:

- In Santo Domingo a widow is supposed to wear black until she remarries.
- In Ecuador men wear a black armband.
- In Vietnam people sew a black square of cloth on their clothes and wear it for a year. They are not supposed to remarry for three years.
- In South Carolina people wear black.
- When a person in Hong Kong dies you buy a wreath made of flowers. Family and friends go to the house and pray.
- In Vietnam you go to the person's house and bring money for the family. The dead person is dressed in a white suit and a long white sheet. If the family is rich they stay home and pray for a week or 10 days. If the family is poor they stay for 3 days. They beat a gong and make so much noise, you can't sleep at night.
- In Hong Kong the family wears black.
- In Santo Domingo rich people make much music and noise, but poor people only pray.

The question, "whose classroom is this," comes up often in different guises, sometimes in the form of requests, at times demands, for "banking" teaching, sometimes in silence, periods when participation in class dialogue is limited, sometimes in lack of disclosure of misgivings about the Mothers' Reading Program approach. This dialogue developed after a woman who had been quiet in class disclosed that she felt lost.

CLASS DISCUSSION: WHOSE CLASSROOM IS THIS?

Problem: Some people feel lost in this class, yet, they say nothing about it.
  Why is this?
• Who remembers a time when you used to feel lost in school?
• Who remembers that sensation?
• Try to remember, when you were a little girl in school to whom did the class
  belong?
• Who was the grownup and who was the child?
• What does it mean to have power?
• Whose class was it?
• Now, think about this class—what is the difference between now and grade
  school?

Feeling Lost in Class

• When the teacher talks and you don't listen, you don't understand.
• In second grade, I was scared of the teacher. He hit me with a ruler.
• I was very scared. I was taught to read by being hit with a ruler.
• In fourth grade I was always lost in History class.

What I Did About Feeling Lost

• I didn't do anything.
• I was too scared.
• I felt like crying but I didn't cry. I couldn't cry every day.
• I would ask for help when I was lost in class.
• I thought it was my fault. The teacher couldn't help it if I was a donkey.
• It was the teacher's fault. His job was to teach.

Who Did Your Class in Grade School Belong To?

• The class belonged to the teacher.
• It was her class because she knew. We didn't know anything.
• The teacher screamed, she had no patience.
• She was the adult. We were the children.

Who Had the Power?

• The teacher.
• She had the power because she teaches the children.
• Power is control.

Why Don't People Say Anything About Being Lost in This Class?

• We are scared to ask.
• If I knew I would ask.
• We're afraid the other women would laugh.
• But no one can laugh about people not knowing because we're all here to
  learn.

- We are all here to learn and teach.
- In this class teachers and students bring the different things we know and teach each other.

Whose Class Is This?

- It is our class.
- It belongs to us.
- The teacher and us. It belongs to both.
- We are adults.
- We know things.
- We understand more, faster than when we were children.

The conversations also had humor, affection, affirmation. As a teacher I steered conversation to dialogue, a deeper, exploring form of conversation in which we focused on a particular strand of the talk in order to analyze it, take it further, develop the ability to observe our own language and our own thought, develop the skill of critical thinking. One woman's anecdote of a childhood exploit let to a dialogue on the subject: "Something I did as a child I thought was great but the adults thought was terrible," that produced, among others, Flor's Bundle and Juan's Spirit. These stories were both told by older Puerto Rican women, one of them nearly blind from cataracts, who had entire successful adult lives behind them without ever reading (one of them had created her own system of notation so that she could run numbers). They were deeply bound to their self-images as nonreaders, almost proud of them, and never tested on the abhorred TABE (Test of Adult Basic Education) above grade one. Only occasionally would they allow themselves to recognize a written word they had just said. Yet, their experience enriched our shared literature. They were a vital part of the literature we crafted together and of the support network the group created to assist its learning.

FLOR'S BUNDLE

I was born in a small "barrio" of Bayamon called Santa Ulaya. My mother Nicolasa and her sister Marta used to go to their cousin Eulalia's home to sew.

I used to play with cousin Eulalia's six daughters from her first marriage to a very handsome man.

Cousin Eulalia was tall and very good looking. She got divorced. Later, she had five children with another man.

Cousin Eulalia didn't want anyone to know she had a new boyfriend named Flor Gonzalez.

One evening when I was six years old I was playing with my cousins while the women sewed.

I saw Flor arrive carrying a bundle. My other cousins didn't see Flor arrive. I watched him hang the bundle under the eave.

I was only six but I had the idea that Flor was sleeping with my cousin Eulalia.

Flor was a big landowner and owned a grocery store. The Catholic church was on his land. On Sundays, when the farmers came down the hills for mass, Flor would sell roast suckling pig, morcilla (blood sausage), codfish fritters and maví, a drink made with sugar and the bark of the mavi tree.

Almost everyone knew that Flor would leave his home at night and go visit Eulalia who lived nearby. Everyone but Jobita, Flor's wife. Eulalia used to sew Jobita's clothes.

People knew Eulalia would go to the nearby farms to dig up "yautias" and that she sold her body for a sackful. She had nine children to feed.

She was a joyful person, full of life and fun. Flor was a charming man but none of us children liked him. He scolded us all the time for taking guavas, mangos, avocados and bunches of bananas from his land.

After Flor hung up the bundle he came inside to chat with the women while they sewed. The women sewed at three machines with foot pedals.

I started out the door. My cousin said, "Stay in, it's dark."

I said, "The moon is out and I'm hot."

Outside, I found the long rod for prodding the bull. I poked at the bundle until I knocked it down.

There was a crash of broken bottles.

Flor snorted, "That good-for-nothing little girl knocked down the wine and anis bottles."

All that was left was a loaf of bread and a round, red cheese.

I ran and hid.

My aunt yelled after me, "You'll get it when I catch you."

I hid until my aunt was ready to go home.

But my aunt didn't hit me. Instead, she said, "Well done, so Eulalia can't keep denying she's got something going with Flor."

My aunt would ask me, "Why did you do it"

I said, "I don't like them doing secret things."

JUAN'S SPIRIT

After my godmother's husband died, I used to put his shoes on at night and cough like him to scare her.

In the morning she would say, "Nena, I heard Juan coughing last night."

I would laugh.

I was about nine years old.

People were telling me that Juan's spirit would come after me because I was naughty.

My godmother had punished me for talking back to her. She'd made me kiss my dead godfather's feet and pray on my knees for an hour nine nights in a row during the Novena.

Later, when everyone was in bed, I would get up and make sounds like my uncle.

People in those days believed spirits came back all the time.

People used to bury their gold before they died. They believed the spirits would come in a dream to tell someone they loved where the gold was buried.

After things were in the ground, they believed they belonged to evil, to the devil.

My grandmother went with her sister to dig up some gold. Her sister said, "The devil is standing right behind you." They say my grandmother dropped dead right by the road where they had been digging.

There was praying in my house every day because my godmother, Fidela, was a "rezadora," a woman who prayed. People would ask her to pray for the sick, the dead or to help solve a problem.

I used to go with her. My job was to close the people's eyes and light the candle. A child, an "angel," had to do that. I was never afraid to do it.

I used to like visiting the sick, or the women who were giving birth.

Fidela was a midwife and I used to get the water for the birth and help out. After the birth I was sent to the river to wash the bloody clothes.

I would walk downhill to the river past the vegetables and the orange groves.

While I waited for the sheets and the clothes to dry I talked to the lizards. I climbed the trees to find the nests of the "reinitas."

No one else was there but God.

These dialogues usually took place informally at the beginning of the three-hour class as the women were arriving. Several strands of conversations went on at the same time; several stories were always unfolding; over time recurring themes gelled. Much of the conversation was transcribed on the blackboard—and later typed—and used for skillwork: reading together, personal dictionaries, personal diaries.

(Latin, Italian, African and African-American participants)

I bought aloe vera juice for my arthritis. I make my own remedies at home. I put aloe in the blender and add herbs. When I make it I add cod liver oil and rum.

Alfalfa is good for arthritis too. You can get tea, sprouts or pills.

In Puerto Rico when a child's belly button popped out we would find a tree with resin and draw the outline of the child's foot on the bark. We would cut the bark and hang it up in the house. As the bark dried up the belly button would go back in.

We used to wrap a half dollar in cloth, put it against the belly button and wrap a cloth all around.

My grandmother was a midwife. She used to burn the umbilical chord.

The first time I worked in the maternity ward the nurse asked me to boil water. I had seen a woman in position to give birth.

I thought, "My God, it's like this?" and crossed myself. I went off to boil the water.

I knew babies came out through there, but I had no idea.

I had been told babies came out through the mouth.

I was told babies come from flowers.

Nowadays, kids know everything about babies. I knew a girl who ran away all the way to New York because her mother never told her she was supposed to sleep with her husband.

She thought she was only supposed to cook, iron and clean.

Once, when I worked in maternity the nurse wasn't around and I had to catch a baby myself. The baby would have died.

We gleaned themes, what Paulo Freire would call "generative themes" (Freire, 1970), from our conversation that became the focus for dialogues—a more structured, directed conversation, that, in turn, led to a more structured group writing activity. This dialogue was the core activity of the class. The difference between the conversation and the dialogue might not at first be immediately apparent; just as at first it might appear that nothing much more was going on than a bunch of women giving each other companionship. But by transforming conversation to dialogue—one of the teachers' biggest jobs—we developed the important skill of observing our own thinking in order to take it deeper and further, in both an empowering and critical sense. This steering of conversation to dialogue by paying careful and respectful attention to the emergent themes, and by being both immersed in the process and observant of it is probably the most important work of the teacher. It can be the most difficult and the most emotionally draining. This work is important because it is only through a combination of participation and observation that the critical function can be introduced into the dialogue. The learners are more likely to be closer than the teacher to the experience the dialogue is exploring. They also have less experience than the teacher with print and with critical thinking itself and will be less detached from the focus of the dialogue. They will rely on the teacher to contribute her greater practice applying critical thinking and her greater experience with print.

The development of a dialogue one year around the constantly recurring theme of plant remedies exemplifies this process. We decided to explore it in depth. We wrote about plant lore. One of the women told us that many of the plants could be bought in the Botanicas but that some grew wild in El Barrio. She took us on a field trip to several empty lots and to Central Park to pick the plants. We had gone from using images to using the community itself as material for our literature. One Saturday afternoon we made a dramatic video in which the women enacted an encounter on the street between two friends, one an herbalist. The video demonstrates the herbalist's recommendation, the picking of the plant in an empty lot, and the boiling of the plant into a tea. The following text became the basis for the video.

PLANT REMEDIES
(Latin, African-American, Italian and African participants)

I know all these plant remedies because before I was a Christian my comadre who was a spiritist taught me.

I learned about plants in Aguadilla from my mother. When we were children and got sick she would go to the yard and bring plants to make us well. In the old days there were no doctors and plants were all the medicine we had.

A lot of these plants you can buy in the Botánicas in El Barrio. A lot of them grow wild in the empty lots and parks.

We picked pasote at 108th and Park Avenue. Pasote we boil in water and use for baths for good luck, and for tea. The tea is good to get rid of worms. You can squeeze the leaves and drink the juice with a tablespoon.

We found dry matuerzo on 105th and Park avenue in the Projects. We found the green matuerzo in Central Park on 110th Street. You can mix the leaves with purple garlic from the Botánicas and with purple onions, and make tea. It's good if you bleed too much from menstruation and good for tuberculosis.

We found mata de gallina or hierba mora in Central Park and at 115th Street between Madison and Fifth Avenue. You boil the leaves with milk and strain the milk. It's good for ulcers. In El Salvador you put it in fish soup. It's good for the lungs.

We found yantén in Central Park. It's all over the neighborhood. You put a few leaves in water and boil them. A few drops of the tea clear the eyes. In Puerto Rico you put the leaves in water out all night in the dew and then put the drops in the eyes.

Yantén tea is also good for the kidneys. You drink it whenever you are thirsty instead of water.

We found altamisa on Park Avenue and 115th Street. Puerto Rican altamisa has a bigger leaf. I was told that plant is alcanfor. It's good to put the leaves in Florida water and rub your body with the mixture to get rid of pain.

It's good to mix it with pasote and boil it for cleaning your house to get rid of bad luck. After your bath you can sprinkle yourself with the tea for good luck.

I would like to find a plant to make me young again.

The best thing for that is tranquility. There will always be problems. You have to learn not to let them get to you. I have a son who is lost. I give him advice. If he doesn't take it, the problem is his, not mine.

A good thing for rejuvenation is to get wet in the first rain of May.

The best thing for rejuvenation would be to live in a high mountain like where my grandparents lived. My grandfather lived to be 98 and my grandmother lived to be 92. It's cool there. They got their water from a spring, water that had never been in a river yet. The spring made a little stream.

An ongoing subplot of our living drama one year was the upcoming marriage of the son of one of the women whose own divorce—after a painful six-year separation—was becoming final. Issues of sexuality and sexual power were central to the women. They led to the following conversations, to the group fiction story "Angelica Maria", and to the dialogues on women and power.

Conversations
(Latin, Italian, African-American and African participants)

- I heard that a long time ago the whole family used to watch the newlyweds make love to make sure the girl bled and was a virgin.
- In Italy the newlyweds' white sheet from the wedding night had to be hung out on the line to show the bloodstains and prove the bride was a virgin.
- In Honduras and Puerto Rico if the husband discovered the girl was not a virgin, the husband took her back to her parents.
- My son is getting married Sunday. For my daughter-in-law's shower they had a male stripper.

My daughter-in-law and my son didn't want it but her friends had the stripper anyway. He showed up, the music started, and he began to take off his shirt, his pants, his bikini. He had tiny underwear underneath.

I laughed and laughed and laughed. It was fun. I had never seen anything like it. The women put money in his underwear. He kissed Adelina, my daughter-in-law, me.

- I saw a male stripper at a shower once and I thought he looked like a dog. I was so embarrassed I hid in the kitchen.
- Yesterday at the beauty parlor I dyed my hair and had my eyebrows plucked. I'd never had my eyebrows plucked that way before. I'm getting ready for my son's wedding.

Sunday, the beautician is coming to my house at 7:00 in the morning to do my hair. I'm nervous and excited. I'm happy about this wedding. It's well planned. When my older son got married it was difficult.

My older son told me, "I have to get married."

I cried and cried and cried.

But then, at the wedding, I got happy. I had a great time, I even danced with my ex-husband.

I don't think I'll dance with him this time, though.

- My son's wedding was beautiful. We danced everything, Greek, Italian, Spanish.
- At my son's wedding I noticed my other son's girlfriend was wearing an engagement ring. I hadn't even met her except on the telephone. Another one getting married!

These conversations led us to write a piece of fiction about a wedding using an image—selected by the women from many images of weddings—of a glamorous soap opera star dressed up in a wedding gown.

ANGELICA MARIA

Angelica Maria looks happy at her wedding but deep inside she's the saddest woman on earth. Just before the wedding she found out her boyfriend, Juan Carlos, is having a child with another woman.

She remembered her friend Rosario. First, her new husband told her he had one child and later on she found out he had three more.

Angelica feels she is taking away the child's father. She is very much in love with Juan Carlos but she is very hurt.

Before the wedding, after Juan Carlos told her the truth, Angelica ran away to Rosario's house. She wanted to clear the way for Juan Carlos to marry the other woman.

One day, she ran into Juan Carlos on the street. He thought Angelica might change her mind. He had been on his way to kill himself, but he didn't.

Angelica went to visit her parents. Her father said, "You aren't leaving this house again until you resolve this situation. Look at how I have lost weight worrying about this. Juan Carlos comes to cry here every night."

That night both Angelica's and Juan Carlos' families got together and planned the wedding. Angelica did nothing, not even buy her underwear.

She adored Juan Carlos but she was bitter. She asked everyone she knew, "Do you believe that love exists?"

Her 79-year-old grandmother said, "No, it doesn't last. There's only companionship."

Rosario said, "Women can love more than men, but when men hurt you, women lose love."

Her mother said, "As long as there is consideration, love lasts."

Her Aunt Manuela, who never got married, said, "Love exists but it doesn't last. That's why I've been afraid to marry."

Her cousin Patricia, who was a few years older and just married, said, "Love exists but people don't know how to nurture it. It stops growing if people let it become routine."

Angelica didn't think she had much choice but to get married. In the old days the parents would decide who the woman would marry. Her parents pressured her into getting married. They had already decided she should marry Juan Carlos.

Angelica remembered that her grandmother's parents didn't like the man she loved because he was poor and a vagabond. Her grandmother had run away with the man. If families have a little bit of money they think they can decide who the daughter should marry.

For years now her grandmother had lived alone. Angelica walked over to visit her. As she walked she thought of the stories she'd heard about her grandmother's husband. He took another woman. He used to beat her grandmother up when he got drunk.

"What do you really think about marriage?" Angelica asked her grandmother.

"Why did I ever get married?" her grandmother said. "There's nothing better than the freedom I have now. I come and go as I want. I don't spend days grating "yuca" to make starch for his clothes, washing, starching, ironing, cooking."

Angelica tried to think of someone who was happy in marriage. She remembered her mother's friend Laura. She got on the bus to visit Laura in her beautiful home.

"Laura, tell me how you've been able to be happy in marriage?"

Laura said, "You have to understand each other and every problem you have, consult one another."

"Let me tell you about my friend Carmen. She used to gamble all the time. She would play all the rent and food money. She was addicted to the numbers. Finally, the landlord told her he was going to tell her husband she had gambled away the rent. Carmen told her husband the truth herself. She thought her husband would want to divorce her."

"But her husband tried to understand. They talked about the problem and Carmen discovered she felt her life was empty. She had expected marriage would make her happy as if by magic. But it didn't. It couldn't. She was disappointed in marriage and she gambled to hide her pain."

"She decided she needed to do something to give meaning to her life. Carmen decided to get a job and pay her gambling debts."

"Understanding saved her marriage."

Dialogue

Why do women do most of the work in the house?
• Some men are lazy.
• She's in the house most of the time.
• Some men don't know how to do housework.
• Women have more experience.
• The men like the house clean.
• Men don't do housework well enough.
Do men have more power than women? Why?
• Yes, it's true.
• He is sexist.
• Men think they are strong.
• He thinks his wife is a slave.
• Men like to fool around with other women.
• Men support women. They give the family money.
• The women need the men to support them for food and rent.
• Some women are scared because the men have more power.
Men can do things women can't?
TRUE
• A man is stronger.
• A man rapes.
• A man has a job without being accused of abandoning his home.
• A man can go out and stay out all night but if woman does it she's a whore.
FALSE
• A man can't have babies.
• Anything a man does a woman can do too.

MEN
- Stronger.
- The society thinks men are more important than ladies.
- People believe women should stay in the house, take care of the kids.
- Husbands used to buy their wives' clothes, even panties.

WOMEN
- Now a woman likes to go out to work and be liberated.
- Women don't have to follow men's orders anymore.
- During World War II the men were fighting and the women went to work.

The literature we created reflected the many languages and cultures of origin within the group. When the program moved to the Lower East Side of Manhattan from East Harlem many Asian women joined the class. The conversations and dialogues began to reflect the concerns and experiences particular to the Asian women as well as issues that emerged when Latin and Asian women came together.

FISH
(Latin, Chinese, Vietnamese, African-American and African participants)

I wonder about fish for the Chinese people. I see fish in restaurants. I see
   Chinese children draw fish.
Maybe they like fish.
Funny, I always see my granddaughter's Chinese classmates drawing fish.
Oh, maybe it's good luck! Every New Year Chinese families buy a fish. They
   eat the fish a few days later. This is to get a lot of food and good things in the
   New Year.
The name for fish, "yu," sounds like the Chinese word for "something left,"
   yau yu. The fish is for having something left from the old year in the new
   year.

NEW YEAR'S DAY (Group Story)

Tat is a 28-year-old man. He was visiting his Aunt Hung who lives in England.
   For the English New Year they went to the Chelsea Arts Ball.
Tat enjoyed the show. He was not comfortable in such a big crowd. There was
   no space to stand. He missed his girlfriend, Phung.
"Oh, look at all these people," he thought. "They look so different." He was
   happy to be there.
His Aunt Hung explained to him, "This New Year is the new calendar, our
   New Year in China is the old calendar."
The celebrations are different. In China, people dance in the street. They shoot
   firecrackers. In London, everyone started to shout at midnight. In China the
   celebration starts when you get up in the morning New Year's Day.

Tat went back to Hung Hon, his village. "For the Chinese New Year I'm going to dance wearing the Big Monk's Head. He teased the lions. The lions chased him. There were a lot of people on the street.

Tat wondered if the people would like his dancing. He hoped they would. He could see their happy faces. He was glad. "Now, maybe when a businessman is having a grand opening he will ask us to dance."

One year no one smiled. Tat's dancers finished their show last. When Tat got home he was sad.

His mother, Phen said, "Next year you will do better."

His father, Shun said, "You will practice some more."

His girlfriend, Phung, said, "Why did you do bad?"

Tat said, "I don't know, I did my best."

That year was the Year of the Tiger. Tat practiced a lot during the Year of the Tiger. For the Year of the Rabbit his dancing was good.

"I feel proud and happy," he thought.

Fiction stories were developed in various ways. At times abstract scenarios were used to present a story outline. Other times the stories began with a character. Freire (1970) used codifications, often visual images that encoded generative themes to initiate dialogue. We often used graphics—photographs, drawings, reproductions of paintings as codifications. The following story was developed by bringing a series of graphics into class for the group to choose from. Although most of the graphics depicted some kind of idyllic setting, our students chose the one where a young man was crouched low, holding a gun, wearing a hanky over the lower part of his face and staring anxiously out at the world. People milled around in the background of the picture, some armed with sticks, and a machete suggested some kind of action. The women responded with great animation to the image. For many it resonated with similar experiences of their own.

THE REBEL

This is an assault. In this country there's a war. The man has covered his face so he won't be identified, so he doesn't breathe the terrible smell and the contamination of a shoot out. Behind the man with the gun and the covered face there are other men with sticks and a machete. They are alert, waiting for the enemy.

The man with the gun is Valentin Gonzalez. He is very nervous right now, very aware and watchful of what is happening, in suspense, anxious. He is scared. He is thinking of his family, his neighbors that are all around him. He thinks of his parents for only an instant. They are young and healthy, hiding in their house. He thinks of Miriam, his girlfriend. If he dies another man will have her and enjoy her.

But his attention is mainly on the enemy that might come. Valentin sweats. He trembles. His hands are moist. The veins in his face are up because he is tense, angry. He hears a noise. He looks. Maybe someone is coming. It is only Raul, his friend. Valentin is a bit calmer now. There is no enemy yet. He does not need to aim his gun and shoot. Valentin is a good shot. Where he puts his sight, he puts his bullet. He learned to shoot from his father. They went hunting together.

The men are fighting over rising prices, over gasoline. That's why they burn tires. They are fighting the police. This fight has been going on about a year.

A fight like this could happen in Texas, Nicaragua, Ecuador, in El Salvador. It could happen in New York over jobs, over people taking advantage of people, over housing, over civil rights.

Some of our dialogue analyzed how to teach using our method from the students' point of view. We asked our students "If you were teaching a new teacher how to teach using the Mothers' Reading Program method, how would you teach the teacher? What would you tell her to do? What steps? Is there a main idea you could tell her? What should she avoid doing?"

I will tell her to have a lot of patience with the students and relax with students.

First, we tell her what we do. We make up stories, and the teacher puts the words on the blackboard. We read together, the students copy the words from the blackboard.

When the students read from the blackboard they try to understand. They ask the teacher the words they don't know. They put the words in their dictionary.

The teacher teaches us by writing on the board; asking us what we don't know; explaining things. The class is from 9 to 12. At 11 we get a 10 minute break. She needs to say things in Spanish and say them softly.

I would like her to teach us verbs. I would tell her to explain some things in Spanish so we understand more.

Because we put all the words together ourselves it makes it easier to understand the language. We do this this way because the words that we know already when we talk, we learn how to read them.

The idea is that by practicing we hold on to more words and at the same time learn how to use a dictionary.

This method makes it easier to learn to read and write more quickly. It is not complicated. It's the best method for adults.

She has to avoid getting angry; avoid upsetting the students; be careful with touchy subjects; avoid too much noise. She needs to make sure no woman leaves without saying something, without participating in the class. The teacher has to avoid teaching something the students don't understand. She needs to avoid the student losing interest and falling asleep.

All these words and these stories we share among ourselves because we are united. What I don't know I can ask from one of my "Compañeras." I learn a little. What another one teaches me. I can teach somebody else.

These students clearly have taken ownership of their learning process and their classroom. They know they have something to teach their teacher. And, they know whose classroom this is.

REFERENCE

Freire, P. (1970). *Pedagogy of the oppressed.* New York: Seabury Press.

9

Teaching How to Read the World and Change It: Critical Pedagogy in the Intermediate Grades

Robert E. Peterson
La Escuela Fratney
Milwaukee, WI

INTRODUCTION

Monday morning a child brings a stray dog into the classroom.

The traditional teacher sees that it is removed immediately.

The progressive teacher builds on the students' interest; perhaps measures and weighs the animal with the children, has the children draw and write about the dog, and eventually calls the humane society.

The Freirian teacher does what the progressive teacher does but more. She asks questions, using the dog as the object of reflection. "Why are there so many stray dogs in our neighborhood?" "Why are there more here than in the rich suburbs?" "Why do people have dogs?" "Why doesn't the city allocate enough money to clean up after the dogs and care for the strays?" While accepting stray animals into a classroom isn't the bellwether mark of an elementary Freiran teacher, engaging children in reflective dialogue on topics of their interest is.

Not surprisingly, the classroom of an elementary teacher applying a Freirian method is markedly different than that of a traditional teacher. What perhaps is not as expected is that a Freirian approach also differs significantly from the methods of many progressive teachers, that is, those who organize their classes in child-centered and holistic ways.

Going to public school in the 1960s I became a proponent of progressive education as a student, but it was only when I read Freire as a junior in high school, that I realized education could be more than just "relevant" and "student-centered." However, the political reality of being a high school student activist in the late 1960s and early 1970s made me doubt the likelihood of a Freiran method being used in the public schools.

It wasn't until a decade later, that I came back to Freire and reexamined his applicability to the public school setting. I was on the other side of the teacher's desk, now looking at things as an educator rather than a student. I had traveled to Nicaragua and observed the week-long celebration that concluded the National Literacy Campaign in August of 1980, and the experience convinced me that I should look again at Freire's work. I knew that the conditions of teaching and learning in the United States differed greatly from those encountered by Freire in the Third World, and yet I felt that the essence of Freire's approach would be appropriate for an urban school setting.

Throughout the 1980s, I worked on applying Freire's ideas in my fourth and fifth grade bilingual inner-city classrooms. My approach contrasted sharply with the numerous "educational reforms" being tried elsewhere. These mainstream proposals were often state and system mandates; their goal was to "teacher-proof" the curricula through the use of basal reader programs, direct instruction, the methods of Madeline Hunter and an expansion of standardized testing (Fairtest, 1988; Gibboney, 1988; Levine, 1988). Under the banners of "back to the basics" and "improving student achievement" these efforts further reinforced and strengthened what Freire calls the "banking" method of education, whereby the teacher puts periodic deposits of knowledge into the students' heads. Such classrooms are very teacher- and text-centered. Little discussion and reflection take place. While the relevance of a banking-type approach appears to go counter to what recent research on literacy suggests (Calkins, 1983; Goodman 1986; Goodman, Smith, & Meredith, & Goodman 1987; Graves, 1983; Smith 1985) this model continues to be the most prevalent method in public school classrooms. Goodlad (1984), for example, found that not even 1 percent of the instructional time in high schools was devoted to discussion that "required some kind of open response involving reasoning or perhaps an opinion from students." As he notes, "the extraordinary degree of student passivity stands out" (p. 229).

Freire posits a dialogic "problem posing" method of education as an alternative. Here, teachers and students both become actors in figuring out the world through a process of mutual communication. In the banking method of education the teacher and the curricular texts have the "right answers" which the students are expected to regurgitate periodically onto criterion referenced tests. However in Freire's model, questions and not answers are the core of the curriculum; open-ended questions prod students to critically analyze their social situation and encourage them to ultimately work towards changing it.

To apply Freire's approach in the elementary classroom one has to have a perspective about the learners and learning which runs counter to the dominant educational ideology. A Freirian approach relies on the experience of the students and implies a respect and use of the students' culture, language, and dialect. It values dialogue and reflection over lecture and repetition. It means constructing a classroom in which students have the maximum amount of power that is legally permitted and that they can socially handle. It means challenging the students to reflect on the social nature of knowledge and the curriculum, to get them to think about why they think and act the way they do.

Ultimately a Freirian approach means moving beyond thought and words to action. This is done on the one hand by teachers themselves modeling social responsibility and critical engagement in community and global issues. On the other hand it means constructing with the students an atmosphere in the classroom and the school where students feel secure and confident enough to interrogate their own realities, see them in a different light, and act on their developing convictions to change their own social reality. In order to do all this, the teachers themselves have to go through a transformative process, breaking the ideological chains of their own formal education, of past training, and the inertia of habit of past teaching.

TEACHING ORGANICALLY

Freire uses generative words and themes in his teaching, words that invoke passion and feeling among his students. In North American jargon this is sometimes called a "language experience" approach for it utilizes students' own language and experiences as the basis of instruction. An example from European literature and from the experience of a New Zealand teacher illustrate the significance of this approach.

In Bertolt Brecht's (1978) famous play *The Mother*, which takes place during the 1905 revolution in Czarist Russia, the mother and a metal worker go to ask a professor to teach them to read and write. The professor, begrudgingly and condescendingly, agrees and proceeds to write two words on a slate board: "Branch" and "nest." The two workers immediately become frustrated by the irrelevance of the situation and demand to know how to spell "worker," "class struggle," and "exploitation." Not clear as to why his initial words were inappropriate, the professor obligingly changes his plans. And, thus, through the power of their own words, the workers learn how to read and write rapidly.

In her work with Maori children in New Zealand, Sylvia Ashton-Warner (1965) developed an educational approach very similar to that of Freire. She understood that the failure of the Aboriginee children in New Zealand schools was mainly due to their cultural clash with the Anglosized system. She drew on the interests and experience of her students, within the context of the culture they brought to school. Her use of "organic vocabulary" to teach reading, spelling, and writing was based on the belief that words significant to the learner would motivate the learner into learning. As she explained:

Pleasant words won't do. Respectable words won't do. They must be words organically tied up, organically born from the dynamic life itself. They must be words that are already part of the child's being. (1965, p. 33)

The proof of her method was in the students themselves. While it took four months for them to learn words like "come, look, and," in four minutes they could learn words like "police, bulldog, knife, cry, yell, fight, Daddy, Mummy, ghost, kiss, and frightened."

The meaningfulness of these words stands in sharp contrast to the first words taught to many children in urban school settings in the United States. One widely used basal company chose eight words as the primary starting point for reading: "red, yellow, blue, girl, boy, the, a, has." In fact, an entire kindergarten workbook is devoted to the word "the." The Commission on Reading of the national Council of Teachers of English (1988) documents how basal reading programs control vocabulary and syntax to such an extent as to make the initial exposure to reading irrelevant and boring to most children.

Children's learning should be centered in their own experience, language, and culture. For this to happen, the classroom environment should be "language rich," allowing the children to develop their language and thinking abilities in as natural a setting as possible. This applies equally to first and second language learning (Krashen & Terrell, 1983; Goodman, 1986). A generative theme approach fosters the development of such an environment.

Practical application.   A generative theme is an issue or topic that catches the interest of students in such a way that discussion, study, and project work can be built around it. Themes may come from an incident in a particular student's life, a problem in the community, or an idea that a student latched onto from the media, the news, or a classroom activity. Writing, reading, talking, acting, and reflecting are the key ways through which generative themes develop. I start the year with a unit on the child's own family and background—placing their birthdates on the class timeline. The second day we place their parents dates on the timeline, the third, their grandparents. We put pins in a world map indicating the places of birth. I ask them to talk to their parents or other family members and collect at least one story, joke, or memory from their family and either write it down or prepare to tell it orally.

The first day of school I also have the students in my class write a book. Inspired by Ashton-Warner's (1965) continual construction of books based on her children's writings and drawings, I do the same. Quality is not important on the first day. I want to show students that we can write, draw, and accomplish things they would not have dreamed of. We choose a topic or topics together, write, draw, and put the unedited papers into a plastic theme binder creating an instant book. This action of collaboratively producing a book based on the students' own experiences provides both a model of what can be accomplished the rest of the year and a benchmark upon which the teacher and the students can judge growth in their abilities. "If we can accomplish this in only one day by working together," I tell my students, "Just imagine what we can do in an entire year!"

Throughout the year I use the "writing process" approach (Graves 1983, Calkins, 1986) which focuses on production of student generated and meaningful themes. Students write for a purpose, whether it is for publication, a pen pal or display. We publish in the school newsletter, the city newspaper, children's magazines,[1] or our own books. Never have I seen students think so much about a piece of writing than when they know it is to be published.

The most ambitious writing we do is for the publication of our own books. Usually this is in the form of anthologies of students' prose, poetry, and drawings—*Kid Power*, *Colors Laugh*, *Splashing in Action* are the titles of a few that we have produced. I especially encourage writings on the students' own communities and families (Wigginton, 1989). At times children have written entire booklets—legends, adventures, autobiographies—that they may give to a parent or sibling as a gift for a birthday or holiday. These booklets validate the children's lives, give them self-confidence in their ability to do projects, help focus reflection on our common field trips and areas of study, provide an inspiration to write and a motivation to read. They are also useful for me, not only as the basis for future writing lessons, but because I learn more about my students and their communities.

Generative themes can be discovered and reflected upon not only through writing in the classroom but through a variety of other language and performance arts activities. Mime, drama, role playing, reading aloud from their own writings, chants, and oral story telling allow students to describe and reflect on their world while improving their basic first language and second language abilities.

Even when standardized curricula must be used, a teacher can utilize the life experiences of their students. For example, if by state law or local decree a teacher must use a basal reader, approaches can be taken that downplay its segmented skills orientation. A student could: Write or tell about what would happen if she were to take the main character home for dinner; write a letter to the main character comparing the student's life to that of the main characters; or write a version of the story that draws on some comparable

---

[1] Publications which accept children's writings include: *Children's Album*, PO Box 6086, Concord, CA 94524 ($10/year); *Rethinking Schools*, 1001 E. Keefe Ave., Milwaukee, WI 53212 ($10/year); *Stone Soup*, PO Box 83, Santa Cruz, CA 95063 ($17.50/year); *Reflections*, Box 368, Ducan Falls, OH 43734 ($3/year); *The McGuffy Writer*, 400A McGuffey Hall, Miami University, Oxford, OH 45056 ($3/year); *Chart Your Course*, PO Box 6448, Mobile, AL, 36660, ($20/yr); *Creative Kids*, PO Box 637, 100 Pine Ave., Holmes, PA 19043 ($10, yr.). *A Young Author's Guide to Publishing* lists submission guidelines for children's magazines; send $2.50 to Dr. Nicholas Spennato, Delaware County Reading Council, 6th and Olive St., Media, PA 19063.

situation in their school community. Teachers can also supplement basals by having students read quality children's literature in decent anthologies[2] or in whole books. My experience has shown that if children shelve the basal a few times a week and instead read classroom sets of entire novels, they are more likely to think longer and more deeply about a piece of literature and how it relates to their lives.

But there are some problems with this organic style of teaching. Given class oppression in our society, poor children usually have a narrower range of experiences than those from more affluent homes. This does not mean they are culturally or experientially deprived—as spending the summer in Mexico or the Mississippi delta or even playing in the back allies of one of our big cities can be a rich experience. Their culture and experience is just different than that of many teachers; it is also in discordance with the texts of the dominant curricula. I believe though that we should stretch what is organic in the children's lives by taking them out into the world and by bringing the world into the classroom (Searle, 1977). Field trips, speakers, movies, and current events studies are obvious ways to do this.

Poetry and music can also bring the world into the classroom. For example, Langston Hughes' poems "Colored Child at the Carnival" or "The Ballad of the Landlord," speak to the experience of many African-Americans and poor people and spark critical discussions. I have had similar success with songs such as "Harriet Tubman" and "I Cried" sung by Holly Near, "Lives in the Balance" and "Lawless Avenue" by Jackson Browne, "Sambo Lando" sung by Inti Illimani, "El Pueblo Unido Jamas Sera Vencido" by Quilapayun. Whenever I use poems or songs I reproduce the words so that each student can follow along and keep a copy.

As we delve deeper into the nature of students' experiences in urban America, new problems with the application of Freire's theory confront us. Freire (1970) assumes that what will most inspire the learner is discussion and reflection on his or her own experiences, particularly his or her own oppression. In my eyes, many children in urban America are oppressed by a few key institutions: school, family, and community.

For an elementary teacher to apply Freire by focusing on such oppression raises difficult problems. The degree to which a teacher can "deviate" from the standard curriculum depends on a number of factors—the amount of peer and parental support, the political situation in the school and district, and the sophistication and maturity of the particular group of students, to name a

---

[2] One excellent anthology is called *Embers: Stories for a Changing World* edited by Meyers, Banfield, and Colon J. (1983) distributed by the Council on Interracial Books for Children, 1841 Broadway, New York, NY, 10023. For a bibliography of children's books that have young people as protagonists who are working for social justice see Peterson (1987). Books to empower young people. *Rethinking Schools Vol. 1, No. 3.* Pp. 9–10, available from *Rethinking Schools*, 1001 E. Keefe Ave., Milwaukee, WI 53212.

few. But there is deviation and there is deviation. To study the Plains Indians instead of the Pilgrims is one thing. To help students become aware and critical about how they are being oppressed in society can be quite another. I have found two ways to approach this problem. First is to deal with power relationships and "oppression" within my own classroom. The second way is to bring the world into the classroom, so that children start reflecting on their own lives. I will first explain the latter.

One year I showed my students the video *The Wrath of Grapes* (United Farm Workers, 1987) about the current grape boycott and followed it up with a field trip to see Cesar Chavez speak at the local technical college. All sorts of good things came out of this activity, but the most interesting was that on the Monday after our trip my students came to school and the first thing they yelled was "Mr. Peterson, Sixth Street is on strike."

"What?" I replied?

"Sixth and National Ave. Is on strike!"

Now the streets in Milwaukee have a lot of pot holes after the long winter but I had never heard of a street being on strike. What had in fact occurred was a strike by workers at a local factory. Later that week during art period I took six students armed with a tape recorded over to the company so they could interview the workers. I believe they learned more during their half-hour interview than they had in years of social studies lessons. We debriefed in the teachers' lounge. When we were reviewing the reason for the strike—a wage cut from $7.00 down to $4.00. Cecilia said rather unemotionally, "That's more money than my mom makes now." We examined where each of the children's parents worked and if they were in a union. "Grievance" became a spelling word the next week and pretty soon there seemed to be grievances about all sorts of things in the children's lives. By bringing the world into the classroom they were better able to reflect upon their own lives.

But as I enlarge the world in which my students operate through sharing of such experiences, always tying issues to and building upon the students' own realities, I habitually confront another problem. The "generative themes" of many media-saturated children often seem to have more to do with life on the cathode ray tube than life in our community. During writing workshop or group discussions I sometimes feel I am in another world of professional wrestlers, super heros, and video games. The average child watches television six hours a day and in one year sees 800 war toy commercials, 250 episodes of war cartoons; the violent commercials and episodes being the equivalent of 22 days of school (Liebert & Sprafkin, 1988).[3]

---

[3] Marie Winn (1987) offers some innovative ideas to both parents and teachers to help children kick the television habit, including plans for classroom and school wide television turnoff campaigns.

One consequence of this television addiction is physical atrophy, but the deadening of the child's imagination and the imposition of a violent, consumeristic ideology are other results that have a direct affect on a "generative theme"-based classroom. When my kids moan about the President their solution is to kill him. A child doesn't like gangs—solve the problem by machine gunning them down or by sending them to the electric chair. There is no simple or short-term solution to this problem, and certainly a single classroom teacher is not going to solve this problem alone. I challenge these ideas through dialogue attempting to get children to think about why they think the way they do (which I explain in more detail in the section on critiquing curriculum and the media). I take what I hear and try to rework it from a different angle—codify it to use Freire's term—and bring it up again in the future in the context of other curricular areas.

In a generative theme-oriented classroom, the tendency is often to try to cover too much too fast. My most successful experiences have been when I've had the class concentrate on one thing in depth. The concept of "less is more" (Coalition of Essential Schools, 1984) applies equally well to a single classroom as it does to an entire school curricula. I have ensured this by using a variety of methods: a word for the day, a quotation of the week, a short poem, a graphic, a cartoon, story, or news article.

When I have a special word for the day it often relates to a topic the children have been discussing or studying. I or one of the students present it in both English and Spanish, explain its epistomology, teach the others how to sign it in American Sign Language, discuss its significance and use it as a "password" as we move through the day's activities. Sometimes the word comes from the conversations I hear, or from a topic of interest that we have discussed in our studies. The focus on one word, particularly in a bilingual setting, helps students become aware of language in a metacognitive sense. Through word webbing or semantic mapping I help connect this word again to the life experiences of the students.

Regardless of whether it's a word, a scripted dialogue, a story, or a discussion which serves to organize classroom dialogue, the focus of instruction and locus of control is learner- rather than teacher-centered. The essence of an organic theme-based approach thus lies in the connections it builds between the topic at hand, the students' lives and broader world around them (Ellwood, 1989).

THE EMPOWERMENT OF STUDENTS

Since students have so few rights, they rarely develop responsibility. By fifth grade I get children who are so damaged by society that they are only able to behave if they are given no rights—even going to the pencil sharpener without having to ask permission is too much for some to handle. This irresponsibility is rooted in the teacher-centered and textbook-driven curriculum which serves to disempower children. Because students are denied rights and kept from decision making throughout their school life and subjected to tedious worksheets and boring curriculum, school life prevents them from developing the responsibility and self-discipline necessary to be independent thinkers and actors in our society.[4] Freire (1970) maintains that through this subjugation students become *objects* acted upon by the authoritarian school system and society. He argues, instead, for a pedagogical process of dialogue, reflection, dramatization, and interaction, whereby students move towards being *subjects* capable of understanding the world and their social context, and ultimately engaging in activity based on this new understanding. Again, the realization of students as subjects is not always easily attained.

I want my students to take responsibility for their own learning, when I begin to encourage this many see it as license to goof off. Shor and Freire (1987) speak of the need to develop transitionary models and activities to train people to be more responsible. In making the transition to empower students, one must therefore be prepared for a sometimes enormous struggle.

The first step in this transition is to enhance the students self-esteem and reduce the anxiety level. This is done through creating an overall positive atmosphere in the classroom and by planning very specific activities which stress self-awareness, respect, and cooperation. Activities like those suggested by Canfield and Wells (1976), Prutzman, Stern, Burger, and Bodenhamer (1988), and Schniedewind (1987) help students become more aware about their own attitudes about themselves and others while developing skills of listening, speaking, and cooperating.

I have children interview each other at the begining of the year and report on it to the whole class. This shows them that they should take each other seriously and it practices public speaking and careful listening. I play circle games involving drama, storytelling, and physical activity as well as small group activities which stress brainstorming, problem solving, and creative writing and dramatics. Instead of segregating affective education activities off into an afternoon corner of the curriculum I try as much as possible to

---

[4]This generalization ignores the class, race, and gender factors which profoundly affect school structure and student self-esteem. For example, Wodtke (1986) found discrepancies between instructional approaches received by suburban kindergarten and those in poor, working-class settings. The suburban kindergartens tended to encourage children to participate in show-and-tell and speak in front of the class, while the predominantly poor and working-class kindergartens rarely utilized such activities instead relying more heavily on worksheets and drill because of the pressures to cover standardized curriculum and the emphasis put on direct instruction. This differentiated approach tends to inculcate certain habits and outlooks in children based on class and race factors.

integrate group process and self-esteem-building activities into the curriculum as a whole. No matter where such activities are during the day; however, I have found that I need to model, role play, and teach many of these social skills. I model something, involve a small group of students with me doing the activity in front of the class, then have another small group do it again in front without my participation. Finally, after a short discussion with the whole class everyone becomes involved in the activity. Later, it is important for the class to discuss both the content and the process of the activity, with both strengths and shortcomings being highlighted. Modeling and discussing with students how to manage their time and to stay organized—from one's desk to one's three-ring binder—are also very powerful tools for the development of independence and high self-esteem.

Finally, I have found that I can reach even more students by linking my attempts at developing self-confidence and responsibility to history. For example, each year I make sure to focus for a while on the fact that in our nation's past females were not allowed to attend many schools, not allowed to speak at political meetings or vote. Through role play, storytelling, discussion, and project work about the past, some students are inspired to take a stronger and more self-conscious role in the classroom.

Beyond the building of self-esteem, students need to be involved with establishing and periodically reviewing the rules and curriculum of the classroom. Students' ability to do this depends on several factors including their maturity and previous schooling experience. At the beginning of the year, I carefully plan lessons which give students a taste of what it would mean to have a large say over what happens in the class. At the same time I am quick to restrict student decision making at the first signs that students are using the increased power as a license to goof off. As I restrict it, I go through a long process of explanation: discussion, role playing, and a lessening of the restrictions. After several cycles of this process, students usually become better able to take on increased responsibility and freedom. Sometimes such restrictions must be done on an individual level. For example, if the desks are arranged in clusters, those students who demonstrate they are capable of sitting close to their classmates and yet still listen to class discussions are permitted to stay in the clusters, while those who are disruptive have as a logical consequence their desk being place in a "row."

Empowerment does not mean "giving" someone their freedom. Nor does it mean creating a type of surface "empowerment" in which one gives the students the impression that they are "equal" to the teacher. The challenge for the teacher who believes in student empowerment is to create an environment which is both stimulating and flexible in which students can exercise increasing levels of power while regularly reflecting upon and evaluating the new learner-teacher relationship.

One element of this environment is class organization. We arrange our classroom according to our needs: Rows for presentations, a circle of chairs for large group discussion, and clusters of desks for small group discussion and work.

For class meetings, for instance, desks are pushed to the walls and the chairs are placed in a big circle. Such meetings form the basis of demo-craticizing the classroom (Glasser, 1969, 1986; Schmuck & Schmuck, 1983) through discussions, voting, and class problem solving. At the beginning of each school year, I chair the meetings but eventually the students take over. One person takes notes each session into a spiral notebook that we keep hung on the wall. I have a special rock which is passed from person to person so we know whose turn it is to speak. The first part of the year is often spent just improving our listening skills so that we can have an interactive dialogue instead of a series of monologues. I do this through modeling what a good listener does and playing listening games, such as having each person repeat one thing or the main idea of the person who spoke immediately before them prior to them speaking.

I start the class meetings with a circle game and then pass the rock and let people state the concern or problem they would like to discuss. I note these and then decide what will be discussed that day, usually starting off with a smaller, solvable problem and then moving into the hot and heavy ones. We use a five-step plan:

1. What is the problem?
2. Are you sure about it?
3. What can we do about it?
4. Try it.
5. How did it work?

Through this five-step process, students begin to work collectively, re-flecting upon the problem and together seeking solutions. While many of the problems poor and minority children and communities face cannot be easily or immediately "solved" a "problem-posing" pedagogy can encourage a ques-tioning of why things are the way they are and the identification of actions, no matter how small, to begin to address them. Inherent is a recognition of the complexity and time needed for solutions with individuals and commu-nities" (Wallerstein & Bernstein, 1988).

A DIALOGICAL INSTRUCTIONAL METHOD

If "student empowerment" is going to be meaningful, students not only need to be involved in some of the problem-solving and posing practices outlined above, but teachers must fundamentally change their methods. Education should not be viewed as the transmission of knowledge by trained technicians, but rather as an interactive process through which problems are posed and answers collaboratively sought. Dewey (1916) felt similarly and spoke of a conception of instruction for knowledge as opposed to instruction for habit. Like Freire, he saw education as an interactive process based on the history, experience, and culture of the student. Dewey said a mechanic taught mechanically would not be able to solve a new problem that might arise, but one taught to understand the whole machine and machines in general would be able to adapt to the new situation. The difference between Dewey and Freire is in part defined by the kinds of activities they advocate as ways for students to gain knowledge. Dewey took a deliberate apolitical stance. The practical educational activities he advocated usually involved students transforming the natural world, that is, gardening or laboratory experiments. Freire, on the other hand, defines practical education activities as critical discussion and collective action aimed at solving political and social problems (also see Walsh's Introduction, this volume).

The centerpiece of Freire's method, and what distinguishes it so sharply from the dominant practices in classrooms of most of North America, is its emphasis on dialogue. Dialogue, as Freire defines it, is not just permissive talk, but conversation with a focus and a purpose. Dialogue shows that the object of study is not the exclusive property of the teacher; knowledge is not produced somewhere in textbook offices and then transferred to the student. By discussion and extensive use of open-ended questioning by the teacher, students begin to think about the object or topic under study. Freire (Shor & Freire, 1987) is not opposed to lectures per se and in fact suggests the use of a variety of formats in the classroom. Since factual knowledge is the foundation upon which many discussions and opinions should be based, short lectures are sometimes important even at the elementary level. However, with the recent trend towards direct instruction, teachers too often demonstrate an overreliance on lecture to convey knowledge, even though only a small amount of such information is retained.

To initiate dialogue, I may use a motivating drawing, photo, cartoon, poem, written dialogue, oral story, or piece of prose. These dialogue "triggers" are useful for full classroom or small group discussions. Wallerstein and Bernstein (1988) have used a simple acronym "SHOWED" as a way to help students systematically respond to such a trigger.

S   what do you *See*?
H   what's *Happening* to your feelings?
O   relate it to your *Own* lives
W   *Why* do we face these problems?
E
D   what can we *Do* about it?

The students are encouraged to use this format to help facilitate their dialogue. It helps to direct students away from spontaneous conversation to a progression that moves from personal reactions to social analysis to consideration of action. A few examples from my class serve to illustrate this process.

One year as my class played at recess, a student slipped and fell on to a broken bottle, putting a ghastly wound into the back of her thigh—over 50 stitches. After the police and ambulance had carried her off on a stretcher, we tearfully retreated back into the safety of our classroom and I thought, "What the heck should I do now?" I sent two kids out to retrieve the guilty piece of glass. We put the piece in an open box and passed it around. The rest of the afternoon we discussed everything from the high school students who share our playground, to the bottle manufacturing companies who have prevented the Wisconsin state legislature from passing a bottle deposit law. One of my students, Fernando Valadez, put his thoughts to poetry:

Pig Pen
Nobody likes to live
in the pigpen of broken bottles,
muddy papers and squished cans.
In our neighborhood of
lonely streets, messy parks,
dirty alleys and dangerous playgrounds
you might get hurt like a friend
of mine who got a big cut on the back
of her leg when she was running
by the swings and fell on some glass.
The ambulance came
and took her away.
Who's going to take the junk
away?

At times the triggers I use are more explicitly value-laden and often cut across the curricula integrating language arts, history, and other subject areas. Some of the best dialogue in my class has come from discussions following the reading of poems or short historical pieces. Will Fisher's poem, for instance, helped initiate discussion of history and justice. The context is ice cream cones and mud, one that a child can relate to and understand:

A Command to Drive Horse Recklessly
    The first warm day in May, a line of common folk in front of the Dairy Queen shop. A carriage dashes by, spraying mud. Women curse and shake their fists. Two men rush after the carriage. It has been stopped by a traffic light. The men angrily threaten the coachman. Clutching his fifty-cent cone, a child catches up and, ignoring the others, flings the cone through the open window into the face of the nobleperson.

Utilizing the "SHOWED" question format with this simple poem has enabled my students to discuss a wide variety of topics ranging from racial and class discrimination, inflation, splashing each other on the playground, to the invention of traffic lights and cars.

CRITIQUE THE CURRICULUM AND SOCIETY

There is more to Freire than generative themes of the learners' lives and a dialogic style. He speaks of the need to illuminate reality to the student, as opposed to the standard curriculum which obscures reality. Freire (1985) suggests that the "question is a different relationship to knowledge and society and that the only way to truly understand the curriculum of the classroom is to go beyond its walls into the society." (Walsh expands on this relationship to knowledge and society in her Introduction.)

In most schools, facts are presented as value-free. Conceptual analysis—to the degree it exists—does not make contact with the real world. History is presented as a series of nonrelated sequential facts. Scientific "truths" are presented without historical context with little regard to the ramifications such matters have on the learners' environment or global ecology. Students are expected to learn—usually memorize and occasionally "discover"—such facts without regard to the values or interests which inform such perspectives (Shor, 1980, 1987).

As stated previously teachers should help students draw connections between their own lives, communities, and environment. But we must also help them reflect upon why they think the way they do; to discover that knowledge is socially constructed, that truth is relative not only to time and place but to class, race, and gender interests as well. Students need to know that what they have before them in their textbooks, in the newspapers, or on the television is not always true. We should thus engage our students in thinking about the validity of texts (Bigelow, 1989). In fact, this is one of the few uses I have found for them in my classroom.

The third-grade basal reader, *Golden Secrets* (Scott Foresman, 1980), for example, has a story on inventions. The anonymous author states that the traffic light was invented by an anonymous policeman. Actually it was invented by the African-American scientist Garrett A. Morgan. I give my students a short piece on Morgan that is from a black history book (Adams, 1969) and we compare and question. Some of my classes decided to write to Scott Foresman and complain.

The problem with textbooks is also what they omit (Council on Interracial Books for Children, 1977a). The Silver Burdett Social Studies Series, *The World and Its People* (Helmus, Arnsdorff, Toppin, & Pounds 1984), used in over two-thirds of the nation's school districts, has a 502-page fifth-grade reader on U.S. History. Only five paragraphs of this text deal with labor unions and working-class struggle, only one labor leader, Samuel Gompers, is mentioned and most of the text is written in the passive tense. "Why?," I ask the students, as I provide interesting stories and we role-play the true history of working-class struggle in our country. I connect this to local history, like the several-day general strike for the eight-hour day in 1886 which ended with the massacre of seven people including a 13-year-old boy. I have the students survey their parents and neighbors as to knowledge of this strike and other important events in our community's history and then we reflect on why people do not know such things. We recreate such history through readers' theater, role plays, simulations, dramas, and special projects.

Similarly, a Heath science text book (Barufaldi, Ladd, & Moses 1981) has a short biography on an African-American scientist Charles Drew, who pioneered blood transfusions and plasma research. Omitted is the fact that Dr. Drew died after a car accident in the south when a southern hospital refused to treat him and give him a blood transfusion because of his skin color.

One example that I particularly like to use in my bilingual class is the story of Sequoyah and the Cherokees. Most history books mention Sequoyah's creation of the alphabet and the Trail of Tears, but few mention that the Cherokee nation had a bilingual weekly newspaper and a bilingual school system with over 200 of their own schools including a normal school— that is, until the early 1900s when the federal government stepped in and disbanded it.[5] I tell the children this story of the Cherokees and say, "Let's see what the history books and encyclopedias say." Usually there are gross omissions and we proceed to discuss why and what impact these omissions have on how we view the world. I ask, "Why didn't the government want the Cherokees to maintain their language?" This is a crucial question in my classroom since, by fifth grade, many of the students have already developed negative attitudes toward their native Spanish language.

There are many stories from the untold history of the oppressed that expose the social nature of knowledge and nurture civic courage and a sense of social justice. I find the history of Shea's Rebellion and the Seminole Wars particularly worthwhile because not only was there a struggle for a just cause but a key ingredient was unity among nationalities, a persistent problem in our nation's history.

Another important way to deal with the socially constructed nature of

---

[5] In 1838, the United States government forced the Cherokee people and other southeastern tribes to abandon their land in Georgia and move to Oklahoma. The Indians suffered such hardships along the way that the path they followed became known as the Trail of Tears. For more information on the bilingual education system established by the Cherokees see Payne (1984) and Weinberg (1977).

knowledge is to directly deal with racist and sexist stereotypes.[6] Around Thanksgiving time I show my students the filmstrip, *Unlearning "Indian" Stereotypes* (Council on Interracial Books for Children, 1977b). It is narrated by Native American children who visit a public library and become outraged at the various stereotypes of Indians in the books.

One year after viewing the filmstrip the students seemed particularly outraged at what they had learned. They came the next day talking about how their siblings in first grade had come home with construction paper headdresses with feathers. "That's a stereotype," the students proudly proclaimed. "What did you do about it?" I responded. "I ripped it up." "I slugged him," came the chorus of responses. As we continued the discussion, I asked why their brothers and sisters had the objects and interrogated them as to how children learn about such things. Finally they decided there were more productive things they could do. They first scoured the school library for books with stereotypes but since they found few, they decided to investigate their sibling's first grade room and look for stereotypes there. They wrote a letter to the teacher asking permission and then went in armed with clipboards, paper, and pens. Results were a picture of an Indian next to the letter "I" in the alphabet strip on the wall. They came back and decided they wanted to teach the first graders about stereotypes. I was skeptical but agreed and after much rehearsal they entered the first grade classroom to give their lesson—rather unsuccessfully I am afraid. But, they reflected on it and later Paco Resendez and Faviola Alvarez wrote in our school newspaper:

> We have been studying stereotypes on Native Americans. What is a stereotype? It's when somebody says something that's not true about another group of people. For example, it is a stereotype if you think all Indians wear feathers or say "HOW!" Or if you think that all girls are delicate. Why? Because some girls are strong.

Another way to show students that knowledge is socially constructed is to get different newspaper or magazine articles about the same subject, from different points of view. Subscribe to newspapers from another country, like *La Barricada*, or use excerpts from papers such as *The Nation*, *In These Times*, *Food and Justice*, or the *Guardian* to contrast the reporting from the established press. Or videotape a children's cartoon or tape record lyrics of a popular tune and then watch or play it, analyze it as a class, and draw out its values. I watch for outrageous stories or advertisements in the paper—these can be real thought provokers—or invite in guests who will shock the students out of their complacency. I also use posters, quotations, and maps.

---

[6] The recognition of the importance of dealing with racism among children has prompted some educators (ALTARF, 1984) to argue that multicultural education is insufficient if it not accompanied by an anti-racist component.

I place a "poster of the week" on a special moveable bulletin board on my classroom wall. By using dramatic, historical, and/or controversial posters I encourage writing, discussion, and critique.[7] I also use a quotation of the week—in English, Spanish, or both. I begin the year providing the quotations myself, but as time passes children offer ones that they have found or created. Some quotations in particular, lend themselves to comparison, analysis and critique:

> When the missionaries first came to Africa they had bibles and we had the land. They said, "Let us pray." We closed our eyes. When we opened them we had the bibles and they had the land. (Bishop Desmond Tu Tu, Nobel Peace Prize Recipient)

Pointing out the biases in maps is also particularly thought provoking. The Mercator projection map, for example, places the equator two-thirds of the way down and depicts Europe as larger than South America although the area of the latter is approximately (6.9 million square miles) double that of Europe (3.8). The newly created Peter Projection may corrects this. Another map challenges the conception that Argentina is on the bottom and North America is on top, by reversing the North and South Poles. Such media invokes considerable dialogue and thinking, including who make maps, why they are the way they are, and how maps shape our thinking about the world.[8]

TEACHING SOCIAL RESPONSIBILITY

As students develop the interest and ability to discuss and reflect on their lives, communities, and the broader world, questions inevitably arise as to how people change the world. This concern and interest in social change can be encouraged by consciously fostering what Giroux (1985) calls "civic courage": stimulating "their passions, imaginations, and intellects so that they will be moved to challenge the social, political and economic forces that

---

[7] High-quality, politically progressive posters can be found through a number of outlets. Particularly good sources are the Syracuse Cultural Worker, Box 6367, Syracuse, NY 13217 and Northern Sun Merchandising, 2916 E. Lake St., Minneapolis, MN 55406. A source for excellent posters of Native American leaders is the Perfection Form Company, Logan, Iowa and for women posters contact: TABS, 438 Fourth St., Brooklyn, NY 11215 (718) 788-3478.

[8] The Peter Projection Map can be ordered from Friendship Press, PO Box 37844, Cincinnati, Ohio 45237. The Turnabout map is distributed by Laguna Sales, Inc., 7040 Via Valverde, San Jose, CA 95135.

weigh so heavily upon their lives" (p. 201). In other words, students should be encourage to act *as if* they were living in a democracy.

One way this can be done is through class meetings and positive reinforcement of socially responsible actions in the classroom. In other words, the first way to build social responsibility is to try to democratize and humanize the educational setting. In my classroom, for example, there is a small quartz rock which is given to the student who has helped someone else. At the beginning of each day, the student who had been awarded for her or his social responsibility the day before chooses the next recipient.

The central theme in my classroom is that the quest for social justice is a neverending struggle in our nation and world; that the vast majority of people have benefited by this struggle; that we must understand this struggle; and that we must make decisions about whether to be involved in it. The academic content areas can be woven around this theme. In reading poetry and literature to children, social issues can be emphasized through books that specifically empower children (Peterson, 1987). Contemporary struggles can be highlighted through curricular materials and readings on Central America, apartheid, and on racism at home.[9] And pictures of real people who have worked for social justice can help children see these struggles as human. In my classroom there is a gallery of freedom fighters, the "luchadores por la justicia" or strugglers for justice that we have studied in social studies and current events. The large portraits—some commercially purchased and others drawn by the children—serve as reminders that women and men of all races have made important contributions to society and serve as keys to unlock our past discussions and studies about people and their struggles. A few years ago one of my students reflected on Cesar Chavez in this way:

> Cesar Chavez is a good man. He is very famous but he is poor. I thought that if people are famous they have to be rich. But this man is poor because he has a group of people and the money he earns he gives to them.

In most curricula, struggle is omitted and conflict forgotten. History is not of social movements or eras but rather the succession of rulers from the

---

[9] I collect and weave into our class curricula parts of progressive curricula such as *Winning "Justice for All"* (Racism & Sexism Resource Center, 1981), *Open Minds to Equality* (Schniedewind & Davidson, 1983) Food First Curriculum, (Rubin, 1984), *Cooperative Learning, Cooperative Lives* (Schniedewind 1987), and a variety of curriculum on contemporary issues such as Central America (contact Network of Educators' Committees on Central America, PO Box 43509, Washington DC 20010-9509. 202-667-2618); apartheid (Bigelow, 1985); U.S. labor struggles (Bigelow & Diamond, 1988); women (contact National Women's History Project, PO Box 316 Santa Rosa Ca 95402 (707)526-5974; peace (contact the Wilmington College Peace Resource Center, Pyle Center Box 1183, Willmington, OH 45177; and racism (see the "Unlearning Stereotypes" filmstrips and guides from the CIBC, 1977a, 1982a, 1982b).

Dolores Huerta, farmworker, leader drawn
by 5th grader Victor Segura.

A heroine not found in most U.S. history basal text books.

Pro-Farmworker drawing by 5th grader Ariel Garcia.

Artwork as an expression of social concern.

Cesar Chavez as drawn by 5th grader Arturo Ibarra.

**"I thought that if people are famous they have
to be rich"—so wrote one student, but he found out otherwise when
he studied Cesar Chavez.**

John Brown, 5th grader, as drawn by Arturo Ibarra.

**Students are fascinated by this white man who gave his life
in the anti-slavery struggle.**

earliest Egyptian pharaohs to the most recent presidential administration. It has been fragmented, distorted, and rewritten. With our common history of struggle denied us, the past rewritten, the rulers of our society find the present much easier to manipulate. When Nixon said, "History will absolve our roles in Vietnam," he knew what he was talking about, for corporate textbook companies continue to write and rewrite our history—at least for the immediate future.

In contrast, Freire points to the positive role of struggle in history. He calls conflict the "midwife of real consciousness" and says it should be the focus of learning (Freire, 1970). The cynic might say that with all the conflict in our schools our students must be of very high consciousness. The key point here is to reflect on and critique conflict, in our daily lives, classrooms, and communities, as well as in history.[10]

Focusing on societal conflict—both historic and contemporary—is not only highly motivating and educational but also helps children, even the very young, to analyze and evaluate different points of view and express opinions as to what they think is just. The study of conflicts can be integrated into social studies units, for example, personal conflicts like Fredrick Douglass's struggle to learn to read; historic conflicts like the wars to take the land from American Indians, slave rebellions, worker strikes, bus boycotts, civil rights marches, antiwar movements; and contemporary conflicts like the United Farm Worker grape boycott, the war in El Salvador, apartheid, the antitoxin "Not in My Back Yard Movement." In my classroom, each conflict studied and any other historical event encountered in the normal course of our school day, is recorded on a 3×5 file card with a couple word description and the date. This card is hung on the class time line which circles three sides of the room. This process provides students with a visual representation of time, history, and sequence while fostering the understanding that everything is interrelated.

Historical conflict is best understood through engaging students in participatory activities. Often I will read or tell a story about a conflict and have children role-play parts of it either during or after the story. Occasionally

---

[10] Simulating classroom and interpersonal conflict through trigger cartoons, scripted dialogues, and role plays helps students to develop the skills and responsibility to analyze and resolve their own interpersonal problems. In classroom conflict, such reflection helps children understand the purposes behind the "misbehavior" and allows them to develop strategies and skills to diffuse and mediate such conflict. For a theoretical and practical approach to helping children understand the reasons for misbehavior see Dreikurs, Grunwald, and Pepper (1982) and for additional ways to mediate conflict see Prutzman et al (1988), Schniedewind (1987), and the curriculum produced by teachers and administrators in NYC Community School District 15 in collaboration with the New York Chapter of Educators for Social Responsibility (New York Board of Education, 1988).

such stories lead to small group or whole class drama presentations. I also use readers theater, that is, scripted plays written so that no acting needs to take place.[11] Sometimes I also encourage students to draw a conflict either together as a mural on large sheets of paper for display or separately for publication.

In addition, each student builds a people's textbook—a three-ring binder in which they put alternative materials. There are sections for geography, history, science, songs, poetry, and quotations. One year after *Rethinking Schools* printed an article on an important Milwaukee event of 1854 when 5000 people stormed the county jail to free a runaway slave the students used the information to write their own bilingual book about the historic incident. By examining local history in which European Americans fought alongside African-Americans for the abolition of slavery, my students began to understand that social responsibility in a race-divided society means working together on issues that might not necessarily be deemed as in ones immediate self-interest.[12]

Freire takes liberating education even one step further—to action or praxis. He believes learners should use their newfound analysis to transform the world. In the school setting transforming-type activities depend on the nature of the group of students, the community, and the school system, and the courage and seniority of the teacher. My students have gone with me to marches that protested police brutality, demanded that King's birthday be made a national holiday, asked that Congress not fund the Contras, and requested nuclear disarmament. Two of my students testified before the City Council, asking that a Jobs with Peace referendum be placed on the ballot. In another instance, the students went to observe the court proceedings in the case of a police killing of an African-American man. Obviously teachers need to be involved in the community in order to know what's happening and what possibilities exist for involvement of children.

Projects that are less overtly political can also stimulate critical thinking: Joining Amnesty International as a class and adopting a political prisoner, adopting a section of beach on a lake or river and keeping it clean, interviewing people involved in a local strike or community struggle, raising money for earthquake or famine relief, writing letters to governmental representatives, having such representatives or social activists visit the classroom, or corresponding with children in other parts of the USA, Puerto Rico, USSR, El

---

[11] Dozens of high-quality reader theaters which deal with a host of conflict in the history of labor, women, and racial minorities are available from Stevens and Shea, Dept. S, PO Box 794, Stockton, CA 95201.

[12] The pamphlet *Joshua Glover: The freeing of a runaway slave in Milwaukee—La liberación de un esclavo fugitivo en Milwaukee* is available from Communicate! Rural Route 2, Pulaski, WI 54162.

Salvador and Mozambique.[13] Discussion, writing, and critical reflection on these activities, however, are crucial so these are not to be just "interesting" field trips or projects.

One year we studied the underground railroad as part of the fifth grade U.S. history curriculum. We also studied the second underground railroad, the sanctuary movement. I invited a speaker to my class who had lived in El Salvador for several years. He showed slides of the people. My children at first laughed at the distended bellies of the starving Salvadoran children, but their chuckles turned to horror and then anger as they began to understand that U.S. bombs are being dropped on these children. The class meeting after the presentation was quite informative. The kids asked "Why?" Why was the U.S. government doing this? Why did Reagan do it?" We asked them "Why do you think?" "Because Reagan supports the rich," said one. "Yeah," agreed the others. But others were still not satisfied. "Why? Why does he support the rich?" Finally the speaker responded. "Because it is the job of the president in this country to support the rich." Paco's hand shot up. "If that's the case," he argued, "what about Kennedy?" The bell rang before the speaker could answer. As I drove him home he said the discussion was better than many he had had on university campuses.

In a group meeting the following day the children decided to write letters to our representatives and the president on the issue. The next day one boy, Michael, came in and said, "Mr. Peterson, we have to send weapons down to Central America or else the Russians will take over and no one will believe in God anymore." I said, "Michael, you've been talking to your mom . . . Great. Keep it up. We'll talk about that later." But that day we didn't get to it and as he left I gave him some *Food First* leaflets about hunger in Central America being the real enemy and asked him to read them with his mom. The following day he did not show up for school—I was a bit concerned. The day after he was back and we talked in detail about the various perspectives on Nicaragua, El Salvador, the U.S.S.R. and the United States of America. The children decided that even if the Sandinistas received money and weapons from aliens from Saturn they had that right because all they wanted to do was run their own country.

A week later at a group meeting, Emma announced that we had to discuss the letters we wrote to the President. "They won't do any good," she lamented, "I bet he just tore them up." She then proposed we go on a field

---

[13] One such telecommunications link up is De Orilla a Orilla (from Shore to Shore) which can be contacted by writing Dennis Sayers, De Orilla a Orilla, N.E. MRC, University of Massachusetts, 250 Stuart St., Rm 1105, Boston, MA 02116. Additional information about communication linkups can be obtained from the book, *School Links International: A New Approach to Primary School Linking Around the World*, by Rex Deddis and Cherry Mares (1988), published by the Avon County Council, Tidy Britain Group Schools Research Project.

trip to Washington DC to meet the President in person and that I, the teacher, finance it. I politely declined. At that point there was what Freire (Shor & Freire 1987) would call an inductive moment—when the students are stalled and need direction—I said that sometimes people protested in Washington DC but often people protested right here in Milwaukee, as the Pledge of Resistance was doing regularly. The kids immediately said they wanted to go, and before I knew it I was sending home letters to the parents explaining that although it was not part of the official curriculum, if they consented, I would supervise a public bus trip after school up to the Federal Building to protest U.S. aid to the contras. I bought tag board and markers from the local bookstore careful not to use the school's supplies. Half the class—12 children—brought back signed notes. The next Monday the students stayed after school and made their signs. At first they asked me what they should say, but I responded that if they were going on a protest march they had better know what they were protesting. They could make the signs themselves. They did. Their signs included:

Let them run their land!
Support the Poor! Not the "freedom fighters" They're the Rich.
Help Central America Don't Kill Them
Give the Nicaraguans their Freedom
Let Nicaragua Live!
Give Nicaragua Some Food Instead of Weapons
We want Freedom and Peace
Stop spending money to make bombs.

When they were finished making their signs we walked two blocks to the public bus stop and during a steady drizzle headed downtown to the Federal Building. They were the only Hispanics at the march of 150 people and were welcomed with open arms. We walked, marched, chanted, and finally went home wet and exhausted.

The next day we had a panel discussion and the kids talked and listened like they were on top of the world. Paula Martinez wrote about it later in our magazine, *Kid Power*:

On a rainy Tuesday in April some of the students from our class went to protest against the contras. The people in Central America are poor and being bombed on their heads. When we went protesting it was raining and it seemed like the contras were bombing us. A week before we had visitor, Jim Harney. He had been to El Salvador. He talked to our class about what was going on in El Salvador. He said it was terrible. A lot of people are dying. He showed us slides of El Salvador and told us its bad to be there. He hoped that our government will give them food and money and not bombs.

Michael, the boy who had come back from home concerned about the Russians and God did not go to the march. He said he had to babysit his little brother. Parent conferences were a week later and I was a bit apprehensive to see his mother—a socially mobile Puerto Rican studying to become a nurse. She walked into the room, sat down and said, "Mr. Peterson, I want to thank you. Michael has become interested in everything. He watches the news, he talks to me about what's going on, he knows more about things than me sometime. I don't know what you did. But thanks." As our conversation progressed it was clear her conservative political views on Central America had not changed, but our differences were secondary, because what was central to both of us was that her son had started to read the world.

REFERENCES

Adams, R. (1969). *Great Negroes: Past and present*. Chicago: Afro-Am Publishing Co.

All London Teachers Against Racism and Facism (ALTARF). (1984). *Challenging racism*. Nottingham, UK: Russell Press. Available from ALTARF, Room 216, Panther House, 38 Mount Pleasant, London WCIX OAP.

Ashton-Warner, S. (1965). *Teacher*. New York: Simon and Schuster.

Barufaldi, J., Ladd, G., & Moses, A. (1981). *Heath Science*. Lexington, MA: D.C. Heath.

Bigelow, W. (1985). *Strangers in their own land: A curriculum guide to South Africa*. New York: Africa World Press.

Bigelow, W. (1989, October/November). Discovering Columbus: Re-reading the past. *Rethinking Schools*, 4(1), 1, 12–13.

Bigelow, W., & Diamond, N. (1988). *The power in our hands: A curriculum on the history of work and workers in the United States*. New York: Monthly Review Press.

Brecht, B. (1978). *The mother*. New York: Grove Press.

Calkins, L. (1983). *Lessons from a child*. Portsmouth, NH: Heinemann.

Calkins, L. (1986). *The art of teaching writing*. Portsmouth, NH: Heinemann.

Canfield, J., & Wells, H. (1976). *100 ways to enhance self-concept in the classroom: A handbook for teachers and parents*. Englewood Cliffs, NJ: Prentice-Hall.

Coalition of Essential Schools. (1984). *Prospectus: 1984–1994*. Providence, RI: Brown University.

Commission on Reading by the National Council of Teachers of English. (1988). *Report card on basal readers*. Katonah, NY: Richard C. Owen.

Council on Interracial Books for Children (CIBC). (1977a). *Stereotypes, distortions and omissions in U.S. history textbooks*. New York: Racism and Sexism Resource Center for Educators.

Council on Interracial Books for Children. (1977b). *Unlearning "Indian" stereotypes*. New York: Racism and Sexism Resource Center for Educators.

Council on Interracial Books for Children. (1982a). *Unlearning Chicano and Puerto Rican stereotypes*. New York: Racism and Sexism Resource Center for Educators.

Council on Interracial Books for Children. (1982b). *Unlearning Asian American stereotypes*. New York: Racism and Sexism Resource Center for Educators.

Dewey, J. (1916). *Democracy and education*. New York: MacMillan.

Dreikurs, R. Grunwald, B., & Pepper, F. (1982). *Maintaining sanity in the classroom*. New York: Harper & Row.

Ellwood, C. (1989). Making connections: Challenges we face. *Rethinking Schools, 3*(3), 1, 12–13.

Fairtest (National Center for Fair and Open Testing). (1988). *Fallout from the testing explosion: How 100 million standardized exams undermine equity and excellence in American's public schools*. Available from P.O. Box 1272, Harvard Square Station, Cambridge MA 02238.

Freire, P. (1970). *Pedagogy For the oppressed*. New York: Seabury.

Freire, P. (1985). *The politics of education*. South Hadley, MA: Bergin & Garvey.

Gibboney, R. A. (1988). Madeline Hunter's teaching machine. *Rethinking Schools, 2*(3), 10–11.

Giroux, H. (1985). *Theory and resistance in education*. South Hadley, MA: Bergin and Garvey.

Glasser, W. (1969). *Schools without failure*. New York: Harper & Row.

Glasser, W. (1986). *Control theory in the classroom*. New York: Harper & Row.

Goodlad, J. (1984). *A place called school: Prospects for the future*. New York: McGraw-Hill.

Goodman, K. (1986). *What's whole in whole language?* Richmond Hill, Ontario; Canada Scholastic TAB. (Distributed in the United States by Heinemann.)

Goodman, K., Smith, E. B., Meredith, R., & Goodman, Y. (1987). *Language and thinking in school: A whole language curriculum*. New York: Richard C. Owen.

Graves, D. H. (1983). *Writing: Teachers and children at work*. Portsmouth, NH: Heinemann.

Helmus, T., Arnsdorf, V., Toppin, E., & Pounds, N. (1984). *The United States and its neighbors*. Atlanta: Silver Burdett Co.

Krashen, S., & Terrell, T. (1983). *The natural approach: Language acquisition in the classroom*. Hayward, CA: Alemany Press.

Levine, D. (1988). Outcome based education: Grand design or blueprint for failure? *Rethinking Schools, 2*(2), 1, 12–13.

Liebert, R., & Sprafkin, J. (1988). *The early window: Effects of television on children and youth*. New York: Pergamon Press.

Meyers, R., Banfield, B., & Colon, J. (Eds.). (1983). *Embers: Stories for a changing world*. Old Westbury, NY: The Feminist Press.

New York City Board of Education. (1988). *Resolving conflict creatively: A draft teaching guide for grades Kindergarten through six*. New York: Board of Education.

Payne, C. (1984). Multicultural education and racism in American schools. *Theory into Practice, 33* (2), 124–131.

Peterson, R. (1987). Books to empower young people. *Rethinking Schools, 1(3)*, 9–10.

Prutzman, P., Stern, L., Burger, M. L., & Bodenhamer, G. (1988). *The friendly classroom for a small planet: A handbook on creative approaches to living and problem solving for children*. Philadelphia, PA: New society Publishers.

Racism & Sexism Resource Center. (1981). *Winning justice for all: A supplementary curriculum unit on sexism and racism, stereotyping and discrimination.* New York: Council on Interracial Books for Children.

Rubin, L. (1984). *Food first curriculum.* San Francisco: Food First.

Schniedewind, N. (1987). *Cooperative learning, cooperative lives: A sourcebook of learning activities for building a peaceful world.* Somerville, MA: Circle Press.

Schiedewind, N., & Davidson, E. (1983). *Open minds to equality: A sourcebook of learning activities to promote race, sex, class, and age equity.* Englewood cliffs, NJ: Prentice-Hall.

Schmuck P. A., & Schmuck, R. A. (1983). *Group process in the classroom.* Dubuque, IA: Wm. C. Brown Company.

Scott, Foresman & Co. (1981). *Scott Foresman reading.* New York.

Searle, C. (1977). *The world in a classroom.* London: Writers and Readers Publishing Cooperative.

Shor, I. (1980). *Critical teaching and everyday life.* Boston: South End Press.

Shor, I. (1987). *Freire for the classroom: A sourcebook for liberatory teaching.* Portsmouth, NH: Heinemann.

Shor, I., & Freire, P. (1987). *A pedagogy for liberation: Dialogues on transforming education.* South Hadley, MA: Bergin and Garvey.

Smith, F. (1985). *Reading without nonsense.* New York: Teachers College Press.

United Farm Workers. (1987). *The wrath of grapes* (video). Keene, CA: The United Farm Workers.

Wallerstein, N., & Bernstein, E. (1988). Empowerment education: Freire's ideas adapted to health education. *Health Education Quarterly, 15* (4), 379–394.

Weinberg, M. (1977). *A chance to learn: The history of race and education in the United States.* New York: Cambridge University Press.

Wigginton, E. (1989). Foxfire grows up. *Harvard Educational Review, 59* (1), 24–49.

Winn, M. (1987). *Unplugging the plug-in drug.* New York: Penguin.

Wodtke, K. (1986). Inequality at Age Five? *Rethinking Schools, 1*(1), 7.

10

Affirming Cultural Citizenship in the Puerto Rican Community: Critical Literacy and the El Barrio Popular Education Program

Rosa M. Torruellas
Rina Benmayor
Anneris Goris
Ana Juarbe
Centro de Estudios Puertorriqueños, Hunter College, CUNY

For the last decade the United States has been involved in a massive adult literacy campaign. The push to "make America literate" responds to a concern for the diminishing competitive power of the United States in the world economy. This is why the business sector has led the recent crusade for the "eradication" of illiteracy. Under the banner "a literate America is a good investment," corporate interests are increasingly funneling money and support for adult literacy programs (Business Council for Effective Literacy, 1986).

Illiteracy is commonly portrayed as a malady with the potential of undermining the very social fabric of the United States. The extent of functional illiteracy (from 17 to 23 million according to recent reports) has been characterized as "frightening" because it "costs billion of dollars each year to our economy in unemployment, underemployment, and diminishing worker productivity" ("The shame and costs," 1986).

Federal, state, and local governments have appropriated millions of dollars for this campaign. "Coalitions for Literacy" and "Governors' Adult Literacy Initiatives" are springing up throughout the country. The availability of funding has resulted in a scramble on the part of public libraries, institutions of higher education, unions, and other organizations to develop literacy programs. Many are oriented exclusively toward imparting basic reading and writing skills, the primary aim being to promote functional literacy.

The narrow bases upon which these efforts are built limit their pedagogical effectiveness, as well as their potential to catalyze more profound social change. Nontraditional educators, practitioners, and researchers have started looking at alternative models that truly address the needs of learners in oppressed communities.

A broader conception of literacy as popular education, developed within the Latin American context, offers a viable paradigm for innovative educational practices in the United States. Within this framework, illiteracy is recognized not as the cause, but as a manifestation of the systematic exclusion of minorities and the poor from economic, political, and educational opportunities. Hence, learning how to read and write becomes a vehicle for developing collective solutions that address the underlying conditions of inequality. Literacy moves beyond decoding printed symbols to developing critical thinking skills.

This chapter will explore the impact of the El Barrio Popular Education Program on a highly disenfranchised sector of the Puerto Rican community in New York City. It foregrounds the experience of four women, examining the different ways in which this literacy for empowerment program mobilizes individual and collective resources for empowerment and change.

The chapter is divided into four parts: The first describes the philosophy, pedagogical practices, and social interaction in the El Barrio Program. The second discusses the objectives, theoretical dimension, and methods of the research component of the Program. Here, we introduce the concept of "cultural citizenship" as a key dynamic in the empowerment process. The third part shifts to personal "testimonies." Narratives of four women, constructed on the basis of life histories, classroom observations, and case studies speak to the changes occurring in their daily lives, in their perceptions of self and future aspirations. The fourth section examines the Program's contribution to the reformulation of gender, class, and national identities and the expression of cultural citizenship.

THE PROGRAM

In September 1985, the Language Policy Task Force of the Centro de Estudios Puertorriqueños, Hunter College, CUNY, initiated a participatory research-educational project in the Puerto Rican community of East Harlem. Inspired by Paulo Freire's educational work in Brazil, it has developed an approach to literacy that draws on people's culture and experience as conduits for learning (Freire, 1970; Freire & Macedo, 1987). Today, "the literacy project" has evolved into the El Barrio Popular Education Program, a full-fledged community-based organization in which the participants are taking increasing directive responsibilities.

The Program was incorporated as a nonprofit corporation in May 1987. It has a nine-member board of directors, which includes four Program partici-

pants and five Latino scholars and educators. Student decision-making power has also been formalized by the creation of a steering committee. This is
the major directive body regarding the day-to-day operation of the Program.
It is composed of six student representatives and the staff. The planning,
organizing, and development of Program activities are more and more in the
hands of the participants.

Membership in the Board and the Steering Committee are important first
steps towards the goal of complete self-management and control of the
Program by the community. A series of workshops, scheduled over the next
two years, are intended to further develop the administrative skills and
leadership abilities of the participants. In the meantime, the Centro continues supporting the growth of this community-based organization, paying for
the director's salary, organizing the research/evaluation component, and
taking major responsibility for fundraising.[1]

In the last two years the Program has attracted an average of 50 participants, mostly women from their early thirties to 83 years of age.[2] The
majority grew up in rural communities in Puerto Rico, and arrived in the
United States as young adults. They live on an average annual income of less
than $5,000, well below the official poverty line. Seventy-six percent receive
public assistance and almost two-thirds are single mothers. Their educational
level ranges from no formal schooling to some high school.

Contrary to most adult literacy projects which emphasize the development of English language skills, we conceived this as a native language
program. The use of Spanish for teaching literacy in this community is
pedagogically sound: People learn better in a language they already know,
and when their culture and knowledge are validated. The Program began
with two and now has three literacy classes — beginning, intermediate, and
advanced — to accommodate the participants' varied educational background. After the second year, an ESL class was introduced at the students'
request. Computers are also integrated into the curriculum as a way to
reinforce literacy acquisition.

Many participants find their traditional notions of education being challenged. Instead of the "banking" approach to learning in which the teacher
periodically deposits information into the students' minds, the goal is to

---

[1] A number of private foundations and two other organizations serving the Puerto Rican
community are contributing to this effort. Casita María provides space at its East Harlem
community center, free of charge. The Continuing Education Program at Eugenio María de
Hostos Community College covers teachers' salaries, counseling, and provides administrative
assistance.

[2] Although this is not exclusively a women's program, its daytime schedule and the fact that
we started working with parents in a local public school has encouraged greater participation of
women than men. Because there are only four male participants, the analysis that follows
concentrates on understanding the impact of popular education on women's lives.

develop "critical literacy." The teachers organize their classes around socially relevant themes: gender relations, work, education, migration, and social history. They encourage highly participatory and collective modes of inter-action, helping to break down traditional teacher–student hierarchies.

In the classroom, the participants are the experts, communicating their own ideas and personal experiences. This learning environment is both exciting and challenging, since it opens avenues for development while potentially setting in contradiction traditional roles and self-concepts. Al-though they sometimes criticize that there is too much discussion and not enough "instruction," students' discourse and practice attest to a new aware-ness emerging from a process of critical thought.

Writing and Testimony

Writing has been an important aspect of the curriculum from the beginning. As an active language skill, writing involves both rethinking and synthesizing ideas explored in class, helping to develop a more analytical perspective. While the participants in the advanced group come to the Program with literacy skills, many do not use them frequently in their daily lives. A strategy used to begin the writing process is to assign each one to write a life chronology. The second step is to flesh out this outline with regularly assigned autobiographical essays. In most cases, the essays are written at home, and read in the classroom. At times, however, it is necessary to do exercises in class, to get students used to writing on a regular basis. In time, the participants no longer associate writing exclusively with school assign-ments. One of the more prolific writers explains that "now I write down everything I do not want to forget."

In the beginners' class, writing is also a central activity. The teacher discourages the common practice of introducing writing through copying. Taking cues from classroom discussion, the participants learn to write key words and eventually phrases on their own. This is the first step in the process of "writing from the mind." By the time they move to the next level, they have already established the relationship between writing and personal expression.

In developing an empowerment pedagogy we are consciously placing emphasis on testimony. Autobiographical writings provide the opportunity for students to "tell" their stories, often for the first time. This helps to dispel the notion, prevalent among working-class people, that history, knowledge, and writing are the exclusive domain of professionals or the rich. Similarly, by giving significance to the participants' daily lives and thoughts, the pedagogy deconstructs gendered ideologies of social roles and capabilities. As their accounts are read out loud in class, participants come to realize that their circumstances are not unique, accidental, or the product of their own errors or "shortcomings." From the individual accounts, a collective "story" and consciousness emerges.

Testimonial literature by other Latin Americans has been presented in class as evidence of the importance of sharing one's life experience in the process of searching for collective solutions and decisions.[3] Inspired by these texts, a Spanish literacy reader was produced for class, based on recorded oral history sessions with a group of women in the first year of the Program.[4] This is an example of participatory education, where students contribute to developing their own pedagogical tools.

Support Systems

The staff believes in each person's ability to learn and to reach beyond the limited "opportunities" traditionally reserved for poor and minority communities. High learning and leadership expectations are conveyed from the very first day. Sitting in a circle, students are asked to articulate their goals and their ideas on how to achieve them. The older members have become the best spokespersons for the Program's philosophy. As one of them told an incoming group: "Here there is no such thing as 'I can't' or 'I don't know'."

The students are themselves starting to define Program priorities and goals. In this context, during a welcoming orientation meeting, student representatives proposed that there be a limit to absences. They suggested that the serious business of "face to face" welfare appointments be scheduled for days when classes are not in session. Despite the fear of bringing up the issue with case workers, the participants have confronted the problem successfully in a majority of cases.

Recently, a group of students from the Bronx visited their local welfare office and succeeded in obtaining carfare and lunch allowance to attend the Program. This request, repeatedly denied to individuals, was approved as a result of this collective strategy of action. Consequently, there has been a drop in absences and an increasing awareness by the participants of their power to negotiate.

The counselor has set up a variety of support mechanisms for the learners. A cross-referral network helps participants obtain needed medical, legal, and social services. She works with each person to identify strengths and set concrete learning goals. She also conducts monthly group "rap sessions" where problems affecting classroom dynamics are discussed and solutions proposed. The sessions always start by focusing on positive events: "Tell us

---

[3] Rigoberta Menchú (*Yo, Rigoberta Menchú*), Domitila Barrios (*Si me permiten hablar*), Bernardo Vega (*Memorias de Bernardo Vega*), Jesús Colón (*A Puerto Rican in New York and Other Sketches*) and the video production *Las madres de la Plaza de Mayo*.

[4] *Aprender a luchar, luchar es aprender*, Centro de Estudios Puertorriqueños, 1987.

something good and new in your life." This supportive environment has played a crucial role in promoting collective interaction and building confidence and self-esteem.

THE RESEARCH

Empowerment and Cultural Citizenship

The research and practice of the last four years have provided better insight into ways of achieving truly empowering education. Part of our research has involved developing a conceptual framework for understanding the empowerment process and the relationship between individual and collective transformation. Beyond the therapeutic impact the Program may have on individual participants is the larger issue of group mobilization.

"Cultural citizenship," a concept we have been developing with other Latino colleagues, articulates empowerment with mobilization and the specific cultural bases for that action.[5] By "cultural citizenship" we mean the practices whereby disenfranchised communities of people actively express and assert their own sense of human, social, and cultural rights.[6] We are defining cultural citizenship as an oppositional practice because it seeks to alter existing relations of power, in the home, the community, or the society.

The concept also acknowledges agency, reflecting the active role of oppressed peoples in claiming what is their own and of drawing sustenance and strength from that claim. In expressing and affirming cultural citizenship, communities, broadly defined, rely on specific cultural referents and social identities. They also depend upon and form social networks as primary means of support.

Cultural citizenship is an affirmative practice. It both contributes to and is a concrete expression of the empowerment process. As we understand it so far, the empowerment process and the exercise of cultural citizenship develop in different stages. Initially, this involves a heightened awareness of the barriers to "moving" and reaching one's goals. Empowerment begins with

---

[5] Our research project at El Barrio is part of a larger, comparative investigation of "cultural citizenship" in United States Latino communities, being carried out by the Cultural Studies Working Group of the Inter-University Program for Latino Research (IUP). This IUP Cultural Studies team includes researchers from the Centro de Estudios Puertorriqueños, Hunter College (CUNY) and from Chicano Studies centers at Stanford University, UCLA and UTexas, Austin. This group has been responsible for developing the term and concept of "cultural citizenship."

[6] The focus on cultural bases for rights expands the concept of citizenship beyond legal, national or state definitions. It also imbues the concept of culture with political dynamic.

the emergence of critical consciousness, when people "change their ideas about the causes of their powerlessness, when they recognize the systemic forces that oppress them, and when they act to change the conditions of their lives" (Morgen & Bookman, 1988). The organizing sense of rights and the concrete action affirming them is what we are calling cultural citizenship.

Individual empowerment is a necessary first step toward articulating collective demands. With some exceptions, the Program has been successful in bringing about individual transformation. To begin with, it is not uncommon to hear many women referring to "school" as a kind of therapy or psychological catharsis. According to one participant, before coming to the Program she "did not know what to do. I was always nervous and at times felt like killing myself." The classes have made her realize that "even though we are old, God has something in reserve for all of us. We can now laugh and have fun."

Gradually, the participants have come to perceive the classroom as a special, supportive niche in which there is a potential for transforming their lives. "School" has also become a catalyst for a complex process of change that transcends the classroom. Along with formal training, it has provided a collective and secure arena for working out personal and social problems.

Since individual empowerment takes place within a highly supportive environment, we can also identify practices of group empowerment underway. The Program is itself a primary locus for developing collective ideology and action. Its continued existence and growth into a community-based/community-directed organization depends on the collective effort and advancement of the participants. In this manner, the Program provides an organized context for constructing and expressing "cultural citizenship."

Research Methods

Classroom ethnography has been a component of the project from its inception. We have amassed a detailed, descriptive account of daily classroom interaction over four years. The research goals have changed over time. The original research design was broad in focus, calling for an examination of literacy needs and practices in the El Barrio community. Once the literacy project got underway, the goals were fine-tuned, and the research put at the service of developing an empowerment educational model for adult literacy. Classroom observation has been critical for identifying those practices that need to be changed, as well as those that should be reinforced. In effect, the research has served to provide an informed basis for constructing a culturally sensitive and socially relevant curriculum for this segment of the Puerto Rican community.

Like the Program itself, research is highly participatory. As researchers, we are not mere "observers" of a process. While in the classroom, we take on multiple roles. Besides documenting classroom interaction, we tutor, help check assignments, participate in the discussion, and substitute when the teachers are ill. Outside, we share with the participants in the lunch room, special outings, and Program activities. The researchers are, in fact, full members of the staff, including the Program founder, its director, and the classroom ethnographer. Researchers, teachers, student representatives, and counselor work closely as a team. The current staff has been in place for two-and-a-half years, affording an important measure of stability and continuity. It meets on a weekly basis to discuss both research and programmatic aspects. The participants are also integrated into this process through the Steering Committee.

Now, ethnographic investigation is moving beyond curriculum development and focusing on the larger issues of identity, cultural citizenship, and empowerment. Through classroom observations and life testimonies, we are attempting to tease out the categories of identity (gender. class, and national/cultural) that seem to be most significant in organizing participants' practice. Through case studies, we will look at reformulations of identities and their practices in light of participation in the Program, and ways in which the Program functions as a primary social network for individual and collective empowerment.

We have begun to work with a select group of women outside the physical space of the Program. Through tape-recorded life histories, we are examining how classroom processes articulate with changes in the domestic and social arenas. This research method draws on cultural and class-specific practices of oral discourse — telling as opposed to writing one's story. Together with the essays women write for class, life histories inform the analysis in vital ways. They provide a view of the past from which to better appreciate and evaluate the changes that are taking place in the present. At the same time, we are witnessing the creation of a new version of that life story, whose content and expression is already marked by the transformations women are experiencing (Thompson, 1978, 1982). In addition, we have begun a series of "case-studies," visiting the women in their homes, accompanying them on their rounds, and engaging in conversations about raising children, marital relations and roles, welfare, hospitals, housing problems, community activities and networks, and education.

The following interpretive narratives are the heart and soul of this chapter. They provide important insights into the process whereby communities affirm and express their cultural citizenship. We have constructed four auto/biographies, drawing from life histories, classroom, and daily life observation and writings of four women.[7] Our long-term relationship with them has

---

[7] The excerpts from oral interviews and classroom compositions that appear in the following section, titled "Testimonies," have been translated from Spanish to facilitate reading for the non-bilingual audience.

nurtured a high degree of mutual trust that informs the following accounts.[8] Because we recognize that oral testimony is as "authored" as written text, we have cosigned the narratives to reflect this collaboration of their words and ours. To paraphrase the Cuban novelist and ethnographer Miguel Barnet (1969), a pioneer in the genre of testimonial literature: These are the stories of Esther, Leonor, Belén and Minerva, as they "told" them to us and as we now "tell" them in return.

TESTIMONIES

Esther Huertas

Esther Huertas grew up in Jayuya, in the mountainous coffee region of Puerto Rico. Her family lived in the conditions of extreme poverty typical of the rural area in the 1940s and 1950s. A number of her 18 brothers and sisters died during childhood. None of the survivors was able to attend school. Esther went to school for one week at the age of 12. But even as a child, her development was secondary to family needs. As the oldest daughter she was responsible for taking care of the home and younger siblings while her parents did agricultural work, so she was not allowed to return. Like her parents and grandparents, Esther reached adulthood without knowing how to read and write.

As a young woman she worked the coffee harvest and migrated periodically to the bigger towns to do domestic work. Esther was expected to contribute most of her earnings to her family, saving only a small portion for herself. She does not recall needing literacy skills for her job as a domestic. Her resourcefulness and good memory helped her along. She would remember the items on a grocery list read to her by her employer, and relied on recognizing the labels in the store. And when her employer sent her and her cousin, who worked across the street, to prepare for their first communion, they both managed to learn the catechism even though they could not read it.

It was during a stroll in a nearby park after the evening lessons, that Esther met her husband-to-be, an acquaintance from her home town. After several months of courting, he asked her to go back home to Jayuya, since he did not want her to work as a domestic anymore. He remained in Bayamón finishing an electrician's training program. This separation awakened in Esther a desire to learn how to read and write. Since she could not do it herself, she had to rely on a friend to read and write her love letters. She still

---

[8] Our research team has been involved in the Program in a variety of ways. Rosa Torruellas is director of the Program, overseeing the adult component; Anneris Goris is the classroom ethnographer; Rina Benmayor and Ana Juarbe are the oral historians. Pedro Pedraza, founder, oversees the children's after-school computer club, a component of the Program not examined in this essay.

vividly remembers the sense of dependency and lack of privacy she experienced at that time. Ironically, her efforts to obtain an education would be thwarted repeatedly by her husband.

Esther migrated to New York in the late 1960s as a young bride. Soon after she arrived, her sister-in-law encouraged her to enroll in a literacy program in the neighborhood. After the first week, her husband forbade her to go. He told her:

> I didn't marry you so you could go off to school and leave the baby in someone else's care. I come home from work and have to be all alone!

Although she had enjoyed the class thus far, she complied with his wishes, setting her own aspirations aside. Several years went by. Esther put all her energies into being the good mother and wife she had been raised to be: "Me dediqué a él y a mi hijo y se acabó." [I devoted my life to him and my son and that was it.] Her husband was the provider, on whom the family depended for economic survival. Since he was a high school graduate he took care of writing or reading letters, a fact that only exacerbated the power he had over her.

Esther remembers having very few friends at that time, going out only to take the children to and from school. She weighed over 200 pounds, but felt content since she was fulfilling the prescribed gender role expectations. Looking back, however, she describes the drudgery of the daily routine: doing household chores all day and running home after picking up the kids in order to have dinner ready by four or five p.m. Her husband would come home, eat, and go to sleep. And that was it, until the next day.

Around this time a Jehovah's witness offered to teach her to read so she could read the Bible. The lady visited Eloisa every day for a week, accompanied by a male Witness. Her husband arrived from work one afternoon and was upset when he saw them: "Aquí el único hombre que puede entrar soy yo." [The only man allowed to enter my house is me.] Esther complied again, asking the woman not to come back "para no causar problemas y pasar bochorno." [to avoid problems and embarrassment.] This time, however, she longed to have another opportunity: "Si Dios quiere yo algún día podré ir a una escuela y quedarme." [God willing, someday I'll be able to go to school and stay there.]

Although Esther was not able to advance her own formal education, she became actively involved in her children's schooling. She describes sitting with them every afternoon while they did their homework, although she could not tell whether they were doing it correctly or not. The purpose, in any case, was not to "correct" their assignments, but to instill in them the importance of education:

I would dictate the letters [to them] even though I didn't know if they were writing them down correctly . . . . I always sat down with them until they finished their homework. I'd talk to them about how important it was to study, knowing that I never had the chance . . . .

The picture we get from Esther at this point in her life is quite different from that of earlier years. Active support of her children's education opened up avenues for her own development. It gave her an incentive to go out and start expanding her social network. She started volunteering at her children's school and assisted the teachers in the lower grades:

I would have breakfast and lunch in school. I'd help take the kids to the bathroom, tell them a funny story when it was nap time . . . I was the first to be present at school activities.

When they were older, she checked on them regularly, visiting their school and making sure they were attending and doing well:

I always stopped by the school. I would say I was going to get a letter and they would let me in. I would ask the teacher or the principal, "I am here to find out how my son, Bernardino Huertas, is doing." They would tell me I was doing the right thing, because there were parents who would not show up even after being sent letters.

Esther's participation in school activities won her the position of treasurer of the PTA. Her natural resourcefulness and wit are evident again in her ability to get ahead and around her illiteracy. She recalls with some amusement how she would memorize the accounts and then confidently stand up and give a financial report in parents' meetings: "Ay madre, ¡yo no sabía leer y escribir y era tesorera de la 121!" [Oh God! I was treasurer of PS 121 and I didn't know how to read or write!] A plaque she received from the school district hangs proudly on her living room wall, and reads in part: "for her contribution to the East Harlem community." Esther's example challenges the stereotype that Latino parents do not support their children's education due to lack of educational credentials or interest.

It was at this specific juncture of her life, when her youngest child was already 10 and she in her late 30s, that Esther decided it was now her turn to obtain an education. She was cashing a check endorsed with a cross and commented how bad it was to be unable to read or write. The cashier woman told her about a literacy program nearby. She enrolled. A few months later, a teacher in the district office encouraged her to go to a new educational program being offered at PS 72, a local school. In the Fall of 1985, she and a group of her female peers joined the El Barrio Popular Education Program. This time she would stay.

A critical turning point in the process of becoming literate is the ability to communicate one's thoughts and ideas in writing. This is a practice the women in the program often describe as "escribir de la mente" [writing from the mind]. For Esther this process has been driven by a strong motivating goal: writing her life history "de mi puño y letra" [in my own hand]. The Program has provided a context and medium for reflection and validation of the participants' lived experience that has encouraged Esther to see her story as a valuable source of knowledge to share. Esther's willingness to take part in this study is related to the desire to leave a legacy that her children and grandchildren can enjoy in the future. She says that her children are enthusiastic about her writing a book about her life:

> My son tells me that he wants me to write my book and that it should have my picture in the front. Then when he gets married and has children, he will show it to them.

Esther conceives her autobiography not just as a personal document, but as having historical and didactic significance. She wants to record the sharp contrasts between the rural Island environment where she was formed and the New York City housing projects where her children are growing up.

> In Puerto Rico we used to walk barefoot. Sometimes when I was going to town I would hang the shoes around my neck and put them on when I arrived. And we wore rags for clothing. And now you [her sons] want new $60 tennis shoes when the ones you have are still in good condition. And I have never worn shoes that cost more than $30 or $40.

But what might be interpreted as a typical intergenerational discourse acquires class-specific significance in this context. Although by many standards present material conditions seem better than in the past, poverty is still the underlying oppressive reality. Esther wants her children to be well aware of this fact and to learn to fight for what they want.

Despite the negative image shed on the poor in this country, Esther is not ashamed of her origins. Her class identity is strong, often expressed in a collective way, "Nosotros los pobres" [We, the poor]. This identity emerges in a context where the traditional values guiding social interaction were "dignidad" and "respeto," [dignity and respect], allowing a measure of self-worth to all. She wants to transmit this knowledge to her children, as a way to prepare them for the tough challenges that lie ahead.

> I remember when I was little . . . . There was a lot of poverty and suffering . . . but despite everything, we were happy. You could see the happiness . . . Not like now. Then, with five cents we could buy a loaf of bread and eat . . . . We didn't care how we dressed or that we had to go barefoot, because everyone got along well and everything was fine. Not anymore.

When Esther joined the Program she had barely learned how to sign her name. Now she regularly brings in compositions of her own inspiration, written at home, and shares them with her peers in class. Although her compositions are still short and written phonetically, they reflect the expressive capacity that signal mastery of literacy. Within the last six months, she has started writing about important episodes in her life, including the following story about her child's bout with meningitis.

> I am going to tell the story of one of my children, the second of my four sons. His name is Edgar, and he was born in Morrisania Hospital in the Bronx; on the 18th of July, 1969. When he was six months old he came down with meningitis. He was in a coma for three months, in a hospital on 14th Street, The New York Infirmary. The doctors would not guarantee his survival. It seemed as if he were dead. He would not move or eat. But I kept my faith, and I promised God that if He saved him, I would go from the hospital to church on my knees. One day I went to see him and I saw him move, and he started living again. I thought I would go crazy when I saw him. I later fulfilled my promise. Edgar was in the hospital for a year and two weeks. But the illness affected his leg and arm. He continued treatment and therapy in a hospital closer to home. And despite everything, thank God, he is 19 today and he graduated from high school with outstanding grades, even though he limps with his right leg, and his right arm is atrophied. But despite everything, he leads a normal life. He likes to do household chores and has four football trophies. That is my story for now. Next time there will be more. Esther. (11/6/88)

Esther's educational development is a highly collective family experience. She keeps a pad and pencil on her night table. After cleaning up the kitchen at night she likes to climb into bed to read or write. Her sons often help her with her homework, sitting around her while she works. They read and help correct her compositions despite their limited knowledge of Spanish. When she gets frustrated for not being able to express something correctly, they tell her to write it anyway and to ask for help in class the next day. Her children are returning the support she has given them, and want her to continue in school. This process has very important implications for reinforcing the importance of education in the home. Two of the children have already graduated from high school.

Writing has become an effective, sometimes cathartic, vehicle for expressing her thoughts and feelings: "Uno se desahoga" [It's a release]. Recently, Esther shared with me a poem she had written one night when she was very depressed. Her children saw her crying and wanted to know what was wrong. They encouraged her to write about it, since they know it helps her feel better. The poem is very lyrical, and concerns love, life and death:

> to be deeply loved
> by someone gives you
> strength

but to love someone
deeply gives you
courage

I'm not afraid to die
but I'd rather not be there
when it happens

but when I dream that
I'm alive, it seems like I'm dead
when I awaken.

                                                    Esther 9/29/88

Esther's writing expresses the conflicting emotions that accompany the process of transformation. As soon as Esther joined the Program her husband tried to make her quit again. But this time she refused. He reacted violently to her demands for respect, accusing her of becoming "fresh" and "possessed by the devil." He has since left her and Esther is now raising their children on her own.

Esther says that people who know her comment that she has changed a lot, and she herself recognizes this has occurred overnight, "de la noche a la mañana." She attributes her new-found assertiveness to participation in the Program:

> One thing I've learned is to demand respect. I've come to realize that I used to let people take advantage of me, even my friends . . . . They would step all over me and I would say nothing . . . . Not anymore!

Having a strong support network in the Program has been a tremendous source of power during these difficult times. It has helped Esther deal with her sense of loss, move ahead in her struggle to fulfill her self-defined needs, and to believe in herself as a person with much knowledge to contribute to her community.

Esther has formed a particularly tight network with two other women who entered the Program with her. Since they all live in the same block of housing projects, they wait for each other and walk together to and from the Program. They also work together in class, checking each other's writings and providing answers to doubts. Learning is a highly collective process in this context as well, as the women take increasing responsibility not just for their own but for their peers' learning.

The staff encourages this collective interaction as the basis where real learning takes place. Esther and her two friends, Rosario and Lila, were illiterate when they started. The three of them have advanced to the intermediate level, and they can all "write from the mind." These accomplishments have raised the women's self-esteem enormously and changed the goals they set for themselves. They also attach a different meaning to their educational process than they did three years ago. When they began they were ashamed of admitting to others that they were attending a literacy class. During a recent case study with Esther I had the opportunity to observe first hand an empowering development.

While walking with the three women to the Program several different neighbors greeted them, in some way making reference to the fact that they were going to school. It is quite clear that the experience of getting an education is now shared with other community members as well. Learning how to read and write is no longer a shameful fact to be hidden from all but the immediate family. It is an activity to be proud of.

Esther aims to go to college and become a teacher. As she recently wrote:

> [If] I had not gone to school I would not be able to write my experiences. I am happy because I have learned to read and write a bit, and I never give up hope that some day I'll be able to go to college. That is all for now. (Oct., 1988)

There is little doubt that she is ready to fight against any circumstance that threatens the realization of this dream.

Esther Huertas and Rosa Torruellas

Leonor Agosto

Leonor Agosto, born in Toa Baja, Puerto Rico, went to New York at the age of 21. Her mother wanted her to migrate to get a job and help support the family on the Island. As she says: "Tenía que hacerlo" [I had to do it]. After working a few years in factory jobs, she returned to Puerto Rico, where she married. Eight years later, she left her two children in her mother's care and went back to New York, looking for work.

Work has governed Leonor's life ever since she can remember. As a young child, she would have to become economically active by participating with other children in what she calls "the *coítre* business." "Coítre" is a fertilizer in which chicken droppings are used. She recalls this experience:

> Well, I remember when I was twelve years old, I would get together with several girls from the neighborhood and we'd go by ourselves to the farm. I was the oldest. We would meet at four in the afternoon, each with a bag for collecting chicken droppings. They paid us 15 cents a bag. I sold *coítre* until I was fourteen.

She also remembers how ashamed she was to do this work: "I stopped doing this when I was older because I got very embarrassed."

Leonor was not the first member of the family to arrive in New York. Her sister already lived in El Barrio and was employed in a factory. As occurs with other immigrants, she depended on her relatives who resided in the "receiving society" for assistance. She was housed by her sister, who provided important social support in the new milieu. Leonor learned how to operate a sewing machine, using the one her sister had at home. Many Puerto Rican women worked in garment factories in New York and Leonor wanted to prepare herself for this. However, her first job turned out to be in a powder-puff factory. Her sister, who worked there at the time, spoke with her boss and convinced him to allow Leonor to come on.

Leonor has worked in several factories in New York City. Her last job was in a laundry, performing a task which as a woman she was well prepared to do: folding shirts. She says that the work there was hard, the conditions terrible, and that she was paid by the piece. Leonor dramatically recounts having to fold "something like one hundred shirts per hour" in order to make what she considered "decent money." After working there for several years, she lost her job. The business relocated upstate. She explains that what happened was that: "they kept only a few workers who had been there for 25 and 30 years."

Becoming unemployed was a tragedy for her. She talks about this with a sad expression on her face:

> Well it affected me a lot. I almost went crazy. I love to work and couldn't conceive of being without a job because I had to pay for my things. I knew the job and the people who worked there, you know, we got along well and I made good money. I made good money at $3.35 an hour.

As a displaced worker, Leonor qualified to collect unemployment benefits which she perceived as a way to get compensated for damages: "I collected, I collected from them." When this benefit terminated, she became eligible for welfare. She felt entitled to this:

> Because I worked. I deserve it. I receive [welfare] because I can no longer collect unemployment and they give me a hand.

Despite her desire and the need to work, Leonor found herself disconnected from the labor market with the only option of "getting a little bit of help from welfare." She accepted the offer as many other women did, but in the process she was transformed from a productive worker to a welfare recipient. After this, Leonor decided to find another type of work:

> Well, to get a good job. A clean job, not like the one I had before. That was a heavy job. I had to do "piece work" and I had to use my back, my chest, my whole body.

Instead, she wanted to work: "in an office, with a computer or something like that, something clean."

She was referred to the Popular Education Program in 1986 by one of the TAP training programs in the area. Her specific goals were to improve her Spanish and English and learn computers, objectives connected with her desire to find a better job.

During the first year in the Program, Leonor did not produce any essays. She had good literacy skills, having completed the eighth grade in Puerto Rico. Everyone remarked that, although she was one of the first participants to arrive every day, she never did her homework. This situation was baffling to everyone. However, at the beginning of the second semester, Leonor announced that she had solved the problem and that now she was going to write:

> I got rid of the man who didn't let me do my homework. I kicked him out. He was the obstacle. Now I can do my homework every night. No one bothers me or stands in my way. Not anymore!

Many of the students felt that it took great courage for her to do something like this. On another occasion in the privacy of her home, Leonor revealed the identity of this person. He was her older brother who had been very abusive since she was a child. Now in her 40s, she felt that the time had come to stop this physical and emotional abuse.

The essays produced by Leonor are extremely important to understand specific transformations in her life. The first example recounts how she was able to apply the English learned in the classroom to a real-life situation:

What I Have Learned in This Class

> I've learned some English in this course. With the little English the teacher has taught me, I was able to deal with a problem at the Telephone Company last month. A Black-American man took care of me. With the little English I have learned in school I was able to deal. I think the man understood everything I said and I understood everything that he said to me. Thanks to the teacher, I understood him well.

The next essay, written in reaction to a classroom workshop on racism, shows the importance of collective discussion in identifying social issues, helping participants rearticulate opinions and finding accurate terms to characterize problems:

> Well, this is a true story that happened in my family. I will start by saying that when my younger sister was 15 she had a black boyfriend. My mother opposed this relationship because he had no work. That was the only reason. But now

comes the full story. My father opposed the relationship because the boyfriend
was black and my sister white. But I don't know whether this was racism or
egotism. My father married my mother who is black. My sister married her
boyfriend. She now has four beautiful children. I want you, my teacher and
my classmates, to tell me whether this is racism or egotism? I want your
opinion so that I can give this story a title. I want your cooperation.

Her writings reveal Leonor's strong sense of accomplishment: Not only did
her English and Spanish improve, but she was able to practice and work on
the computer. Other things happened which Leonor had not planned for.
For instance, she was able to expand her social network which, prior to this,
was limited to her relatives. Also, she had the opportunity to visit different
places in the city such as museums. This is important because Leonor's life
was strictly confined to her apartment and El Barrio. In addition, her self-
image improved, as reflected in a dramatic change in her physical appearance.

Leonor was recommended by the counselor to take High School Equiva-
lency classes at one of the colleges in the city. The possibility of doing this
was not within Leonor's plans when she entered the Program, but she felt
that her potential was being recognized. She seized the opportunity, and
within a few days was requesting the necessary transactions because: "There
at Hunter College one can study nursing and everything."

Leonor has established new future objectives, and her negotiating ideology of "yo voy a mí" [I bet on myself] motivates her to go on in life. Like
Leonor, the program capitalizes on the ideology of "nosotros vamos a ustedes
y con ustedes" [we bet on you and with you] and maximizes people's literacy
skills in the process of empowerment.

Leonor Agosto and Anneris Goris

Belén Resto

Belén Resto's life history demonstrates movement and the desire for change.
Moreover, her story reflects a growing stance of challenge to become the kind
of woman she wants to be and serve as a source of new support for her
daughters and her community.

Belén Resto was born in 1942, in the town of Vega Baja, Puerto Rico
where her father worked as a foreman in the local sugar mill. At the age of
eleven, her parents separated and she and her two brothers went to live with
her maternal grandfather and aunt. The limited economic support provided
by her father and excessive home responsibilities forced Belén to leave school
by the time she was 16 years old.

I lost interest because I didn't have support. I had no one to help me in
anything. If I needed to buy something [for school], I couldn't. So, I didn't

have the drive I have now to progress, to study. But I did take care of my brothers and my mother. So, when I'd come home in the afternoon, I'd have to see if I had any time to do my homework after washing, cooking and scrubbing and all of that. Ay!

Lack of jobs and the family's critical financial situation compelled Belén's aunt to leave for New York on the eve of the great Puerto Rican migration of 1950–60:

> My aunt, with whom I live now, would help us. After 1949, when she arrived in this country, she never returned to live in Puerto Rico. That way, we received more money along with what my father and maternal grandfather contributed.

Many families depended for survival or for a complementary income on relatives that relocated to the United States. Cheap air fares, the institution of a migration bureau, and sterilization of women were organized expressions of an official governmental policy of population reduction and control.

A decade later, Belén too left Puerto Rico because the only opportunity available to her was factory work:

> When I was 18 years old, I needed to work in a factory or somewhere, but my mother didn't want me to, so she decided that I should come to New York to live with my aunt.

Ironically, once in New York City, she started to work in a belt factory, a job that her brother's godmother helped her get:

> [It] . . . was my first [work] experience. I didn't feel out of place because all the workers were Puerto Rican.

However, she says, her work habits created animosity on the part of the other employees. They were conscious of the difference between working at home and working for wages and were not willing to perform as rapidly and productively for the bosses:

> When they would hand me those bundles of work the owners would be so surprised that I would go to get more! They would check them. They couldn't believe how fast I worked. . . . the rest of the workers would spend days on that same amount of work. So without realizing it, I had done something that made them feel bad.

Like her mother, Belén had not worked for wages outside of her home, except for washing and ironing clothes: "una docena, doce piezas, por 75 centavos" [for 75 cents a dozen pieces]. In addition, as is emphasized in her life history, she had plenty of housework to do for the family scrubbing floors and cooking, washing and ironing for her brothers. Some of the same energy and quality of relationships that she describes while working in the factory were actually conditioned by "home work" and home life. The compulsion and sense of responsibility she felt toward her domestic duties were transferred to the work place.

Her relationship with her fellow workers underscored for Belén the kinds of values with which she was raised. She makes reference to her principles:

> I never let anyone lay a hand on me, anywhere I go. Some people actually enjoy that!

She felt that her co-workers' familiarity with the bosses amounted to disrespectful behavior. Consequently, she did not identify with them and when one of her male co-workers sexually harrassed her, she responded with:

> Treat me with respect! I am not the kind of woman you are used to dealing with!

For five years she worked in garment factories. But in 1967, through the poverty programs, she had the opportunity to enroll for office and clerical training in a Manpower agency. She completed her training as a typist and found a job in the Collections Department of a First National City Bank branch. With this, Belén feels she accomplished one of her lifelong goals. This called to mind her feelings as a nine-year-old child, passing by a typing school in her town, Vega Baja, and being embarrassed to look into the storefront because she felt the people in the school were better than her people.

> I feel somewhat fulfilled in the sense that in 1967 I worked in a bank. It made me feel important.

Belén's desire to remain within the bounds of "socially correct behavior" and family-sanctioned roles brings her much grief today when she thinks about her marriage and relationships.

> In Puerto Rico, they raise you . . . [in a way] that for me, the most important thing was the sacrament of my white dress and my virginity.

The strongest expression of Belén's struggle for self-dignity and self-determination can be heard in her explanation of how her first marriage was arranged by her aunt while she was at work:

> So it turned out that when I got home, my aunt had already given her approval, she had given him my "yes." She had given him my "yes!" My aunt kept telling

me, after all the years he'd been coming over, "What would people say?" I didn't have a boyfriend and no one else came to visit. So, worried about what people would think, you know, that there was something going on between us, or that they would gossip about me, I left things as they stood.

Belén is confronted daily by her family for having three daughters "con tres apellidos" [with three different last names]. Her aunt insults her and her sisters-in-law spend time gossiping about her, making Belén's existence unbearable at times. But she overcomes the stigma of having two daughters out of wedlock by maintaining her standards of morality in spite of what others might think:

> It's terrible to be obedient. Then you start thinking "what will they say," the family, the people who know me. You hold it in and hold it in until you explode. That is when you start to lose those customs.

After three years of tolerating abuse and being isolated from her family, Belén was willing to deal with what others thought of her separation from her first husband.

Belén's self-image is also shaped by an unceasing commitment to provide for her daughters. This image has been hard earned because until recently she depended almost totally on their fathers to support her and the girls. However, as she states:

> When my daughter was born I stopped working because of the fear that he [my husband] instilled in me. He would tell me that if I gave her [our daughter] to a babysitter and something happened to her he would take her away from me.

Rather than test her custody rights as a working mother, Belén decided to stay home to raise her daughter. However she takes pride in the fact that she has held her daughters' fathers accountable for their economic well-being. About one of them, she says: "Hoy mismo él se siente orgulloso de que él mantiene a su hija." [To this day, he feels proud to be supporting his daughter.]

In the 16 years Belén was out of the labor force, most of her network consisted of family members, her children's fathers, neighbors, local merchants, Jehovah's Witnesses, and public school personnel. Through her daughters' school activities, Belén's horizons expanded and she began to take an active interest in their education by participating in the PTA. Through parent-organized seminars at the school, Belén's interest in education and child development grew as did her awareness of the importance of communication in the home:

> [I learned] how to talk to our children, and how to listen to them in order to give them a thoughtful answer; to give them attention. Yes, we can help them but we don't listen, we're worried about other things, and when we're not, we are

abrupt. That's the way I used to be. When I was growing up that's the way it was. In truth, we don't pay attention to them. We don't make time for them, because many of us do have the capacity to help our children. At their school, I am working with the people who, in one way or another, have a positive attitude. So I am moving to another stage.

Belén joined the El Barrio Popular Education Program in 1985 when it was still based at PS 72, her daughter's school. She was interested in computer training and quickly acquired those skills. She also acquired new feelings about her potential for learning and contributing to her community:

> Sometimes you actually feel that other people are better than you. I have to stop that. We are all made of the same stuff and if we are really interested and want to [study]; that twenty or thirty years have passed makes no difference. So now, here in Casita María, I have learned alot in Felix's class. I have become enthusiastic about reading. I never liked to read. This program has made me interested in reading. Now thanks to Pedro and Rosa, I am always getting invited here and there. I also try to support the Program by bringing in new people and I feel that I am contributing in this way.

Belén's sense of responsibility earned her several important positions in the Program. After two years as a student, she is now a member of the Board of Directors. She is also a part-time tutor in the Program's after-school computer club for children. Working with the children has been an enriching experience. Most importantly, they give her a great deal of support. As she states:

> I learn a lot from them, from their enthusiasm, from what they write . . . When they don't know something I try to teach them.

Her work with them has given her a sense of worth: "Yo me siento grande, grande." [I feel important, really important.] Moreover, the relationships with the students and other members of the Program have helped her overcome one of her biggest fears: to speak and introduce herself in English.

With her new-found confidence and support network, Belén has become the first woman in the Program to enroll in Hostos Community College. Her original goal of learning to use the computer and find employment has been transformed. She now aspires to a teaching career:

> I think if I achieve this [goal of becoming a teacher] in some way or another I can help my community. [The idea] is not merely to become a teacher, but to know how to teach, you know.

But, in the meantime, Belén is working very hard at setting an example for her daughters and the children she works with. She is giving them the attention and the direction her upbringing lacked because her mother did not foresee Belén's future as linked to anything outside of the home.

Belén is one of many Puerto Ricans demanding and seeking economic and social opportunities in a long-established community which has experienced more than its share of poverty and marginality. Her testimony is offered as a way of breaking down the clichéd images of poor, working-class women. It is also a tribute to the processes and creativity she and other members of our community engage in day to day, as we stretch out to reach our personal goals and fulfill our commitments to the generations to come.

Belén Resto and Ana Juarbe

Minerva Torres Ríos

Age 83, Minerva Torres Ríos' self-appointed nickname in the Program is "la nena," [the baby]. This is not just a playful twist on the fact that she is the eldest but that she is one of the most energetic, socially engaged, and joyous participants in the Program. Minerva was born in Guayanilla, on the Caribbean coast of Puerto Rico, in 1905. At age 16, she completed the eighth grade, which for that time constituted a substantial educational achievement. She then went to work in a local, home garment shop, embroidering linens, lingerie, and blouses until 1929, when she migrated to New York City. El Barrio became her home for fifty-odd years; the Amalgamated Clothes laundry her place of work for 40.

Upon retirement eighteen years ago, Minerva joined the Senior Citizens' Center at Casita María, a former "settlement house" in East Harlem. She has since enrolled in all the special interest courses offered at the Center and so, when the El Barrio Popular Education Program came to Casita, she signed up. She did not need literacy training. As she puts it:

> In Puerto Rico, one comes out of the third grade knowing how to read and write. I don't understand what the problem is here.

So, what did this Program have to offer a woman who reads and writes fluently, who is not in search of better employment or of an avenue to higher education?

Rather than empowering her to propose new life goals, the Program has provided Minerva with a formal context of validation. It has offered her the opportunity to define and fulfill a special role within the collective, that of the "Historian":

> I don't know, Rina. At this Center they've had many programs and I've enrolled in them all. But, I think this Program is really extraordinary. Every

time Felix [the teacher] gives us something to write, it jogs my memory. The other day he showed us a painting of women washing down by a river. Immediately, my mind flashed on the people washing on the riverbank [in my hometown], singing and washing in the river.

This Program, as distinct from the others, has offered Minerva a context for bridging the gap between past and present, allowing memory to become more than personal nostalgia. This has enabled her to reclaim and rename as "history" the experience of living in a bygone period of Puerto Rican culture. Her class essays deliberately document various aspects of her times, for example: "Mi primera enseñanza" [My First Lesson], "Remembranzas" [Remembrances], "El baquiné" [Child Burial]. She frequently qualifies statements with: "hablo de mi tiempo" [I'm speaking about my times], and has expressed the desire to write the history of her hometown.

However, her passion for history is motivated by more than a desire to *document* the past. Because the essays are always read aloud and discussed in the class, they are produced for an "audience," the younger Puerto Rican women in the Program. So, she conceives her writing not as an exercise for improving literacy skills or a vehicle for self-evaluation, but as a contribution of knowledge to her community.

Elsewhere in the interview, I asked Minerva if she had ever thought of being a teacher, to which she replied:

I might have become a journalist because I love to write. Even at my age I love to write.

But writing is not the only strategy through which Minerva expresses her historical and cultural ambassadorship. She actively constructs spaces for political practice. Since retirement, she has become an ardent advocate for the Hispanic elderly and often travels to the State Capital to lobby. She sits on all the major committees at Casita María, has served on the Program's Steering Committee, volunteers on a daily basis in the seniors' lunchroom, collects money, distributes tickets, keeps records, and — together with her equally active 90-year-old friend, Mr. Burgos — periodically volunteers to teach elementary school children about Puerto Rican life and culture.

Again, Minerva does all this not just to keep herself busy, to have company, or to improve the quality of her own life. Her role is predicated on a sense of connectedness. For example, my case study notes of November 16, 1988, record these observations from an informal chat on the subject of benefits for the elderly:

Then, Burgos came along to put four cans of Goya beans into a cart for needy families for Thanksgiving. Minerva pointed out that the two of them are the representatives from Casita María on the Concilio de Personas Mayores Hispanas (the Council for the Hispanic Elderly). They have been active for a long time in this organization, which has been responsible for acquiring benefits for senior citizens. Both Burgos and Minerva stated that they were doing this not for themselves but for the generations to come, so that they would have it easier in their old age.

Both "upstairs," in the El Barrio Popular Education Program and "downstairs," in Casita María,[9] Minerva encounters and organizes contexts in which validation and self-worth is organically linked to the shared terrain of community.

What historical, social, and personal factors helped shape this sense of social commitment? Life history as a method offers us valuable clues. Minerva was delighted to sit down and record her life experiences. We agreed that, together, we would turn her testimony into a little book, as a legacy for future generations. As she constructed this narrative, certain life-cycle chapters — childhood, migration and work — revealed the discourse that organizes her values, identities, and practice.

Childhood in Puerto Rico occupies a major part of her 200-page life history transcript. Although my first elicitation was in part responsible — "Minerva, tell me about your youth in Puerto Rico" — I had obviously hit a central nerve. Minerva projects her childhood in idyllic terms, in which poverty and exploitation are tempered by the physical beauty of the environment and by structures of respect, morality, and order in social life:

> Our lives were poor but happy because there was no violence. Boys and girls used to go swimming together in the river with old clothes on [and nothing ever happened].
>
> I used to love going to the beach. We'd get up early, around 5am and walk down there in a group. Just as we arrived, the dawn would break. That dawn in Puerto Rico is beautiful, the sky gets lighter and lighter and then you see that sun, oh God!

Ever-present in her account is the contrast between then and now. This image of a carefree and wholesome past is reconstructed against the backdrop of fear and urban violence which surrounds Minerva today and which she perceives to be developing, even in Puerto Rico. Her own physical safety is indeed a concern, but she is also preoccupied with social disintegration. The traditional structures of "respeto" — of children for parents, children for teachers, and parents for teachers — allow her to feel more securely anchored in the threatening and changing contemporary environment.

---

[9] Casita María rents two floors in a low-income housing project in East Harlem. The ground floor houses Casita's senior citizens' center and the second floor, the Popular Education Program.

> My mother was a very serious person who brought us up very strictly. We had
> to respect our teachers. I couldn't come home and complain about the teacher
> because she would tell me that the teacher was right. She'd take me to school,
> and in front of all the kids give me a spanking.

School is another major chapter in Minerva's testimony. With great fondness
and precision of detail she paints a picture of a local, multigrade school
house, where children of the rich and poor studied together. She tells us how
colonial rule meant that English became a language of instruction, that
teachers were often "imported," and that the curriculum was largely defined
in the United States:

> We had a book that was called *Rudiments of America* because at that time
> everything came from here [the U.S.]. At that time the Governor was Ameri-
> can, the laws were American. From here they would send them over there [to
> the Island] and they [the laws] were all made here.

Puerto Rican children became well-versed in the major myths and chapters
of United States history:

> I learned all the songs from the South in English. "Old Kentucky Home," 'Oh
> Susana," "Old Black Joe," I know all those songs . . . . I know the story of
> Lincoln, from my schooldays there, they taught it to me in Puerto Rico; I know
> the story of Washington, Benjamin Franklin with his kite . . . . There were
> classes about Puerto Rico but there was no history book of Puerto Rico. They
> taught it orally, you know.

> There in Puerto Rico they never taught us about the Mayas, nor about the
> peoples of South America. I didn't know anything of that. I'm learning it now,
> because Felix gives us that history, about the Mayan indians.

Minerva's present involvement in the Program has undoubtedly led her to
recall and emphasize her grade-school experience. Yet, it was also a part of
her life that imbued her with a tremendous sense of achievement and self-
confidence, as well as with skills and frameworks of knowledge, even though
these were not to translate into fulfilling work.

Migration to New York City at the age of twenty-four was a decisive step.
Also significant was the moment of her arrival - the onset of the Great
Depression. Minerva's words cut a sharp contrast between life "here" and
"there:"

> I was growing up and life was getting more expensive. So I said, "Well, I'm
> going to go to New York and at least I'll be able to help the family financially."
> So I did. My cousin sent me a ticket and I came. The trip took five days and I
> was in New York. That's when hard times *really* began.

After several months working in a scarf factory, she managed to insure herself against the perils of seasonal work by finding a stable job. She recounts with humor and some irony how she bypassed a clerical job in a hospital, commensurate with her level of schooling, because she would have to work Sundays, a factor that at the time she equated with exploitation. As a single woman with no other source of financial support, she opted to work in a commercial laundry because this was steady work. Consequently, she spent forty years pressing cuffs and collars on men's shirts.

> I earned ten dollars a week. Welfare and unemployment insurance didn't exist. It was the Depression. But with those ten dollars I survived until Roosevelt passed the minimum wage law, and I started to earn fourteen dollars. I worked Saturdays, all day, with no extra pay. I worked from 8am to 7 or 8 at night.

The contrast was further marked by what I suspect was an anecdote of unintentional irony. Filling in details of daily life in Puerto Rico, she waxed poetic on how much she loved to iron as a young girl, peppering her narrative with expressive gestures:

> I'd set up a charcoal stove and heat up three irons. Then, I'd set up a board in front of the window. I would take my iron and "lalalala" begin to sing and iron. I loved to iron! And when the iron got cold, you'd put it to heat and grab the other one and test it: "Tá! It's ready."

Work in the laundry was to have a politicizing impact. Six years after coming to work at Amalgamated Clothes, Minerva found herself involved in a mass effort to unionize laundry workers. The success of this action brought her increases in pay, benefits and job protection, convincing her of the importance of standing on a picket line and fighting for one's rights. This experience contrasts with the idyllic way in which Minerva recalls her first job in Puerto Rico embroidering for doña María Rodríguez, whom she describes as a benevolent local entrepreneur.

If Minerva's sense of class and national identity is very much marked by childhood in another time and place, her political outlook and, I would propose, social practice are governed by the New Deal era that brings Social Security and Welfare into being. To this day she sees such programs as positive safety nets for the poor. So, she subscribes to the notions of socially responsible government and the need for public pressure in the claiming of rights. Contrary to most post-World-War-II Puerto Rican migrants, she understands how institutional structures of government and community work in the United States and believes that one must work with or through them.

Minerva cuts her *social* profile through this life-history account. She is less eager to talk about questions of gender and sexuality. She never had children of her own, but does have many nieces and nephews here in New York. About her first marriage she wrote a composition recounting the story of how she eloped with her boyfriend but eventually separated on her mother's insistence. About her second marriage, many years later, she offers little information, quickly pulling the conversation back to topics about life during "her times."

Wanting to account for these silences, I first thought that in gender struggles Minerva may feel less successful, less proficient in dealing with its structures of domination. However, on closer consideration, it is also apparent that these episodes do not fit into Minerva's conception of history and her role as transmitter. They are personal dimensions of her life that in her estimation do not bear the weight of useful or important public knowledge. And so, they do not deserve the same attention. However, silences do provide important clues as to how people perceive the contribution of their life history and how they in turn selectively organize its contents.

The Popular Education Program has given Minerva the opportunity to write, an activity she dearly loves. It has satisfied some of her curiosity and thirst for knowledge. But, more importantly, it has strengthened an identity rooted in class and national consciousness. The Program has provided the space for Minerva to be a *teacher* of Puerto Rican culture for the younger women. She reminds them, through her extraordinary memory, that she is a witness of history. She also shows how through their daily life and commitment to community people also become actors in history. On a more personal note, I asked Minerva if remembering the past makes her sad. She replied:

> To the contrary. It gives me joy, it gives me life. I don't feel at all close to death.

Memory is a strategy for life and for building the future.

Minerva Torres Ríos and Rina Benmayor

IDENTITY, NETWORKS, AND CULTURAL CITIZENSHIP

These testimonies and case studies show that empowerment is not a uniform or homogeneous process. People's personal histories combine with new forms of knowledge in particular ways. What is perhaps most remarkable about the El Barrio Popular Education Program is the extent to which the collective environment generates the opportunity for each participant's self-definition and growth.

These four cases also give us insight into the potential of the Program to stimulate collective empowerment. We are looking at a process in which the very interaction between individuals and their community of peers has an impact in building collective confidence, new identities and goals, and expressions of cultural citizenship.

We chose Esther, Minerva, Belén, and Leonor for this "pilot" study because we identified them as persons who, in different ways, were undergoing a notable process of transformation. We wanted to explore how participation in the Program was impacting their consciousness and lives. As a sample, these four women also represented a range in age, marital arrangements, time of migration, employment histories, educational levels, and reading/writing skills.

The particularities of each woman's life, however, have also made us aware of common dimensions. Each narrative brings to the fore aspects of the collective Puerto Rican experience in the United States: migration, structural relation to work, gender roles and relations, national and cultural frames of reference, and overall social location of this working class population. We understand these to be interrelated spheres, organized by the political economy of capitalism and by the particular colonial relationship of Puerto Rico with the United States.[10]

In all four instances, gender and class oppressions intersect to limit these women's access to education. As daughters and sisters, they were expected to take responsibility for domestic chores and siblings from an early age. Other women in the Program also share this experience, and recall how their brothers were sent to school while they were denied this opportunity. Their education was of secondary concern, since gender roles prescribed that their adult lives would be tied primarily to household and family needs. At the same time, extreme poverty conditions forced them to labor during childhood, further precluding them from obtaining an education.

The same economic conditions that limited these women's schooling compelled Puerto Ricans to migrate to the United States throughout the century (History Task Force, 1981). "Operation Bootstrap," the plan to industrialize the Island, set in motion the influx of U.S. capital, the expulsion of surplus labor, and the arrival of more than one million "Boricuas" to the United States between the late 1940s and early 1960s (Bonilla & Campos, 1982, 1986). Uprooted by poverty and lack of jobs, people came in search of opportunities or, as they express it, "buscando ambiente."

Leonor, Belén, Esther, and Minerva's personal histories illustrate the continuous struggle of Puerto Rican women, tracked into unskilled factory jobs and working under stressful and unstable conditions (Benmayor et. al., 1987). Like Leonor, thousands lost their jobs as a consequence of labor and

---

[10] As researchers of the Centro de Estudios Puertorriqueños we have the advantage of being able to draw on sixteen years of critical analyses of Puerto Rican migration history, political economy, culture, educational. and language policies and practices.

capital flows in the manufacturing sector. Since the 1950s, company reloca-
tion and the mechanization of routine tasks have also contributed to their
displacement (Sassen-Koob, 1981). Minerva, who entered the labor market
in the 1930s and benefitted from several decades of effective union advocacy,
had the job security that later generations of Puerto Rican women would not
have.

Belén, like many other poor women, negotiated her livelihood somewhat
differently, depending on her aunt and children's fathers as providers. But
she dutifully paid the price for this support. Her life would be dominated by
her family's moral pronouncements as to what she should or should not do or
be. To this day, they disapprove of her being in college, telling her she is "too
old." Esther's life has been governed by an oppressive ideology that dictates
that her place as a woman is in the home, responding to everybody else's
needs but her own.

All four women are now increasingly affirming their right to self-defined
goals, despite the constraints of traditional role expectations or conflicting
emotional commitments. These women are now making education a priority
in their lives. By insisting on their right to an education, they are affirming a
cultural citizenship based on a new gender identity. Their daily attendance
suggests that they are exercising increasing control over their own future.
Getting an education is translating into an assertiveness that threatens traditional arrangements of authority and power.

In classroom discussions and compositions, many of the women raise the
issue of domestic conflict in their lives. The phenomenon is not particular to
the Puerto Rican community. The level of domestic violence has escalated
considerably in the society as a whole. Testimonies of conflict abound in our
classroom ethnography notes. Verbally, the women may express a certain
amount of bravado in dealing with these issues. They also acknowledge that
resolutions often involve contradiction and compromise, even the reproduction of old behaviors. Silences can also be suggestive of problematic dimensions, as in the case of Minerva, who does not prioritize gender issues at all in
her life history.

However, as each tries to negotiate and resolve her particular situation,
she is confronting family and spouse resistance to her efforts from a new
perspective. The process has not been easy. It has meant questioning long-
held conceptions and values regarding gender, renegotiating power relationships, and re-forming decision making practices in the domestic sphere; in
extreme cases, the end of the relationship. There is no doubt that understanding gender oppression has not come to the women through abstraction,
but rather through very concrete situations. We see that moving forward,
"superarse," has meant painful breaks with forms of security or dependency
already in place.

These issues pose a challenge to the Program and its ability to address needs arising from domestic conflicts. At a basic level, the goal of community empowerment entails not just working with women, but also engaging more men in reflection and analysis of their reality. Ideally, women and men should find in each other a source of support for personal development. It is important that gender oppression be challenged by all and recognized for what it is: an expression of inequality and a practice that reinforces powerlessness.

While direct intervention in domestic conflict is beyond the purview of the Program, we are dealing with the issue in a number of ways: "affirmative action" efforts to increase male participation, directing specialized workshops on topics like domestic violence, and encouraging more egalitarian classroom interactions between male and female participants, including the teachers.

The Program has been a primary support network in the process of affirming and transforming gender identity and practice. It provides much needed "personal" time and space to debate, question, and formulate alternatives. The high expectations conveyed in the Program impact on the women's self-image. In the process, they are redefining diverse aspects of their identity as women and as learners. Increasingly, they see a wider range of options open to them. The collective atmosphere and interaction nurtures this process. Personal advancement is supported by, and has an impact on the whole. Group support for individual transformation becomes the greatest source of collective empowerment.

The Program has also enabled the women to form new networks among themselves. These are activated in the classroom, further facilitating learning. Women who are more advanced help others in writing, reading, fulfilling in-class assignments, and working on the computer. The participants respond to each other's needs with sensitivity and care. They identify with their "compañeras' " struggles and give each other emotional support. When the women leave Casita María, they take these networks with them, as many come to rely on their peers to deal with extra-educational issues in their lives.

The women also draw strength from other areas of their collective identity. Leonor, Esther, Minerva, and Belén share a common discourse on Puerto Rico that is both culturally and class based. The past is remembered fondly, proudly, because of the human values it represents. At the same time, there is a clear sense of class position. The four of them grew up in conditions of severe poverty, a strong reality framing their collective identification as: "We the poor" Nevertheless, for them class position does not the carry negative connotations of "social deprivation" that exists in the U.S. context. In Puerto Rican society poverty is imbued with the cultural value of "dignidad."

But Puerto Rico is not only an aspect of their past. It is also part of their present and, in some cases, a plan for their future. Migration separates people from family, friends, and community. But ties are not severed; they remain strong and active. The women in the Program travel frequently to the Island for major family celebrations: weddings, baptisms, and funerals. Financial linkages are not uncommon: Esther often sends money to her parents in Puerto Rico; Leonor supports her two children who live on the Island with her mother; and Belén's parents are on the Island as well. Afraid of flying, Minerva returned only once, in 1947, but her national identity remains firmly rooted in the Puerto Rican heritage of her youth, and it is being constantly renewed by her active involvement in the community here.

Esther and Leonor are also redefining a class identity cast upon them as "state-dependent." Both are on welfare, an institution commonly experienced as oppressive. Being on public assistance opens the door for case workers to pry into their private lives. The aid they receive is barely enough to meet immediate subsistence needs. However, they are shedding the stigma this society attaches to welfare recipients. Now they are beginning to view state aid as a *right* that provides them with some space to strategize for their future. Both want to re-enter the labor market and get off the welfare rolls. But they have transformed their short-term employment goals into long-range educational plans. Receiving welfare is giving them a chance to develop and carry forward their objectives.[11] For now at least, they will continue using state assistance to their advantage.[12]

The women are also reinterpreting their identity as workers, challenging their condition of poverty and the position ascribed to them within the labor force. According to current definitions, they fall into the so-called "underclass," a structural version of the "culture of poverty" (Wilson, 1987). They would be commonly described as unskilled, uneducated, and therefore outside the labor pool, dependent on state welfare, and with little promise of being able to pull themselves and their children out of the poverty cycle.[13]

The current responses to structural unemployment focus on training members of the "underclass" to adapt to the new labor market realities (Meléndez, 1988). However, as Torres' critique (1988) sharply points out:

---

[11] Through life history interviews with the unemployed in Montreal, Paul Grell (1985) uncovers a variety of ways people live in and respond to what is now becoming a permanent social space of "non-work." He finds that nonparticipation in the labor market has also served as "a growth point for new networks of sociability, practices and ways of living, of being."

[12] Current welfare legislation in New York provides that persons receiving public assistance may enroll in training programs as an alternative to workfare.

[13] Numerous studies document the crisis affecting the Puerto Rican community in the United States. Statistics show that Puerto Ricans have the lowest median household income, educational achievement, and labor force participation. Forty two percent of families are below the poverty level, as compared to 12 percent of the total U.S. population. Women and children are particularly hard hit. Almost half of all Puerto Rican households are headed by females, who depend on public assistance for their basic needs. See ASPIRA, 1983; Institute for Puerto Rican Policy, 1986; Community Service Society, 1985; N.Y. State Advisory Committee for Hispanic Affairs, 1985; Pérez, 1985.

Another indispensible element is to be found among grassroots movements for community empowerment. Community empowerment means not only building local institutions; it means individuals realizing they are the ultimate agents for change. The best anti-poverty programs will be those which help the poor to empower themselves.

Some participants have come to the Program seeking to improve their employability in what is becoming a dichotomized and exclusionary labor market. However, partly as a result of their participation in the Program, many are now repositioning themselves *beyond* this "underclass" in a way not envisioned by conventional skills-training programs. Belén, Leonor, and Esther have expanded their social and political frames of reference. They better understand how their life situation has been structured by larger social and economic forces, rather than by the "ignorance" or personal insufficiencies for which they once blamed themselves. Today, Esther aspires to become a teacher; Leonor plans to get her high school diploma and is thinking about nursing and about expanding her computer skills; Belén is beginning college studies in elementary education. Although typically female careers, these are not mere jobs, but the type of work *they* want and are learning how to define.

The affirmation process we observe taking place in the context of the Program exposes the disenfranchising nature of generalized social classifications. They ignore how people negotiate, successfully or not, the circumstances of inequality. By contrast, in focusing on how these women have begun to redefine their lives, we are better able to appreciate the depth of the response within each individual. These women are daring to challenge cultural and ideological traditions, as well as state and economic systems that position them as powerless. They are beginning to exercise their "cultural citizenship" as women, as workers, as Puerto Ricans, but ultimately as human beings.

We do not perceive these women to be atypical "success" cases. Regardless of the language, literacy, or job levels they may have attained, none of them has experienced "upward mobility" in any material sense. Instead, they are highly representative of the invisible vitality, strength, and resourcefulness that exist in a community beset by poverty. These four women illustrate how, given the space, the chance, and the right support, people are able to put their assets into action. The ultimate measure of "empowerment" in the Program is not the individual attainment of a white-collar job, but rather the harnessing of people's resources for self-determination and collective equality.

Collective Empowerment

Oppressed people do not passively accept their "fate," but actively search for ways to improve their personal and collective lives. Participation in the El

Barrio Popular Education Program is one strategy for achieving this. Perhaps the most critical challenge to the Program and its participants is making the leap from the level of personal strategy into collective mobilization.

Minerva's assessment of the Program speaks to the fact that literacy has to be defined in broader terms, and that learning cannot occur isolated from students' social referents:

> I have dozens of certificates and diplomas from the educational courses I have taken, but this Program is different because it covers everything. We learn about history and culture, about much more than just reading and writing [our paraphrase].

In the four cases we have examined we can see how a participatory approach to learning frames individual empowerment within a discourse that goes beyond personal gain. Belén says that by becoming a teacher she can "be of more help to my community." Esther sees a teaching career as a contribution to future generations — including her own grandchildren. Minerva came with an already well developed sense of social commitment. The Program has validated her historical and cultural vision, and provided her the opportunity to inspire her "compañeras" to follow her example. Leonor became an active participant in the classroom, having become engaged in the collective learning environment.

This move beyond the self is not surprising, since individual transformation has been nurtured by a pedagogy that privileges the importance of culture and community forms of knowledge and interaction. Relevant class content and shared testimony has allowed identification of common problems and bonds. Participants gain a sense of trust and construct a collective practice that is the basis for real advancement and learning.

Commitment to collectivity — to family and community — is a deeply embedded value in Latino cultures and discourse (Sommer, 1988). The Program reinforces this commitment, offering participants a context in which to express it. In this way, the Program serves as a primary support network for developing and affirming a collective cultural citizenship.

When it started, the major objective of the Program was to involve parents in helping define and demand a liberatory education for their children. In a system where 80 percent of Latino youths drop out of high school, this is vital to the survival of the community itself. Advances is this arena have been made at the personal and program-wide levels (i.e., collective governance of the Program itself, more parental involvement in their children's schooling, participation in community school board elections and in mobilization for Latino representation of the New York City Board of Education).

However, linking collective practices within the classroom to more specific community-wide struggles is still a major challenge. There is no dearth of problems to be tackled — poor health, gentrification and displacement, deficient education, school failure for children, and drugs. The goal is to articulate discussion of these issues to concrete mobilization.

Establishing structured and systematic links to this form of struggle is on our agenda for the future. Our uppermost priority at this point, however, is to move forward the self-management aspect of the Program, and engage participants and the community in running and developing this literacy-for-empowerment model.

Developing consciousness and empowerment is a complex process. It requires putting in place real supports and opportunities: well-funded programs that are grounded in an innovative pedagogy and a holistic view of learning. The cultural and experiential dimensions of this practice are critical (Giroux, 1983; Giroux & Aronowitz, 1985; Standt, 1987; Weiler, 1988).

In this regard, the debate around "cultural literacy" currently underway in the halls of academe (Hirsch, 1987) is not irrelevant to our classroom in East Harlem. Efforts to promote a unified national culture, along with the recent "English Only" movement, threaten the sources upon which "minority" communities build their identities, draw their strength and enrich the fabric of American society. One of the most insightful responses to those who want to bunker education in a homogeneous cultural canon affirms instead that:

> American culture is extremely diverse and is becoming more so every year, and the global community that is increasingly part of our lives is even more multifarious . . . . The final test of "pluralistic literacy" is one's ability to translate from one code to another, to participate in conflicts productively, with understanding and tolerance but without sacrificing one's own meanings. (Armstrong, 1988)

This approach rests on an understanding of and respect for diverse ways of knowing and learning. However, for a community of U.S. citizens who confront life in this country from a subordinate position, the struggle is to change those power relationships. Our objective in the El Barrio Popular Education Program, therefore, is to develop *critical literacy*, as a model and strategy for disempowered communities to affirm their own forms of knowledge, to acquire new ones and to negotiate their position in society on an equal footing. This is a pedagogy not merely for imparting skills, but for bringing about social change.

REFERENCES

Armstrong, P. (1988). Pluralistic literacy. *Profession 88*. New York: Modern Language Association.

ASPIRA. (1983). *Racial and ethnic high school dropout rates in New York City. Summary report*. New York: Aspira.

Barnet, M. (1969). *Canción de Rachel*. La Habana: Arte y Literatura.

Benmayor, R., Juarbe, A., Alvarez, C., & Vázquez, B. (1987). *Stories to live by: Continuity and change in three generations of Puerto Rican women*. New York: Centro de Estudios Puertorriqueños.

Bonilla, F., & Campos, R. (1982). Bootstraps and Enterprise Zones: The underside of late capitalism in Puerto Rico and the United States. *Review, 5*, 4.

Bonilla, F., & Campos, K. (1986). *Industry and idleness*. New York: Centro de Estudios Puertorriqueños.

Business Council for Effective Literacy. (1986). *Newsletter, 1*(7).

Community Service Society. (1985). *Poverty in New York City: 1980–1985*. New York: Community Service Society.

Freire, P. (1970). *Pedagogía del oprimido*. México: Siglo XXI.

Freire, P., & Macedo, D. (1987). *Literacy: Reading the word and the world*. S. Hadley, MA: Bergin and Garvey.

Giroux, H. (1983). *Theory and resistance in education*. S. Hadley, MA: Bergin and Garvey.

Freire, P., & Aronowitz, S. (1985). *Education under siege*. South Hadley, MA: Bergin and Garvey.

Grell, P. (1985). *Etude du chomage et de ses conséquences*. Groupe d'analyse des politiques sociales, Université de Montréal, Canada.

Hirsch, E. D., Jr. (1987). *Cultural literacy: What every American needs to know*. Boston: Houghton.

History Task Force, Centro de Estudios Puertorriqueños. (1981). *Labor migration under capitalism: The Puerto Rican experience*. New York: Monthly Review.

Institute for Puerto Rican Policy. (1986). Puerto Ricans and other Latinos in the United States, *Datanote on the Puerto Rican Community, 4*, 1.

Meléndez, E. (Forthcoming). Towards a good job strategy for Latino workers. In *Proceedings of "Cities in Transition Conference."* LBJ School of Public Policy. Austin: University of Texas Press.

Morgen, S., & Bookman, A. (1988). *Women and the politics of empowerment*. Philadelphia: Temple University Press.

New York State Advisory Committee for Hispanic Affairs. (1985). *New York State Hispanics: A challenging minority*. Albany, New York.

Pérez, R. (1985). *The status of Puerto Ricans in the U.S.* New York: National Congress for Puerto Rican Rights.

Sassen-Koob, S. (1981). *Exporting capital and importing labor: Caribbean migration to New York City*. (Occasional Papers No. 28). New York: Center for Latin American, and Caribbean Studies, New York University.

The shame and costs of illiteracy. (1986, September 13) *The New York Times*.

Sommer, D. (1988). Not just a personal story: Women's "testimonios" and the plural self. In B. Brodzki & C. Schenck, (Eds.), *Life/Lines: Theorizing women's autobiography*. Ithaca: Cornell University Press.

Standt, K. (1987). Programming women's empowerment: A case from Northern Mexico. In V. Ruíz & S. Tiano (Eds.), *Women on the U.S.–Mexico border: Responses to change*. Boston: Allen and Unwin.

Thompson, P. (1978). *The voice of the past*. Oxford: Oxford University Press.

Thompson, P. (1982). *Our common history*. Atlantic Highlands, Humanities Press.

Torres, A. (1988, October 24). *Poverty in the U.S.: A public policy agenda for the 1990's*. Paper presented at New York University, Centro de Estudios Puertorriqueños manuscript.

Weiler, K. (1988). *Women teaching for change: Gender, class and power*. South Hadley, MA: Bergin and Garvey.

Wilson, W. J. (1987). *The truly disadvantaged: The inner city, the underclass and public policy*. Chicago: Chicago University Press.

Author Index

Subject Index